In Pursuit of Big Tench

In Pursuit of
BIG TENCH
Len Arbery

The Crowood Press

First Published in 1996 by
The Crowood Press Ltd
Ramsbury, Marlborough
Wiltshire SN8 2HR

British Library Cataloguing-in-Publication Data
A catalogue record for this publication is available from the British Library.

ISBN 1 85223 933 6

Line drawings by Paul Groombridge

Typeset and designed by
D & N Publishing
Ramsbury, Marlborough
Wiltshire SN8 2HR

Typefaces used: text, M Plantin; labels, Gill Sans.

Printed and bound by BPC Books, Aylesbury

Photo Acknowledgements
All photographs taken by the author except the following:
Angling Times 17, 180; Bob Buteux 155 (upper), 156, 163, colour plate 4 (upper); Kevin Clifford 26, 45; J. Darville 15; Bob Dilley 43; Peter Drennan 57; J. Everard 53, colour plate 7 (lower); *Improve your Coarse Fishing* 28, 112, 141 (left), 153 (lower), colour plate 1 (upper left), colour plate 3 (upper left), colour plate 4 (lower left), colour plate 6 (lower); Pete Jackson 7, 9, 165, colour plate 5 (lower), colour plate 8 (upper left); Bob James colour plate 8 (lower); P. Marriot 18; Bill Quinlan 105, 139, 141 (right), 170, 172, 173, 175; R. Smith colour plate 4 (lower right); P. Stone 10 (upper); M. Tapley 39; A. Wilson 16

Dedication
For all their considerable sacrifice down through the years this book is respectfully dedicated to my immediate family: June, my wife; Karen Bradley and Tony our children.

As inward love breeds outward talk
The hound some praise; and some the hawk;
Some, better pleased with private sport,
Use tennis; some a mistress court;
But these delights I neither wish,
Nor envy – while I freely fish.

I care not, I, to fish in seas,
Fresh waters best my mind do please,
Whose sweet calm course I contemplate,
And seek in life to imitate;
In civil bounds I fain would keep,
And for my past offences weep.

William Basse

CONTENTS

FOREWORD

In the 1989/90 season Len Arbery won the *Angling Times* Drennan Cup. Although my own company sponsors this event, I can say without reservation that it is the top award any big fish angler can receive.

The competition has no points or scoring system, just the ultimate panel of judges: that is, all the country's top big fish anglers who have previously been weekly or annual winners in the event. The structure is such that to win, you have to have had an amazing season and clocked up lots of big fish. You must also have had a long and respected track record of catching specimens by design, because top anglers won't vote for any one fish wonder. The 14lb barbel and 6lb chub that topped Len's 1989/1990 season were spectacular enough to last most anglers a lifetime, but it was his track record of so many big fish over so many years that really pulled in the votes from his fellow experts.

Genuine experts are strange beings, and they are invariably generous with their information; thus instead of jealousy guarding their hard-won expertise, they'll help anyone and tell anyone anything. However, to write an enjoyable book on angling that will actually help the reader catch more fish is very difficult. Angling is such a vast subject, and with so many variables, that few of its rules can be set in stone. To do it properly, the writer needs a broad-based and balanced expertise in order to lead the reader towards more and bigger fish. Len's recently published *Complete Book of River Fishing* did just that, and was both informative and an excellent read. Similarly this new book will definitely help the reader catch more tench.

Some angling writers are all technical, paying minute attention to tackle and technique; others are all watercraft, and their books are full of illustrative examples and anecdotes. Len successfully combines method, watercraft and attention to detail. This book has a balanced approach born of his vast experience of catching tench in all waters under all conditions using a wide range of techniques. It will help anglers at all levels to catch more tench, and will increase their enjoyment in doing so.

Len is unquestionably a genuine angling expert: he is respected and liked throughout the sport; he has the broad-based experience, not just concerning tench, but many species. He is also a considerable angling historian and a first-class engineer. It is this background which gives him the overview, and enables him to write such informative and enjoyable books. This volume is undoubtedly no exception.

Peter Drennan
Oxford
December, 1995

ACKNOWLEDGEMENTS

I would like to thank all those who have enriched my life: Bob Buteux, Bill Quinlan, Kevin Clifford, Ron Chant, the late Jack Hilton, and the late Alec Lewis; My son Tony; Pete Cranstoun; Ritchie McDonald; Bob James and Bob Baker, Roger Smith, Kerry Barringer, Alan Atkins, Les Bamford and Vic Cranfield, all of the Carp Society. Then, in addition, there are those who have helped make fishing so memorable: Dave Ball; Edward Barder; Alan Brown; Stuart Bruce; Brian Culley; Peter Drennan; John Everard; Pete Frost; Richard Graham; Harry Green; Steve Harper; Bob Harrington; Ken Hodder; Stef Horak; Tony Miles; Bob Moulsey; Mick Newland; Pete Reading; Chris Sandford; Jim Soden; Pete Springate; Dave Steuart; Dave Swallow; Alf Tapley; Dave Tissington; Stan Twinane; Trefor West; Newall White; Chris Yates; Pete Young; and last, but by no means least, to living angling legends and great friends, 'Old Uncle Fred' and 'Old Stoney': to the uninitiated, Fred J. Taylor and Peter Stone. To these, and to all those others who have made fishing, for me at least, the most absorbing and enjoyable of leisure pursuits, I extend my heartfelt thanks.

I'd also like to extend my thanks to the following for their invaluable assistance and expertise in the preparation of this book: to the staff of that important magazine *Improve Your Coarse Fishing*, especially Neil Pope, Kevin Wilmot, Andrew James and Bob Atkins. To Colin Dyson, one of the most respected voices in angling and once editor of *Coarse Angler*, not only for allowing extracts from that magazine, but also for the help and encouragement he gave me when my first fishing articles were penned. To Simon Roff of *Coarse Fisherman*. To Kevin Clifford, for allowing me to quote some of his work. To Tim Paisley of *Angling Publications*, and Chris Ball of *Carp Talk*. To Dr Barry Rickards and Martin (Lucky) Locke for all their help. To Marsh Pratley and Phil Smith of NASA, and to the Tenchfishers for their help with

Janet Jackson – the reliable half of the partnership!

the tench lists. Also to Bob Baker of Streamselect for his support through the years.

To the suppliers of photographic material, who include those princes amongst angling photographers Bill Quinlan, Tony Arbery, Bob Atkins, Bob Buteux, Pete Jackson and his wife Janet Jackson (the reliable half of the partnership!), Bob James, Kevin Clifford and Ron Chant.

I am also very grateful to Dr Bruno Broughton, Peter Drennan and Kevin Clifford for their scientific advice, and their help in various other ways.

Finally to the contributors: Bob Buteux, Tony Arbery, Pete Jackson, and especially Bill Quinlan who has been such an inspiration down the years. Bill's piece on estate lakes (Chapter 7) wasn't written for general publication, and I had to 'twist his arm' to get the necessary permission – and it was well worth the effort, also to Peter Drennan, for penning the Foreword. May I take this opportunity to extend my sincere thanks to you all.

Len Arbery
Uxbridge
December 1995

INTRODUCTION

When taking my first tottering steps along the big-fish angling path it was rare to meet another of like mind. In fact, mainly because the pursuit was in its infancy, I listened to a great deal of bad advice and became discouraged. Motor-cycles and motorbike racing captured my interest, then the opposite sex came along and I dropped angling altogether. It wasn't until I was married and with a couple of children that I took up angling again. A chance meeting with Dave Short, an old motorcycling friend, led to us going fishing together.

A couple of years later, through a stroke of marvellous good fortune, I met Bill Quinlan. In those days Bill and his fishing companions – notably Bob Buteux, Jack Hilton and Roger Smith – were at the very top of the tree. That first meeting was an event in itself, because Bill actually turned up: I was to learn, and quite quickly, that for being unreliable Bill was unsurpassed. He didn't turn up for our next meeting, and for the one after that Dave and I arrived early and waited outside until he *did* come; actually we were so keen we'd probably have waited all night. When he showed us his carp tackle, however, we realized ours was totally inadequate; nevertheless he told us where we could purchase equipment and suggested a couple of waters. The upshot is that I am sitting here writing this today – so blame Bill!

Through Bill I met the aforementioned Bob Buteux, Jack Hilton and Roger Smith, and also the other members of the famed Herts-Chiltern Specimen Group. What a tremendous group of anglers to mix with, anglers of the highest calibre: Alec Lewis, Peter Frost, Frank Guttfield, Bob Carter – with friends and mentors like that, who could fail?

Peter Drennan (right) *presents the Drennan Cup to the author.*

Len Head's 1975 brace was such headline news that Anglers' Mail's Roy Westwood *travelled out specially for his pics.*

Big carp were, and are, my first love, but any big fish, apart from eels, excite me; and particularly big tench. I am also interested in the historical side of the sport, and sit on the British Record (rod-caught) Fish Committee. The highlight of my fishing career was winning outright, for the 1989/90 season, the most prestigious and coveted award in big-fish angling, the Drennan Cup.

Learning to appreciate and cope with the problems involved and associated with catching big fish consistently, takes much time and effort, and involves a certain amount of hard work. With the present hectic pace of life, many anglers have no wish to go to such lengths – but all I can say to such people is that they are missing a great deal, and hope this book will provide an insight, and some shortcuts, to the delights of big-fish angling. My own angling career has been spent in the pursuit of big fish in both still and running water, and I wouldn't have missed either for anything!

Since time immemorial great catches have excited, influenced and fired anglers' imaginations, but it is only in relatively recent years that tench have really 'troubled the scorers'. I am old enough to remember the incredulity and rumpus

Blaber's Kennet monster of 12½ lb caused in the angling press, back in 1951; and then there was Laing's eleven-pounder of 1959, from a small pit at Wraysbury. But it was Pete Thomas' lost 'record' tench, described in print by his friend Dick Walker, and Fred J. Taylor's catches that first caught my interest. Then Barry Rickards' and Ray Webb's exploits fanned the flickering flame; and when Len Head caught *that* brace of Bures Lake tench in 1975 it was fully aroused: weighing 8lb 2oz and 7lb 1oz these fish might appear 'nothing special' by today's standards but, believe me, there were those that believed Len's great brace would never be equalled, let alone surpassed, and some wise heads were amongst them.

I realize that success within angling, as with most other matters once you are past the beginner stage, means different things to different people. Nevertheless, the main purpose of this book is still to try to help the angler who has already made the transition from being a 'novice', no matter what his age, who not only wants to succeed with tench, but also has the desire to catch much bigger fish than the norm. It is assumed that the reader will have at least a rudimentary knowledge of angling, therefore some everyday

Probably the last photo of Dick Walker; seen here with his long-time friend, Peter Stone.

angling terms are not explained; such explanations would increase unnecessarily the bulk of this work.

In his classic fishing book, *Still Water Angling*, Dick Walker laid down five basic essentials for the catching of big fish. As these 'essentials' are just as relevant today, it is important that we remind ourselves of them:

1. Locate the fish.
2. Don't frighten the fish.
3. Use the right tackle.
4. Fish at the right time.
5. Use the right bait.

As Dick explained, 'These are the five essentials, from what one might call a material point of view. I know that they do not cover the problem completely; what I want to stress is the importance of feeling your way to success, step by logical step. If you fish in this way, you are bound to succeed sooner or later.' Very wise words indeed, and ones which will be enlarged upon where appropriate.

If the hints, tactics, wrinkles and tips contained herein – the result of more than a quarter of a century spent hunting big fish – help you to put some big fish on the bank, my main purpose has been achieved. However, I hope this book also shows my respect and high regard for my family and for my friends. I may not have caught as many big fish as other anglers, but I've certainly been blessed with the very best of friends, and these are more important to me than any fish, no matter how big that fish may be. My best friend is June, my wife: she puts up with all manner of comings and goings both by night and by day, and she is so tolerant and understanding of the reasons behind me leaving her alone so often when I've been at the waterside.

So, may you all catch the tench of your dreams – as long as it's not as big as mine!

June Arbery brought the camera out to the lake for this shot.

1 MEMORABLE BIG TENCH

In answer to the question 'When was England's first double-figure tench caught?' most of England's tenchmen would almost certainly tell you that it was in 1975. However, although there is a degree of truth in this, it doesn't tell the whole story.

THE THORNVILLE ROYAL TENCH, 1801

We have to go back a very long time indeed to find the first reported double-figure English tench, right back to 1801, and this was perhaps the most famous big tench of all, the Thornville Royal. Without exception modern writers quote the account of the capture of this great tench given in William B. Daniel's three-volume work, *Rural sports*. In fact there is a different account in volume XI of Sir Charles Linnaeus' monumental work, *Natural History*, an account which is interesting enough, I think, to repeat here:

A piece of water at Thornville Royal, Yorkshire, which for several years had been ordered to be filled up, and for which purpose logs of wood, roots of trees, rubbish, etc had been thrown into it, being found useful, the steward was ordered to clear it out in November 1801. Persons were accordingly employed, and though almost choked up by weeds and mud, so that little water remained, and no person conceived any fish, except possibly a few large eels would be found; yet about two hundred brace of tench, of all sizes, and as many perch, were found; about ten brace of which were from three to four pounds weight each. After the pond was thought to be quite free, under some roots there seemed to be some animal, which was conceived to be an otter: the place was surrounded; and on opening an entrance among the roots, a tench was found of extraordinary form, having literally assumed the shape of the hole, in which he had, of course, for many, many, years been confined. His form was an irregular semicircle; his length, from fork to eye, was 2ft 9in; his circumference, to almost the tail, 2ft 3in; his weight, 11lb 9oz, his colour was also singular, as his belly was vermilion. This extraordinary fish, there being a sculptor in the house, was sketched, and a model taken of it. After being shown to many sporting men, it was carefully put into a pond; but either from confinement, or age or bulk, it only floated, and with difficulty, at last swam gently along. It was alive and well, when this account was taken at the end of the year 1801.

Being somewhat of a sceptic by nature, there are a couple of points which I find myself questioning in the Linneaus account. Twenty perch between 3lb and 4lb each seems rather too many big ones, and how does a tench measuring 2ft 9in (83cm) long, with a 2ft 3in (68cm) girth, weigh so little as 11lb 9oz? Compare these dimensions with those of a 14lb 3oz tench caught in June 1987, which were 2ft 1½in (64cm) long by 1ft 11½in (59cm) girth! The caption to the engraving in *Rural Sports* states that both length and girth of the Thornville Royal tench were 2ft 3in (68cm), which is somewhat more believable, but still rather more than I find credible. Perhaps the

5lb 14oz River Kennet tench.

then resident of the Thornville Royal estate, the famous – or should it be infamous? - Colonel Thornton himself, supplied the dimensions. For in 1805, in his book describing his angling in Scotland, he claimed to have caught a pike of almost 50lb, *and* perch of over 8lb!

MR BLABER'S 'RECORD' TENCH, 1951

Now let us move on 150 years, and from York-shire to Berkshire's River Kennet, where we find my second memorable tench. On Sunday 11 February 1951, a roach angler from Willesden, London, caught a fish whose renown was to reverberate around the angling world for years to come – in fact in some circles it still does. The angler in question, Mr R. Blaber, reported to the *Anglers' News* (sadly now defunct) that on that winter's day he had caught, on a redworm, a tench whose stomach was distended 'almost to the size of a football' and which weighed no less than 12lb 8oz. As if a spawn-filled tench from a river in mid-winter wasn't unusual enough, Mr Blaber went on to say that he hooked a second huge tench, though subsequently lost it after a prolonged battle.

Because the fish was witnessed by three inde-pendent anglers and the weighing scales were checked and found to be accurate, it was accepted by the *Anglers' News* as the new record tench. But a storm of protestations invaded the letter pages, with two main areas of dissension emerging: one school believed the fish wasn't a tench, the other that the fish was diseased, prob-ably dropsical. Because no photographs were available and the fish was returned alive, these matters could not be determined and, indeed, remain unresolved to the present day.

Personally I believe that an error was made somewhere along the line. During the past twen-ty-five years I have fished the Berkshire Kennet regularly and, unlike many other venues, its tench have not shown much, if any increase in size. In fact my friends and I have accounted for plenty of Kennet tench, but apart from one soli-tary specimen of 5lb 14oz, have yet to witness or catch any other over 5lb. Now, the Kennet and Avon canal is another matter entirely, and it is a strong possibility that Mr Blaber was fishing close to a junction of river and canal, which cir-cumstance could throw an entirely different light on his fish. Unfortunately we will never know.

Whatever the truth of the matter, there was bound to be a certain amount of scepticism. Just consider the following analogy: at the time of Mr Blaber's twelve-and-a-half-pounder the record stood at 8lb 8oz, a tench caught from a Leicester canal during a match by Mr M. Foode the previ-ous August. Could you imagine the incredulity today if someone was to claim a new tench record with a fish *50 per cent* heavier than Gordon Beavan's current best? Even in the existing climate of rapidly increasing records, a tench in excess of 20lb would take some believing, don't you think?

In the 28 July 1951 issue, although remaining at the head of their notable fish list for the season 1950–1, the *Anglers' News* stated that despite Mr Blaber's conformation to all the rules the committee had decided that, since the tench had been abnormal, it could not be accepted as a new record, and Mr M. Foode's fish remained at the head of the list.

DONALD LAING'S UNACCEPTED ELEVEN-POUNDER, 1959

My next memorable tench is one of 11lb exactly. It was caught on breadflake by a seventeen-year-old from Moor Farm Wraysbury, Donald Laing, who had never caught a tench in his life before. Donald was using an old rod, 10lb bs line, and fished in 10ft (3m) of water. Unlike the case of the Blaber tench, photographs were taken, one being published on the front page of *Angling Times*, in the issue of Friday 7 July 1959. This proves the fish was indeed a tench, heavy with spawn. Even though the Record Fish Committee's rules at the time did not cover such a contingency, it was decided that fish suffering from abnormal conditions would not be awarded 'record' status. They decided tench carrying spawn were indeed abnormal, so young Donald Laing's fish was denied record recognition on a technicality.

LEWIS BROWN'S TEN-POUNDER, 1975

Finally a double-figure tench was caught in 1975 whose authenticity did satisfy the British Record Fish Committee and, indeed, every tenchman in the country. I refer, of course, to the 10lb 1oz 2dr specimen caught by Lewis Brown, of Peterborough. Here, at long last, was a healthy 'double' caught intentionally.

The venue was a brick pit not far from Lewis' home. He arrived shortly after dawn on Sunday 3 August, which turned out to be an exceptionally hot day. By 6.15am he was fishing the near bank drop-off, with float tackle – I nearly said with traditional float tackle, but in fact there was very little which was traditional about his set-up: his line was no less than 8lb bs and he employed a size 6 hook because he knew the pit contained enormous tench. Fishing about one-and-a-half rod lengths out, and overdepth so that his worm bait lay hard on the bottom, Lewis missed the first two bites. He then switched to a small section of worm which promptly produced a nice sailaway bite and one with which he successfully connected. Five anxious minutes later his prize was safely netted and dragged ashore, the landing-net handle bent beyond repair in the excitement. Later Lewis told Len Head that he expected his record to be short-lived, beaten by another tench from the same water; but that event did not materialize.

THREE GREAT TENCH FOR 1981

It was not until June 1981 that the next double-figure tench was caught, and then there were three of them! The largest at 10lb 10oz fell to the rod of Denis Kelly, and came from a Cheshire mere. Denis was employing maggot and feeder legering tactics, using 6lb bs line and a size 12 hook. The huge tench was by far the biggest specimen in a bag made up largely of tench in the 5–6lb class. It was heavy in spawn and, commendably, immediately returned to the water after weighing to prevent unnecessary stress. An unselfish act that ruled out any record claim. Denis said later that in his view, no fish in such condition should be considered for record status anyway.

Nor did the next biggest tench of 1981 figure in the record books. It came from Wilstone Reservoir but was unfortunately foul-hooked in a ventral fin. The captor, Richard Francis, having established with the committee that fish hooked outside the mouth were ineligible, made no claim.

Almost a week earlier Tony Chester had also been fishing Wilstone Reservoir for its giant tench. Tony used to fish local waters only, until a friend captured a 7lb 9oz tench from Wilstone the previous year. He was with two friends, Roy Ecob and Dick Wollaston, as well as Lester Strudwick whom they met on the bank. This was to be a longish session of several days' duration, so all four anglers employed 'bed-and-buzzer' tactics, bivvies pitched in a line along the 'poplars' area, with worms and maggot the main baits.

On the opening morning Roy was the first to score with a fish of 6lb 9oz. About twenty hours later, in the middle of the night, the second tench came to Lester's rod, and upped his personal best to 9lb 2oz. Within minutes of sorting everything out after this capture it was Tony's turn, at 7lb 3oz his biggest tench yet. Tony was ready to return home there and then – but I'll bet he's glad he didn't because an hour later his alarm sang out again. The fight lasted about four minutes and Lester, wielding the landing net, soon had an enormous tench gasping on the grass. Two sets of Avon scales gave identical readings: 10lb 2oz. The fish was claimed as a record, and accepted at 10lb 1oz 4dr.

JOE DARVILLE'S 10lb 10oz RECORD, 1984

Three years slipped by before Tony's big tench was surpassed. This time it was Hertfordshire big-fish specialist, Joe Darville's, turn for tench fishing glory. The weather was evidently diabolical, teeming rain driven by strong westerly winds. As evening approached it improved, however, and by six o'clock it was muggy and quite oppressive.

Joe was fishing alone, using 11ft carbon rods, ABU Cardinal 54 fixed-spool reels, loaded with 6lb line and size 6 Jack Hilton hooks. His bait was high-protein paste on the right-hand rod, whilst an air-injected lobworm completed the left-hand outfit. The paste was fished on the top of a bar about three rod-lengths out, in 3ft (1m) of water, the worm at the nearside bottom of the bar in 10ft (3m) of water.

Joe had waited some time and was pondering a change when the left-hand buzzer sounded and line trickled slowly off the spool. After first flicking over the bailarm, Joe struck and the rod slammed over. The hooked tench made three or four determined runs before being subdued, and as it at last slid over the net Joe thought, 'A nine-pounder, at last!' But it didn't weigh 9lb, in fact

Joe Darville and his 10lb 10oz ex-record tench.

list only exists. For information on the BRFC, and guidelines for claimants, see the Appendix.)

NASA accepted Joe's claim and his fish held the record for a year. His ambition was to regain it, but it was not to be: sadly, Joe Darville died prematurely.

ANOTHER RECORD TENCH FOR WILSTONE RESERVOIR, 1985

In June 1985 Wilstone Reservoir regained its record tench status, the fortunate angler this time being Alan Wilson, from Blackpool. Alan arrived at Wilstone on 23 June 1985; he teamed up with Tony Chaffey from the Isle of Wight, and together they fished the famous 'point' swim. From here Alan had considerable success in the past, in fact taking a personal best tench of 9lb 6oz from this very pitch the previous year.

Alan and Tony made use of a small boat to position their groundbait accurately; this consisted of breadcrumb, sweetcorn, maggots and lobworms. Alan's tackle consisted of 1¼lb test 11ft carbon rods, ABU Cardinal 55 fixed-spool reels loaded with 8lb bs mono; he used lobworm and maggot hookbaits, whilst Tony tried lobworm and sweetcorn. After Tony had unaccountably missed a slow, steady bite on sweetcorn, Alan switched to corn himself, nicking two grains on the hook and placing it tight to a snag in 9ft (2.7m) of water. In his own words:

At 6.10am the indicator on the corn rod flickered into life and climbed deliberately to the butt ring. My strike brought a big thump on the other end, but I didn't know whether it was a tench. After seven or eight minutes I had it halfway back, and then it took off on a really determined run for the snag; I was thankful for the 8lb line because I had to clamp down hard and only just turned it away from danger at the last minute. Then I saw it for the first time, and knew that at least it was a tench , and not a bad one! It set off on further deep, short runs, but at last began to tire, giving us a much better look at

the balance didn't stop until it read an amazing 11lb 3oz! After deducting 9oz for the weighsling, the actual weight of the tench, a female, was 10lb 10oz.

Joe first managed to contact his close friend, Steve Howard, who in turn contacted three other experienced Lea Valley anglers to act as witnesses. All four together with Joe witnessed a reweighing, and photographs were taken. There followed a short discussion as to whether Joe should claim the British Record (rod-caught) Fish Committee (BRFC) record, or that of the National Association of Specialist Anglers (NASA); eventually they decided on the latter since all NASA required was a photograph and an affadavit, plus independent witnesses of course. This course of action meant the fish wouldn't have to be retained any longer. (In those days there were two separate and distinct lists for coarse fish, but since then common sense has prevailed and NASA now provides – through the good offices of the National Federation of Anglers (NFA) - delegates to the BRFC, and one it – and it did look huge! Eventually it came up to the surface and lay on its side gasping. For an anxious moment or two it balanced on the rim of the net, then at last Tony coaxed it into the mesh.

Climbing back up the steep bank sides at Wilstone with only one hand, with a big landing net and a big fish clutched in the other, isn't easy! But between us we managed to get fish and netsman to the top. Tony carried the fish to a soft, grassy place to unhook it, and then we put it into the weighbag, hooked it to the scales and hoisted it up. We counted in unison 'eight, nine, ten, eleven, twelve!' Until finally it came to rest between 12lb 8oz and 12lb 9oz – and with that I gave out a mighty whoop of delight!

The late Peter Tombleson was at that time secretary to the BRFC and came out in person to weigh and witness Alan Wilson's fish; so obvi-ously, there was no room for dissension when this huge tench was accepted as the record at 12lb 8oz 11dr.

THE MONSTER FROM WRAYSBURY 1, 1987

Some predicted that Alan Wilson's record tench would last for years, perhaps for ever; but two short years later, in June 1987 it was shattered in no uncertain terms. Phil Gooriah was the fortu-nate captor and here is his own account, as told to me at the time:

I arrived at Leisure Sport Angling's water, known as Wraysbury 1 fishery, on Friday evening, 25 June 1987. Having first raked the chosen swim and set up the rods, I sat down to recover from my exertions. A cigarette had a calming influence and set me dreaming of a double-figure tench which my

Another of Alan Wilson's Wilstone whackers.

'No room for dissension' – Alan Wilson's ex-record tench was weighed by BRFC Secretary, Peter Tombleson.

brother Vigay and I had often considered a possibility from this venue – I could see it in my mind's eye, swimming in the water just before me. Vigay and I had concluded that a 10lb-plus tench was a realistic objective – but neither of us had the slightest notion that the dream was soon to become a reality.

Saturday morning came and went, and despite regular baiting up, we had only one immature perch to show for it. By mid-afternoon I had stripped down to just tee-shirt and slacks because it was so incredibly hot and humid – conditions which nevertheless gave me renewed confidence, as this was the sort of weather I believed was needed to get the tench to move onto the shallows where I was fishing.

I had a couple of line bites which I suspect were from bream and had me striking at thin air, then a brief tussle with a nice fish which ended prematurely when the hook pulled

out: a great disappointment. So ended that period of action.

The expected evening feeding spell didn't materialize, and in the oppressive heat, and no doubt helped by a lack of sleep the previous night, I dozed off. Then a single bleep from the Optonic on the left-hand rod startled me, and as I roused myself, I noticed two things at once: the soft half-light of dawn; and the beta-light butt-indicator as it shot up to the rod, accompanied by a continual scream from the Optonic. As I stood with the hooped-over rod in my hand, a smile came over my face – when I'm fishing I do like to be woken by the 'dawn chorus' or, better still, by the Optonic's song, and this particular day was heralded by both.

My watch read 4:45am. The fight at this stage was not really typical of tench, and my first thought was that a bream was responsible. When the fish came to the surface I drew

Phil Gooriah and his 14lb 3oz, Wraysbury 1, ex-record.

it gingerly towards the waiting landing net, and in the gloom saw it was no bream but a huge tench, its belly the size of a football. At this moment the fish righted itself and the line, which somehow had caught round its fins, came free – this, I suspect, is what drew the fish to the surface prematurely – and it shot off to the right, under my other rod, obviously trying to reach the cover of an overhanging tree whose branches trailed in the water just there. To cut a long story short, it tried to reach this refuge three or four times, but each time side-strain from my end defeated it; after a fight lasting about five minutes, I managed to land it.

As I opened the mesh to gaze upon my prize, I was absolutely staggered by its sheer size; my hands were shaking so much it was a minute or two before I could steady them enough to remove the hook which was lodged in the left-hand corner of its mouth.

Once this operation was accomplished, I put the landing net together with the tench onto an old set of Thomas Salter scales ... whack! the pointer went down, and down, until it read an incredible 15½lb. Allowing for the weight of the landing net, I knew the tench must be around 14lb, a new record – and by a mile! No words of mine will ever express how I felt at that moment; total elation enveloped me!

The big tench was taken along to where my brother was fishing and we weighed it again, only more accurately this time; we now made it 14lb 5oz. [Subsequently, the balance used in this weighing was checked by a weights and measures inspector and found to be 2oz (57g) out, so the actual weight was 14lb 3oz.] Neither my brother nor I, nor any of the other witnesses – Peter Springate, Dave Goy, Peter Welford, Peter Thatcher and others – who eventually assembled to see the fish, could believe the tench was so heavy, so it was weighed yet again, this time on a set of Kevin Nash scales: these made the weight 14lb 3oz. For the record, its length was 25½in (64cm), and its girth 23in (59cm).

The capture of this fish confirmed my belief that Wraysbury 1 has a relatively small head of very big tench, a contingency which is due. I think, to the large number of specimen-sized pike present – these keep the stock density of tench low, allowing the survivors to grow to record proportions as a result.

Perhaps not surprisingly, many experienced big-fish men stated categorically that Phil Goori-ah's monster could not be bettered, anyway not in the foreseeable future. However, I for one believed the 14lb 3oz record to be anything but inviolable, and said as much in *Angling Times*. And so it proved when in September 1993, Londoner Gordon Beavan caught the current record of 14lb 7oz from a Colne Valley water. A report of this fish's capture will be found in Chapter 10.

SPECIMEN TENCH – A RECENT PHENOMENON

It is clear that tench are now bigger than they have ever been before; in fact the sheer size of tench caught nowadays is astonishing to many long-time tench anglers. As far back as 1954, Harry Brotherton listed just thirty-three known tench of 6lb and over, the biggest being M. Foode's 8lb 8oz specimen, and had this to say:

The minimum weight for entries of tench in the Notable Fish List, published annually by *The Anglers' News*, is 3lb 12oz. From 1946 to March 1953, 238 such tench were entered, the season 1952–3 providing the greatest number, that is, fifty. This number included one fish of 6¼lb and one 6lb fish; two 5¾-pounders; one of 5lb 9oz; five of 5½lb; one of 5¼lb, and one of 5lb 2oz. There were also

four five-pounders and eight of more than 4½lb.

Even up to and including the early 1970s five-pounders were the target and a six-pounder the fish of a lifetime for most tench anglers. I well remember my very good friend Bill Quinlan's years of frustration trying to catch a six-pounder without success and Bill was, and still is, one of the very best tench anglers around. When at long last Bill succeeded and caught his elusive six-pounder in 1977, the gilt of the occasion was tarnished somewhat because I'd caught our first-ever seven-pounder earlier that very same morning! It was then that Bill and I knew for certain that big tench were being caught in greater numbers than ever before.

The overriding questions at present must be as follows: have these larger specimens always been here just waiting to be caught? Or has a relatively recent occurrence (or occurrences) caused an explosion in the optimum size of tench? Remember, the first fully authenticated 9lb-plus tench was caught in 1963 (9lb 1oz, by John Salisbury of Cambridgeshire, from Eggetts Lake at Hemingford Grey) but there have been hundreds of over 9lb caught since then. I have put these questions to tench anglers up and down the country, and some of their ideas make interesting reading:

1. The late coming of spring in recent years accounts for the tench spawning later, therefore more fish are carrying eggs when the season begins and so more gravid, heavier fish are caught as a result. (Despite the law being changed in 1995, the close season still remains sacrosanct on many stillwaters.)
2. Increasingly anglers have a more rational approach to tactics, and have more available time; this new generation is searching for and catching bigger tench.
3. Baits are better, and their application is better understood. Home-bred maggot, caster or sweetcorn, fished in conjunction with feeder tactics, account for a good many of the very big tench caught nowadays; so do well thought-out HNV boilies and pastes.

4. The nation's insatiable appetite for sand and especially gravel to build longer and wider motorways and suchlike has resulted in the excavation of many pits that provide a more suitable environment for the growing of 7lb-plus tench than the longer-established, more natural waters.

5. Anglers as well as other predators are reducing the stocks of all fish, and tench possibly being affected least of all are taking full advantage of the reduced competition for the food available. The effects of pollution or the infamous 'perch disease' which decimated the stocks of this species countrywide, must also be included in this theory. Furthermore newly created waters are usually less than fully stocked for many years. Another circumstance which probably means a surfeit of food for the relatively few fish that do exist in such waters.

6. More and more tench are being moved from one area to another by water authorities, associations, angling clubs and fish farmers to supply the demands of anglers the length and breadth of the land. This provides a source of new blood to local strains which over countless generations may have become too interbred for optimum growth.

Faster growing and therefore perhaps potentially bigger tench may also have been introduced from abroad. After World War II, before import regulations were imposed to restrict the importation of fish and so also possible fish diseases, fish, including tench, were brought into England on a much larger scale. It has long been reputed that much bigger tench than ours exist in waters in Europe's mainland: J. Travis Jenkins in his book *The Fishes of the British Isles* (Frederick Warne, 2nd edition 1958) makes this statement: 'The tench attains a weight of 8lb in England; on the Continent it grows to a length of 28 inches and a weight of 17lb'. I consider that a 28in (71cm) long tench really *would* be some fish, particularly if you remember that Phil Gooriah's 14lb 3oz ex-record tench was just 25½in (64cm) long!

Perhaps all the foregoing ideas – plus others not mentioned – have some bearing on the phenomenon. However, none except the last two (5 and 6) explain the fact that tench appear to be outstripping the potential size of other species in the same water. For example, although there certainly has been an increase in the numbers of 25lb pike and 10lb bream taken in recent years (these weights, I feel, are roughly comparable with 7lb tench), several fish of these proportions always have been caught. However, this just isn't so in the case of 7lb tench: prior to 1960 there were only four authentic seven-pounders recorded, but recently I've had five over this weight in one session.

The Top Fifty Tench Lists – 1983 and 1995
To further illustrate that the existence of really big tench in this country is a relatively recent phenomenon, compare the two lists shown of the top fifty tench, the first was published in *Coarse Angler* magazine in July 1983; the other was collated and compiled for NASA by the Tenchfishers, accurate as at 29 September 1995. I am indebted to both organizations, and Marsh Pratley in particular, for supplying the latter and permitting its reproduction here. From the 1982 list only three tench have retained their status some thirteen years later: Denis Kelly's 10lb 10oz fish, in the list proper, plus Blaber's Kennet fish of 12lb 8oz; and Laing's eleven-pounder from the footnote. Moreover nowadays it takes a fish of 10lb 5oz or over to make the list at all, so the record in 1982 – Tony Chester's fish of 10lb 1oz 4dr from Wilstone – doesn't even qualify.

The late Colin Graham was responsible for compiling a 1982 'Coarse Angler's Top Fifty Tench' list; a year later the list was revised and updated by my good friend Kevin Clifford. In his article published at the same time, Kevin also had something to say regarding the possible reasons for the undoubted increase in the size of tench:

Whilst attempts have been made to ensure that the *Coarse Angler* lists are as comprehensive as possible, it is obviously a fact that there are bound to be some omissions for one reason or another. With almost all other species I feel these omissions have been kept to a minimum, but with tench the list is incomplete to a much greater extent.

Could it be that big tench are becoming so prevalent that some people have become blasé about reporting them? Be that as it may, the existing list does show clearly and undeniably that the general size of tench has dramatically increased in recent years. It is sobering to realise that prior to 1950 only two tench over 7lb had been recorded. There are of course some examples of the same fish appearing more than once in the list, as we have seen in the lists of other species. For example Roy Ecob's 9½-pounder from Wilstone was the same fish caught a year later at 10¼lb, and a fish just hovering under 9lb was caught on a number of occasions from the A40 pit at Oxford, before being killed intentionally in 1982.

However, it is the overall increase in numbers of fish over 6lb, not long ago considered exceptional and now commonplace, which shows unquestionably that some sort of change has taken place.

There have been various theories put forward to explain why tench should suddenly increase in size within the last ten to twenty years or so, but none in my opinion offers the complete answer. I think it would be fair to say that these theories can be summarized as follows:

1. Improved tactics and baits: for example, long-range feeder techniques, HNV 'boilies' and sweetcorn (while it lasted).
2. Recent increased angling pressure on productive big-tench waters, for example the A40 pit, Tring Reservoirs and Yateley.
3. Better strains of tench being stocked since the early 1970s when fish imports suddenly expanded.
4. More natural food becoming available during the late 1960s and early 1970s due to the decimation of some roach and perch populations, caused by disease. For example the 'Marsh' in Norfolk, and Drax pond in Yorkshire.
5. Further enrichment of fisheries with nutrients from increased use of fertilizers.
6. Large-scale baiting campaigns offering readily available, quality feed.

I tend to feel that all these reasons, and perhaps others, are the cause of the increase in the size of tench, and that no one factor is generally responsible. Jim Gibbinson, whose authoritative writing has enriched (couldn't resist that) angling for so many years, suggested in the June 1982 issue of *Coarse Angler*, that the reason was the sudden eutrophication from agricultural chemicals in the late 1970s of understocked gravel pits. Whilst it is true that there has been a degree of eutrophication, I do not feel that the scientific evidence substantiates the view that this could be the main cause, although it may be on specific waters.

Allow me to elaborate. There has been a fairly steep increase in the use of fertilizers by farmers since the late 1960s. The constituents of these fertilizers which are mainly involved in eutrophication are soluble nitrates and phosphates. It is generally accepted that the dramatic rise in nitrate levels in our rivers runs parallel and is caused by the increased use of fertilizer on the land.

Phosphate is much more readily taken up in the land, and there appears to be little evidence to suggest that very much is lost through drainage run-off. Levels of phosphate have increased in our rivers in recent years, more dramatically than those of nitrate, and this is almost certainly derived from treated sewage effluent. The phosphate comes in the main part from the breakdown of domestic and industrial detergents. Since most sewage is discharged directly into the river systems, it is difficult to see how it could end up in enclosed fisheries. There may be, however, cases where rivers flood into nearby pits and lakes, or seepage takes place through the gravel strata.

COARSE ANGLER'S TOP 50 TENCH JULY 1983

	Weight	Captor	Bait	Location	Date
*	10.10.0	D Kelly (Stoke-on-Trent)	maggot	Cheshire Mere	June 1981
**	10.4.0	R Francis (Pinner)	lobworm	Wilstone	June 1981
***	10.1.4	A Chester (Melton Mowbray)	lobworm	Wilstone	June 1981
	10.1.2	L Brown (Peterborough)	worm	Peterborough pit	Aug 1975
	9.13.0	unknown angler		N Yorkshire pond	July 1980
	9.11.0	R Seal (Farnborough)	sweetcorn	Frimley Leisure Sports	June 1978
	9.11.0	B Blower (Manchester)	maggot	Pickmere	Sept 1979
	9.8.4	R Taylor (Rugby)	sweetcorn	Lake at Newbold	June 1980
	9.8.0	R Fisher (East Malling)	bread	Johnson's lake, Kent	June 1981
	9.8.0	D Sharp (Whitchurch)	maggot	Salop lake	July 1981
	9.7.8	R Ecob (Melton Mowbray)	lobworm	Wilstone	June 1980
	9.6.0	P Lambert (S Harrow)	sweetcorn	Harefield lake	June 1978
	9.6.0	K Potten (Selby)	sweetcorn	Pond near Drax	July 1981
	9.6.0	F Guttfield (High Wycombe)	swan mussel	Whitbread's lake, Bedfordshire	July 1981
	9.4.0	P Goddard (Hitchin)	swan mussel	Whitbread's lake	June 1980
±	9.3.4	P Martin (Chertsey)	paste	Chertsey lake	Aug 1960
	9.3.0	L Strudwick (Cuffley)	lobworm	Wilstone	June 1981
	9.3.0	P Clements (Bradenhall)	sweetcorn	Yateley Leisure Sports	June 1982
	9.2.0	S Plumb (Banbury)	maggot	A40 pit, Oxford	July 1981
	9.2.0	J Parker (Kenley)		Wiremill lake, Surrey	Oct 1959
	9.2.0	S Clarke (Hatch End)	worm	Stocker's lake	Sept 1982
¥	9.2.0	B Wiseman (Kelvedon)	bread	Rivenhall lake	Sept 1963
¶	9.2.0	P Davidson (Bridgend)	paste	Kenfig Pool	June 1976
	9.2.0	A Burton (Luton)	crust	Bedfordshire lake	June 1980
	9.1.0	J Salisbury (Chatteris)	worm	Eggett's, Hemingford Grey	July 1963
	9.1.0	A Russell (Bracknell)		Folly's Pit, Berkshire	July 1979
	9.1.0	R Caldwell (London)	maggot	Broadwater lake	July 1982
	9.1.0	N James (Comberton)	maggot	Middlesex lake	July 1981
	9.1.0	K Mowberry (Guildford)	bread	Kent lake	June 1981
	9.0.0	G Young (Basingstoke)	paste	Berkshire pond	Oct 1964
	9.0.0	S Smith (Stockport)		Redesmere	Sept 1976
	9.0.0	S Barker (London)	worm	Cobham lake	July 1977
	8.14.0	J Shuksmith	particle	Southern gravel pit	July 1982
	8.14.0	S Plumb (Banbury)	lobworm	A40 pit, Oxford	June 1981
	8.13.0	G Elkington (Leicester)	lobworm	Home Counties stillwater	June 1982
	8.13.0	A Gidley (Maidstone)	particle	Johnson's lake, Kent	July 1982
	8.12.0	P Goddard (Hitchin)	swan mussel	Whitbread's lake, Bedfordshire	June 1980
	8.12.0	D Holmes (Telford)	maggot	Cheshire pool	Sept 1981

8.12.0	C Tyler (Witney)	sweetcorn	A40 pit, Oxford	July 1982
8.12.0	A Parker (Ditton)	sweetcorn	Johnson's lake, Kent	Jan 1983
8.12.0	P Pilley (Harrow)	snail	Middlesex lake	June 1970
8.12.0	C Tolley (Brierley)	maggot	Fen's pool, Staffs.	June 1974
8.12.0	D Boulstridge (Coventry)	maggot	A40 pit, Oxford	June 1980
8.11.0	F Jenkins (Broadstairs)		private Surrey lake	July 1978
8.11.0	D Turner	sweetcorn	Johnson's lake, Kent	July 1980
8.11.0	A Nickolson (Oxford)	worm	Dean's Farm	June 1981
8.11.0	D Clifton (Doncaster)	paste	Broxholme pond, Drax	Aug 1977
8.10.8	P Lindsey (Gillingham)	H. protein	Johnson's lake, Kent	June 1979
8.10.0	J Corrigan (Abingdon)	lobworm	Oxfordshire pit	July 1974
8.10.0	I Huckstepp (Ashford)	maggot	Radnor Park, Kent	Oct 1977
8.10.0	S Barrow (Leicester)	flake	West Orielton, Pembrokeshire	Aug 1980
8.10.0	M Pardoe (Liverpool)	maggot	Cheshire lake	June 1981
8.10.0	P Hammond (Sevenoaks)		Johnson's lake, Kent	Sept 1981
8.10.0	R Bone (Goole)	flake	Pond near Drax, Yorks	June 1976
8.10.0	P Goddard (Hitchin)	swan mussel	Whitbread's lake, Bedfordshire	June 1980
8.10.0	M Voller (London)	maggot	Long Life pit	June 1982
8.10.0	E Lucia (Barnhurst)	protein	Kent lake	July 1982

*   No record claim as Dennis feared that his fish, heavy with spawn, might die.

**   Record claim said to have been withdrawn when the fish was declared foulhooked.

***   Currently accepted as the record tench by the British Record (rod-caught) Fish Committee.

±   A record at the time . . . but no claim made as rules at the water demanded that all fish caught be returned immediately.

¥   Another potential record at the time but no claim was made. Fish reputedly slipped through the captor's hands when being transferred from scales to keepnet.

¶   The biggest Welsh tench.

Other large tench reported

*	12.8.0	R Blaber (Willesden)	red worm	River Kennet	Feb 1951
	12.0.0	Found in a lake		Burnham-on-Sea	1947
	11.9.8	Found when the lake was drained		Thornville Royal, Yorks.	1801
**	11.0.0	D Laing (Wraysbury)		Wraysbury pit	July 1959
***	9.9.12	W Dearsley		Wraysbury pit	July 1959

*   Returned to nearby pool. Not accepted as a record fish at the time as it was assumed it was in some 'abnormal condition' due to its swollen belly.

**   Again returned to the water, but subsequently not accepted for the same reason as the River Kennet fish.

***   This fish taken to the Zoological Society of London and kept in aquarium. It, too, had a distended belly and died some time later. It, too, was invalidated from Record status.

THE NASA TOP 50 TENCH AS AT SEPTEMBER 1995

No	Weight	Captor	Location	Date
1*	14.8.0	Gordan Bevan	Herts Lake	Sept 1993
2	14.4.0	Gary Newman	Bury Lake	Aug 1994
3**	14.3.0	Phil Gooriah	Wraysbury 1	June 1987
4	14.0.0	Alan Wilson	Wilstone Reservoir	June 1992
5	14.0.0	Gordan Bevan	Herts Lake	Sept 1993
6	13.7.0	Gary Newman	Bury Lake	Sept 1994
7	12.15.0	Gary Newman	Bury Lake	Sept 1994
8	12.13.0	Dean Franklin	Wilstone Reservoir	Sept 1995
9**	12.8.11	Alan Wilson	Wilstone Reservoir	June 1985
10***	12.8.0	R Blaber	River Kennet	Feb 1951
11	12.8.0	Cathy McCorkell	Startop Reservoir	June 1990
12	12.6.0	Alan Wilson	Wilstone Reservoir	June 1993
13	12.0.8	Rory Adair	Surrey Lake	July 1995
14	11.10.0	Bob Henderson	Wilstone Reservoir	June 1991
15	11.10.0	Roy Woodford	Wilstone Reservoir	June 1993
16	11.8.0	Larry Reeve	Surrey Lake	July 1994
17	11.8.0	Chris Stothard	Surrey Lake	July 1994
18	11.8.0	Del Smith	Horton Church Lake	July 1995
19	11.6.0	C Wylot	Home Counties Pit	1988
20	11.6.0	David Harman	Kent Water	Aug 1995
21	11.4.0	Graham Marsden	Cheshire Mere	July 1995
22	11.3.0	M Perkins	Kent Water	1988
23	11.3.0	G Stewart	Kent Water	Aug 1991
24	11.2.0	George Clark	Dorchester Lagoon	July 1994
25	11.1.0	S Lambard	Herts Pit	1985
26	11.1.0		Dinton Pastures	Sept 1987
27	11.0.0	D Laing	Wraysbury	1959
28	11.0.0	Andy Nellist	Wilstone Reservoir	June 1991
29	11.0.0	D Wood	Redesmere	July 1991
30	11.0.0	Bill Bowden	Queenford	July 1995
31	10.15.0	Chris Mayo	Wilstone Reservoir	July 1993
32	10.14.0	Chris Sullivan	Hampshire Pit	July 1995
33	10.14.0	Bob Bronger	Larkfield Fishery, Kent	June 1995
34	10.13.0	Alan Wilson	Wilstone Reservoir	June 1988
35	10.13.0	Martin Webb	Alder Lake	July 1994
36	10.12.0	K Machelti	Tottenhill Pits, Norfolk	Aug 1988
37	10.12.0	M Clements	Yateley	June 1990
38	10.12.0	Shaun Simpson	Wilstone Reservoir	Sept 1995
39	10.10.0	D Kelley	Cheshire Mere	June 1981
40**	10.10.0	J Darville	Herts Pit	June 1984
41	10.10.0	A Willis	Oxford Pit	June 1987
42	10.10.0	Chris Burt	Southern Water	June 1990

43	10.8.0	S Scales	Wilstone Reservoir	Aug 1986
44	10.8.0	D Head	Johnson's Lake	Jun 1990
45	10.8.0	Barry Harrod	Startop Reservoir	Aug 1992
46	10.8.0	Warren Gaunt	Wilstone Reservoir	July 1993
47	10.6.0	I Tester	Sutton-at-Hone	July 1987
48	10.6.0	D Penny	Berks Pit	June 1988
49	10.6.0	A Dempsey	Larkfield	Jan 1993
50	10.5.0	Ken Downes	Hollowell	July 1995

NOTES:
* Current British Record
** Previous British Record
***Not accepted due to 'abnormal condition'
(Thanks to members of the Tenchfishers for assistance in compilation of this list.)

Nitrogen levels in stillwaters are rarely limiting factors in their productivity, since most, if not all, can be assimilated from bacterial fixation. Indeed it has been proposed that additions of nitrates may stimulate denitrification and thereby work against eutrophication. Phosphate levels, however, are almost always the limiting factor, since they are rarely present in quantity naturally, and phosphate is easily and readily taken up in the bottom deposits of a water. Therefore it is almost invariably an increase in phosphates, primarily originating from sewage disposal, that is the direct cause of eutrophication. Enclosed waters which receive a direct input of treated sewage effluent, such as Tring Reservoirs, will obviously show effects of eutrophication. Gravel pits and lakes in close proximity to rivers, or those which derive their supply of water from rivers and streams carrying sewage effluent deriving from domestic, industrial or intensive livestock production, will again show varying degrees of eutrophication.

The last four seasons have produced 39 tench from a total of 57 on the second *Coarse Angler* list, suggesting that the 1983-4 season can produce another bumper crop, with a new record a distinct possibility. No doubt new waters will be 'discovered', but I expect already established big tench fisheries to dominate the forthcoming catches – Hertfordshire's Tring Reservoirs, Johnson's Lakes in Kent, the A40 pit at Oxford, Southill Park in Bedfordshire, Cheshire's Reedsmere, and that magnificent conglomeration of big fish waters centred around the sewage disposal carriers of the River Colne and Colne Brook, from Rickmansworth to Staines. And I nearly forgot the famous Yateley complex, situated alongside the tiny River Blackwater, which carries the effluent from at least four sewage works, those from Sandhurst, Camberley, Farnborough, and Aldershot. Reckon I might stop going in for those snagged up fish!

Kevin's reasoning is, as ever, logical and persuasive, and yet there are anomalies. Even bearing in mind all other possible reasons for the dramatic increase in size of tench given in this chapter, none stands up to close scrutiny when certain specific waters that produce large tench are considered. For example it may be that stocking with better strains of fast-growing tench is considered to be the most likely cause. However, this theory does not hold good for Southill Park Lake (also known as Whitbread's Lake or Twitchalot Pool). Southill has been renowned as a big-tench water since at least the 1950s and as far as can be

A Southill Park 'biggie' for Kevin Clifford.

ascertained hasn't had a relatively recent introduction of new tench stock; so why was it that in the summer of 1980 it started producing tench of 8lb and 9lb? This from a lake where, although fished by such notable tench anglers as Dick Walker, Peter Thomas, Bill Quinlan, Bob Buteux, Frank Guttfield and John Simpson, a 6lb tench was once considered to be a very notable capture. In fact from 1960 to 1965 the average weight of tench caught from Southill by Bob Buteux was almost 4lb; said, at the time, to be better than from any other water in the country!

Kevin Clifford tells me that it is his belief, formulated when he fished Southill in the early 1980s, that the bigger fish captured in that period are probably the same individuals as were caught previously at lesser weights. To substantiate this view it is as well to realize that Southill tench are no greater in length now than they have ever been, around 21 to 22in (53 to 56cm) for the biggies.

Then again, if rivers are carrying the chemicals that are responsible, why is it that *they* are not producing 8 and 9lb tench in numbers? A look at the lists again will confirm that, apart from Blaber's mystical Kennet monster, not one river fish is included. In fact in my experience of river tench, which I readily admit is limited, they are not getting any heavier at all. Although we have not fished it specifically for tench very much, the river Kennet has produced quite a few for my friends and I over the past thirty years, but in all that time I have witnessed only one tench over 5lb: a 5lb 14oz specimen which I caught in the winter of 1994–5. As an aside, and interesting enough for its own sake, is the fact that the Kennet's barbel and chub are indeed increasing in size, a fact which is also true of some other rivers.

Yet another question I've long pondered concerns the Colne Valley pits, which I do know fairly well having fished one or other of them for tench since about 1968: why is it that one water grows big tench, when an adjacent one, perhaps only separated from the first by a narrow spit of land, produces tench of only average proportions? Of course the stock each particular fishery contains must have some effect. For example a big head of carp may mean the tench don't get a surfeit of easily available food, preventing them reaching their full potential. And yet some of these pits with the most carp also grow the biggest tench.

All this I find very puzzling, and unless some carefully controlled experiments are carried out, perhaps of several years' duration, it seems unlikely we shall ever know for certain just why tench are getting so much heavier. As tench anglers, however, we should count ourselves fortunate in the extreme that the situation exists now, and take full advantage of it because, quite possibly, it could be a fleeting phenomenon, never to be repeated.

Because Kevin Clifford has been so much a part of this chapter, his is the final word:

There is a natural increase of nutrients in stillwaters regardless of anything man might do. Pure water, without nutrients and dissolved gases, exists only in the laboratory and is incapable of supporting life. Run-off from surrounding land, no matter how poor, the accumulation of sediment from surrounding trees and plants, the excreta of bankside and water-resident animals, even rain falling through the atmosphere: these all increase the availability of nitrogen, potassium and phosphate, and other nutrients, to the aquatic environment. This is a form of pollution in the strictest sense of the word, but is usually referred to as eutrophication. Human activity often speeds up this process and sometimes increases it to such an extent that obvious damage is done. Clearly, the level at which nutrients are added is important. In the right amount it can enrich an otherwise barren fishery, increasing its productivity, and making available vast quantities of food items for fish. Too much, and all the fish die, either due to de-oxygenation or by direct poisoning.

The eutrophication of stillwaters by man does have some benefits. Specifically, for instance, gravel pits, which often start life as poor in nutrients, often end up as highly productive fisheries. This usually means the fishery can support a greater biomass, usually reflecting itself in either more fish, or fewer, larger fish than would be the case otherwise. On the other hand, man-made eutrophication of some of our large lochs in Scotland and our lakes in the Lake District, is having serious detrimental effects upon the fish species and other forms of aquatic animal life which have evolved in that particular environment.

TENCH RECORDS SINCE 1950		
Angler	**Weight**	**Year**
M Foode	8lb 8oz	1950
John Salisbury	9lb 1oz	1963
Lewis Brown	10lb 1oz 2dr	1975
Tony Chester	10lb 1oz 4dr	1981
Joe Darville	10lb 10oz	1984
Alan Wilson	12lb 8oz 11dr	1985
Phil Gooriah	14lb 3oz	1987
Gordon Beavan	14lb 7oz	1993

2 PHYSIOLOGY OF THE TENCH

The famous Swedish naturalist, Linnaeus, gave the tench its scientific description in 1758, though it was known and used for food much earlier than that. He chose the name *Cyprinus tinca*, thus clearly recognizing its close relationship to carp. subsequently, however, the tench was considered far enough removed from other carp to be given its own generic name, and so became *Tinca tinca*, probably the best known, and most revered scientific name of any of our freshwater fish.

It seems inconceivable that anybody could confuse the tench with any other British species, and yet though not commonplace, errors have undoubtedly been made. I can only think of one reason, and that is that the people involved had never before seen a tench, or even a picture of one. Two distinct varieties occur in British waters: the golden tench, and the common or green tench, but it is the latter that is usually meant when referred to simply as 'tench'. There is also the rare vermilion tench; I have not witnessed this fish, and it is not clear to me whether it is a third distinct variety, or whether the colour of its tummy, from whence it gets its name, is an environmental factor. The famous Thornville Royal tench, mentioned in Chapter 1, was said to have been of this variety.

Vermilion tench should not be confused with common tench carrying the red blotches they sometimes do, especially around spawning times or if they have been crowded into keepnets. At one time this condition, which is known as 'red pest', seemed more prevalent than it is now. Probably the situation has improved these days because keepnets, retaining sacks and landing

Tinca tinca *(female)*.

nets are designed and manufactured from materials which are much more sympathetic to the welfare of fish.

THE GOLDEN TENCH

Golden tench are relatively rare, so much so that I have never seen one except in pictures or in a glass case. They are small fish, rarely attaining 4lb, but very beautiful, more yellow than golden, with a few irregularly shaped black spots situated haphazardly on body and fins.

The golden tench is not indigenous. According to the noted Victorian naturalist, Frank Buckland, it was introduced to this country by Sir Stephen Lakeman in 1862. Frank Buckland evidently acquired a quantity of these imports, reputedly from Germany, because in a letter to him in October 1880 Higford Burr of Aldermaston Park writes:

My Dear Buckland, – Do you recollect being here when I dragged the pond and gave a *déjeuner* to the Volunteers in September, 1862? It was shortly after that you sent me three gold tench, which if I recollect right, you told me were given to you by Sir Stephen Lakeman. I put those three tench into a pond by themselves; only two lived, but the survivors were luckily male and female. In November, 1864, I let the water off the pond in which they were, and I sent you several fish of 3in or 3½in long, the fry of 1864, evidently the fry of 1863, and a number the size of minnows.

The first time I ever saw gold tench was in Bohemia, between Eger and Carlsbad, in the year 1856. Whilst the horses of the *eilwagen* were changing I walked round the garden of the post, and there I saw two or three shoals on the surface. I saw they were not carp, and never before having seen or heard of gold tench, could not make them out; but subsequently talking of them to friends, I discovered that they were gold tench.

It was fortunate you gave these gold tench to me, for being quite by themselves they bred faster than if mixed with other fish; at least so it seems to me, for I do not hear from the many friends and others to whom I have liberally distributed them, that they have met with the results that have risen from the one pair you gave me. I have now two large ponds full of them, too full, in fact, for them to grow to a large size, but I have had them, from a small pond where there were but few, of 4lbs weight.

Higford Burr.

Higford Burr did indeed attempt to increase the distribution of golden tench; an extract from another of his letters, received by the Reverend W. Houghton on 8 May 1878, reads:

I have now a great number; what we catch with rod and line in summer I place in a small pond until cool weather sets in, when I am happy to distribute them to any gentleman who may apply for them.

It is therefore quite likely that the occasional specimens caught these days are descendants of the fish first introduced by Sir Stephen Lakeman so very long ago – although the Reverend W. Houghton in his book *British Freshwater Fishes* (Webb & Bower, 1981 edition) reports that a Mr Masefield set apart one of his ponds at Ellerton Hall for the breeding of golden tench. Frank Buckland in his work *The Natural History of British Fishes* (Society for Promoting Christian Knowledge, 1883) states: 'Golden Tench have also bred freely at Woburn Abbey and also in Norfolk.' What both Houghton and Buckland fail to tell us is where these fish originated from.

Zyg Gregorak's angling complex, Anglers' Paradise, at Beaworthy in North Devon, provides the chance of catching golden tench; and according to Barry Rickards and Bob Church, they inhabit some of the pits around Cambridge. It is a great pity there aren't more about, for most anglers, myself included, would regard such a beautiful fish as an asset to any stillwater.

THE COMMON TENCH: A DESCRIPTION

As anglers, it is the common tench that demands our particular attention. The adult is the most distinctive and easily recognized of all British freshwater fish so a full scientific description is not necessary here; a few brief notes may be helpful, however.

Tench vary in colour, and not only according to their environment or locality. A single water may produce tench where the body colour in different individuals spans all the more usual shades from almost black, through brownish-bronze, dark green, to a light golden-green – almost yellow. The scales of the latter seem to have a silhouette effect, enhanced by what looks like a very thin black border drawn round the extremities of each scale. This is a particularly attractive variety.

At one particular water where the difference between individuals was particularly noticeable, some anglers believed the darker-coloured specimens to be the patriarchs; the wizened appearance of these fish certainly added to the impression. This belief was erroneous, however: inevitably over the years we fished that water, some fish were repeatedly recaptured; but the lighter-coloured tench never did get noticeably darker with the passage of time. In my view it is more likely that the water in question was stocked more than once, from more than one source in its formative years, so the tench were of different backgrounds and, of course, genetically different too.

The colour of the tummy also varies: in some fish it is creamy-white, in others buff, and still others have a warm yellow to their underparts. The fins are all rather thick and 'fleshy'; they are ordinarily dusky blue or almost black, the female's neat and delicate, the male's larger and more powerful. The dorsal fin is short, and very high and rounded; the tail is shovel-like with hardly any noticeable vee. The eyes have a jewel-like, golden-red iris, and are proportionately rather small. The down-turned mouth has a single small barbule on each side, situated at the extremities of the top lip. A prominent lateral line runs the full length of the flank.

It really is fortunate that tench are so distinctive because if we had to rely on scale counts, used to define and distinguish some other fish species, we'd be in a great deal of trouble! Most authorities differ on even the most basic measurement, that being the number-range of scales in the lateral line. Holcik (1968) gives 87–115, Jones and Tombleson (1964) give 95–110, whereas the *Angling Times* publication, *Know Your Fish Guide* gives 95–120. What we do know for certain is that the scales are extremely small: Richter estimates that each individual has up to 30,000. These are covered with a copious coat of mucus which is not unpleasant to the touch, giving the tench a velvety feel.

The Visual Differences between the Sexes

In tench, the visual differences between the sexes is plainly evident, yet even with first-class photographs to help, some anglers still have difficulty. This is an important matter because the female grows so much bigger than the male, and the capture of, say, a 6lb male is therefore a more

This is a fine example of a male tench, caught by Bill Quinlan.

This fish is easy to recognize.

noteworthy event than that of a female of similar size.

Unlike any other British coarse fish, the differences can be seen at any time of the year. Although the females grow larger, they are neater and more streamlined in appearance than the male. Males have a distinctive lump on each flank immediately above the ventral (pelvic) fin; these lumps are evidence of the internal reproductive organs, the gonads. Males also have larger fins, particularly the ventrals which extend to, and sometimes beyond, the vent; they are of an exaggerated spoon shape and are equipped with a powerful first ray. Overall the appearance of the male could be said to resemble an underwater bulldog, with a heavy head set on powerful shoulders, and they certainly fight with the tenacity of a bulldog. The heaviest male I've seen on the bank weighed exactly 7lb, and was caught by

Kevin Clifford: Kevin doesn't mess about when it comes to playing big fish, but it still took him about twenty minutes to land this particular specimen.

The Recognition of Individual Fish

Nowadays the fact that individual fish can be recognized is well known, but it hasn't always been so. Way back in the late 1960s and early 1970s I, amongst others, noticed that individual fish could be recognized quite readily. In I think 1976 at the British Carp Study Group conference at Guildford, my friend Kevin Clifford and I presented a paper on the subject. Briefly, a fish's scale arrangement is rather like our fingerprints, in that each and every one is unique. Fully scaled fish are, however, difficult in the extreme to identify by scale arrangement alone, and tench are downright impossible.

The situation is eased somewhat by the fact that fish have a second set of 'fingerprints': their fins. The shape, position, colour, and the number of rays in the fins make identification reasonably certain, if not easy. Other miscellaneous features not already mentioned are facial lines, warts, spots, scars and other healed injuries; all of these aid identification – besides which the scientific community keeps reminding us that 'There is nothing unique in uniqueness!'

Good quality photographs are the key to all this, because a protracted and detailed examination at the time of capture will put an end to the subject's life and the phenomenon under discussion. In recent years anglers have become much more aware of the fact that the same fish is likely to be caught more than once in its lifetime, and some will be captured many times. Consequently, as I have already said, fish recognition is now accepted, and practised more widely than ever before. This is a positive and good reaction, for it underlines the need for conservation, and makes anglers aware just how relatively few big fish are in our waters. And if it does anything to minimize the number of fish stolen and/or illegally stocked elsewhere, that will be an invaluable bonus.

Hermaphroditism
Because the weight differential is so huge at one time I proposed that male tench should have their own 'record', separate and in addition to the existing list. As males are so easily distinguished from the females, I argued, what is the problem? The problem as I have since found out for myself, is that things can be very different from what they appear to be at first glance: the sexing of tench is no exception and there are anomalies to be considered.

In his excellent book *Tench* (The Crowood Press, 1986), Len Head tells of the heaviest 'male' tench caught from Bures Lake in Suffolk. This specimen was witnessed by several very experienced and knowledgeable tench anglers as well as by Len himself, so there could be no

A possible hermaphrodite caught by Bill Quinlan.

Male and female tench – the lower fish being the female.

doubting its sex ... So why was it that when this same fish was caught the following season, it was carrying spawn!

My very good friend, Bill Quinlan, once caught what was regarded by the informed anglers present (including yours truly) to be a very big male; photographs of this tench clearly show bulges on the flanks indicative of the gonads. However, the photographs also clearly show what we had not noticed at the time of capture: the small, neat fins belonging to a female. Len Head has recounted witnessing tench displaying similar conflicting characteristics on two separate occasions.

Are these and other fish like them, hermaphrodites? Perhaps we will never know for certain, even though instances of hermaphrodite carp have been scientifically examined ('Abnormalities of the gonads of carp', by S. Gupta and Ch.

Meske in *Journal of Fish Biology*, 1976, **9**, 75–7). It has been demonstrated that some of these fish have contained fully developed male and female organs, and that in these self-fertilization was possible. Experimentally (Kossman, 1971) it has been shown with carp that some 10 per cent of these self-fertilized eggs developed, and that some of the second generation were also synchronous hermaphrodites. (Synchronous hermaphrodite fishes are those in which both sperm and ova in the ovatestis mature and become active simultaneously.)

I am indebted to Kevin Clifford for first bringing these scientifically noted examples to my attention. From this evidence, and not forgetting the observations quoted earlier, I now willingly cede that a separate 'record' for each sex of tench is neither practical, nor feasible.

THE REPRODUCTIVE CYCLE

Most authorities say that tench spawn in June, and it is probably true to say that the majority of tench do indeed achieve this important event at this time. It is my experience, however, that some tench spawn earlier, and some later than others: I have never yet seen an opening to the season (16 June) when at least some of the tench are not carrying spawn; and there are also some which have always spawned, as their distended vents bear witness. And this holds true no matter what the spring weather has been.

There are several factors which may have a bearing on just when tench spawn, such as barometric pressure, water temperature and water levels, but it is probably the female's ripeness or otherwise, which determines the actual timing for a particular individual. It would never do for all the females to synchronize exactly: survival is the name of the game, so it is in Mother Nature's best interest to stagger important events such as spawning of tench, because if a calamity did befall the water, this way she has less chance of losing the whole batch of offspring for any one year.

Fecundity in tench is prodigious; Dr Gunter of the British Museum, circa 1900 records the astonishing number of 297,000 eggs stripped from a single female, and it has been suggested that the total weight of ripe spawn carried can equal 40 per cent of the normal bodyweight. I cannot confirm that, although it wouldn't surprise me unduly if that were proven to be the case. I can, however, vouch for the fact that two known tench from different waters certainly did carry in excess of 25 per cent of their 'clean' weight in spawn. Survival rate, as with most creatures with such high fecundity figures, is likely to be less than 1 per cent.

The apparent barrenness of an occasional female tench I find particularly intriguing. In at least two different waters the biggest and heaviest individual tench caught has been a female, but this is only surprising in that although caught on several occasions and in different months, these fish have never shown any evidence of carrying spawn, or of having recently shed spawn.

One of these fish weighed more than 10lb on the last occasion it was caught, and was heavier than any fish caught from that water.

Could it be that this particular individual has been barren all her life, and that her large dimensions were due to the fact that she could utilize all her energy for growing, instead of in egg production? For argument's sake let us agree that this is likely. But what if such a fish's reproduction problem became cured, and she produced a full belly of spawn: is that one plausible explanation of how potential record-status tench come about? This is purely speculative, of course, but it nevertheless seems a fairly reasonable proposition to me.

THE LIFESPAN OF THE TENCH

I really can do no better than to quote from *Redmire Pool* (Beekay, 1984) a book written jointly by Kevin Clifford and myself, to explain something about the ageing of fishes:

The age to which fish may live is a subject which has long fascinated those who study or catch them. Icthyologists of the past suggested that carp lived to be a great age. Tate Regan (1911) mentions 150 years, whilst Frank Buckland (1883) quotes Wheeler, the professional fisherman at Windsor Great Park, who claimed that a particular carp in a stew pond was nearly 100 years old. Flower (1935) recorded that a carp lived for 47 years in captivity. Nowadays, however, the generally accepted maximum life expectancy of carp and most other non-salmonoid fish is about 15–18 years. Scientists have come to this conclusion through the study of the scales, operculae, and otoliths of fish. In the same way that the age of a tree can be assessed by counting the number of rings on a cross section of the stem, so certain parts of a fish, such as the scales, can be read by counting the checks caused by a slowing down of growth during the winter. The success of this technique for accurately establishing the age of fish has never before been

Recognizable by its unique dorsal fin, this tench was caught on several occasions over the years.

seriously challenged. There is now very strong documentary evidence to propose that some fish or species of fish, notably carp, live considerably longer than conventional ageing methods would imply. Indeed, like human beings, they continue to live long after growth has ceased.

Tench are certainly no exception. At one pit near Chertsey in Surrey, a pollution decimated the tench population in the summer of 1987 and my son, Tony, had the unenviable task of burying the fish. One tench he recognized from its distinctive tail as being a fish I'd caught in 1976; interestingly, it measured the same length in 1987 as it had done eleven years earlier: 22in (56cm). Being full grown in 1976 it was, say, around fifteen years old; at the time of its death it was therefore at least in its 'mid-twenties', but probably much older still.

THE SENSES

Sight
The habits of the tench depend to a great degree on the power of its senses, and it may be safely assumed that its sight is well adapted to its natural environment, water. It has been suggested, however, its sight through air is indistinct: I don't know about that and remain open-minded about it, but what I *do* know, from observation, is that movement definitely catches the fish's eye, whether beneath, on, or above the surface. Thus the angler standing in full view of tench may observe them going about their business, even in gin-clear water and from close range, provided he keeps movements to a minimum and carries them out stealthily. Sudden movements, even one so innocent as brushing a fly from one's face, will certainly startle them, and they will move away. By remaining stock still, I've often observed tench feeding almost within arm's reach, but the least sudden movement or noise has sent them scurrying off. Perhaps this is the reason why gently moving baits such as worms, maggots or pop-ups are so effective: they are obviously more noticeable to the tench.

Because of their keen vision, Peter Drennan invented a float with a transparent body. Peter was fishing a pit containing some very big tench in crystal-clear water. One day he found some of them feeding on a fairly shallow gravel drop-off, close to his own bank: the drop-off extended for several yards in either direction and the tench

Peter Drennan still occasionally finds the time to go fishing.

regularly patrolled back and forth, but always returned to feed in the same spot. Peter waited until the tench were well out of the way, and only then furtively placed his float tackle in the hot spot – but they refused to recommence feeding whilst it was there. As soon as he removed it, back they would come. Plainly what was needed was a float which he could see, but one the tench would find invisible or would not notice. Hence Drennan's range of crystal-bodied floats: these have proved themselves countless times, in all sorts of differing situations. In fact there is no doubt at all that when float fishing for shy fish in clear water, the crystal patterns cannot be bettered.

Just how well tench can distinguish colour is not at all apparent; at least my experiments with different coloured baits have so far proved inconclusive. Furthermore, the more successful tench baits cover a wide range of the spectrum, from the bright yellow of sweetcorn to the subdued browns and reds of casters; in other words, a considerable colour range. However, the angler should bear in mind that these baits will not look the same underwater, and the difference will be more marked the deeper and/or murkier the water.

Smell

A perennial question still raised by anglers is this: when two anglers are fishing together, using seemingly identical tackle, methods and bait, why does one catch lots of fish whilst the other struggles? In extreme cases the successful angler will pull out fish after fish whilst his companion remains biteless, and the situation persists even if they exchange tackle and/or fishing position.

A great many theories have been offered to explain this phenomenon, and some certainly have a degree of merit, but the most plausible explanation has always been overlooked: the fishes' extreme sensitivity to smell. Experiments have indicated that fish are better at detecting small traces of chemicals in water than any scientific instrument yet devised for the purpose, and one such chemical is an amino-acid called L-serine. This is present in the surface of the skin of mammals, including humans, and some individuals exude more, or a stronger type (I'm not clear

which) than others. So it may be mooted that in waters where fish are wary of human L-serine, the angler who imparts more evidence of it on his bait or tackle suffers a disadvantage.

Such anglers should not be disheartened, however, because the current practice of adding extra synthetic flavour to baits will effectively mask or disguise the presence of L-serine. Further, other contaminates or taints that may repel fish are also likely to be concealed by the addition of flavours that they find attractive. For example, in the USA carp are considered to be a major pest in certain waters and are poisoned, and the most effective mask for the poison was found to be maple syrup flavouring. Moreover, maple-flavoured baits have proved to be a winner on countless carp waters in this country.

To give an idea as to just how sensitive to smell some fish are, tests have demonstrated that for example salmon, swimming upstream through fish-ladders to get to their spawning grounds, will turn round and swim back downstream if a man, some distance upstream, rinses his hands in the water. Copper also acts as an extreme repellent to salmon: they can detect 1 part copper to 200 million parts of water – roughly equal to six drops thoroughly mixed in enough water to fill an Olympic-sized swimming pool – even though they could survive in water containing twenty times that dilution.

Further tests have been conducted to try to establish what smells stimulate feeding in fish. One such test involving a freshwater species of catfish (possibly channel catfish) showed that the three most powerful feeding stimulants were, in order: extract of earthworms, extract of ox liver and human saliva – so perhaps the old belief in the efficacy of spitting on your bait is more than just superstition!

Wounded and/or frightened fish give off an alarm substance known as *shreckstoff*. This is instantly and instinctively recognized by other fish, and it is generally supposed that its main function is to warn a wounded fish's fellows that danger threatens – indeed it may even help predatory fish in their search for meals. It is wise therefore not to return or retain fish adjacent to where one is fishing, but to carry out these activities further along the bank.

Baits will be all the more effective if they appeal to the fish's sense of smell, and this is best achieved by including protein in their make-up. Proteins are composed of simpler molecules known as amino-acids, and these contain the elements carbon, hydrogen, oxygen, nitrogen and occasionally sulphur, all of which are whitish powders in their pure state with (to humans) faint but distinctive smells. Equally important, they are soluble in water. Enzymes are globular proteins which are extremely soluble in water, and the axiom is clear: they are important to a bait's effectiveness largely because the more soluble the bait, especially its smell, the more readily it can be detected by the fish.

Nevertheless, just how fish use their sense of smell to detect such weak concentrations remains a mystery to this day. Again, however, the important point is that they do. Furthermore, it has also been demonstrated, by scientific means, that hungry fish are much more sensitive to smell than those which have recently fed.

Hearing

Water is 780 times denser than air, and sound travels through it five times faster than through air, i.e. one mile (1.6km) per second. In a lake of 'normal' size sound can therefore be considered instantaneous. And because water is such a good conductor of sound, a noise made at one end of the lake can be detected at the other end more clearly under the water than above it.

Fish have acute hearing, and if their sight is impaired the auditory system adapts to compensate, in much the same way as it does in humans. It is probably true to say that, of all its sensory systems, the fish's hearing is the most versatile. The Americans have long since recognized that certain sounds – such as made by the popping lures of their pike and bass fisherman – can attract as well as repel feeding fish.

Sensitivity to Temperature

The fish is a cold-blooded creature and as such its body temperature is governed by the temperature of the surrounding water. However, temperature adjustment for a fish is not an instant process, and any rapid external temperature change is likely to prove fatal, simply because the fish cannot adjust quickly enough; although fortunately, water temperature does not change as rapidly as that of air. Fish can detect very small changes in temperature: for instance it has been shown in tests that the cod can detect a temperature change as small as $\frac{1}{50}$ of 1°F, and is therefore very much more sensitive than any mammal. The general belief among biologists in the USA is that temperature is the single most important factor governing the occurrence and behaviour of fish.

Another point worthy of note is that fish digest food more quickly in warmer water than in cold; in fact for the carp, this process happens four times more quickly at 79°F than at 50°F. Add to this the fact that carp can consume as much as 16 per cent of their bodyweight per day during bouts of peak feeding, and it's no wonder the top carp boys get through plenty of bait! However, as mentioned elsewhere, tench are nowhere near so gluttonous – I only wish they were!

THE RESPIRATORY SYSTEM

In order to survive, fish must have abundant dissolved oxygen in the waters in which they live; oxygen is therefore a critical ecological limitation. It gets into the water either from the air above the surface or from the plant life below it. The air also acts as a 'buffer' in the other direction, absorbing oxygen from the water should saturation levels be too high.

The air we breathe is 18 per cent oxygen, but fish must exist by breathing in water that, on average, contains only 0.0006 per cent oxygen (six parts dissolved oxygen per million parts water). When the dissolved oxygen content is diminished below the normal amount by around 25 per cent, fish have trouble with feeding, growth, self-protection and other vital activities. If dissolved oxygen is lowered by around 50 per cent or more – to 0.0003 per cent, or less – the fish die from suffocation. Such is the narrow margin between all being well and certain catastrophe.

3 LOCATION

More than thirty years have slipped by since I first hunted tench. In those days venues which contained large tench were few and far between, and unless you were among the fortunate few to live close to one of these waters, the seeker of big tench had to undertake long journeys, generally on public transport or by pushbike, if he was to stand any chance of success. Big tench were in fact much smaller then, between 4lb and 5lb, and a single six-pounder was all one could realistically hope for in a lifetime of tench fishing. It is true that the record for the species had stood at 8lb 8oz since 1950 (M. Foode, Leicester Canal), and in 1963 was raised to 9lb 1oz (J. Salisbury, Eggett's Lake, Hemingford Grey) but no more than a handful of tench over 7lb had ever been caught, so it was only the most optimistic of tench men who believed it possible to catch one of similar size. Fortunately none of these restrictions applies now, and tench of 7lb, 8lb, 9lb, 10lb and even bigger are being caught each and every year.

THE POTENTIAL TENCH WATER

Location and Character
Wherever its situation and whatever its size, a shallow lake is more productive acre for acre than a deep one, simply because sunlight can penetrate to the bottom more readily, warming the water in the process. Also clarity enhances productivity because clear, silt-free water allows maximum sunlight penetration. Thus waters occurring within regions which enjoy longer hours of daylight are usually best at producing more and bigger fish. Water temperature comes into this as well, of course, because the longer the

period of suitable – that is, warm – conditions, the longer the growing season. Hence it is not surprising that most of the more prolific and productive of Britain's waters are situated in the south. Nevertheless, in spite of this undeniable fact, big tench are becoming increasingly widespread each year, and there must be around twenty counties in the British Isles which have waters containing tench of 7lb and over. Nor would this be anywhere near a complete list, and with only a modicum of research anyone sufficiently interested could name many more.

Finding Out About the Better Waters
Discovering waters which provide better-than-average fishing – either big bags of average-sized fish, or fewer but bigger individual fish – is a continual process, and it is important to be constantly alert for any snippet of information, however insignificant it may at first appear. My memory is notoriously unreliable, so I make notes on anything to hand at the time, and then enter them in a notebook kept specifically for the purpose.

To begin the search for a water with good tench-fishing potential, the angling press has much to offer; sometimes reports will mention everything, even the name and location of the water in question. However, this is not usually the case and more often the information will be disguised to some extent, which is understandable because the successful angler will not be prepared to reveal his secrets too freely, particularly if he, and perhaps one or two friends, have spent time, money and effort in realizing the water's potential in the first place. Nevertheless, useful information can often be gleaned from angling reports, and pieced together constructively.

More reliable information may be gleaned from people with a similar interest. While it is certainly true that you can learn of promising venues from matchmen, pleasure anglers (whatever that term means), occasional fishermen and even non-anglers, this is far outweighed by the knowledge which can be provided by those who are seriously interested in tench. The 'Tench-fishers', as the name implies, is a recognized society whose membership extends countrywide, and whose aim is to increase overall knowledge of the species. Non-members would do well to apply for membership – although don't think for one minute you can join and learn all about everything without putting something back in return! (To contact the Tenchfishers, *see* Useful Addresses.)

A Water's Desirable Features

Obviously, checking our reports of potential waters entails visiting them, primarily to see for yourself the stamp of fish you seek, whether caught or still in the water. And even if the fish themselves are not to be seen, there are other factors to look for which may suggest the presence of large tench:

1. *Weed Growth*: During the summertime, weed growth of abundant proportions in sparklingly clear water are both essential requisites for tench, although there are a few exceptions (usually estate lakes or reservoirs). What kind of weed is present probably doesn't matter so long as there is plenty of it, because profuse plant life provides both an abundance of oxygen in daylight and sanctuary to all kinds of life: insects, immature fish and, most important, crustacea. I firmly believe the various crustaceans, water snails, mussels and suchlike are a vital ingredient in the diet of tench – this is not to discount other species – if they are to grow big, strong and healthy.

More than likely such a water will be a mature gravel pit, but don't rule out an estate lake or reservoir without good cause. Every good lead

Correct location on this large gravel pit was obviously achieved by Alf Tapley.

needs following up, and don't ever act too hastily or you might miss out on another Southill Park or Wilstone reservoir!

2. *Islands*: The presence of islands is an advantage, especially if they are remote and inaccessible, because they offer the tench undisturbed margins in which to feed in safety. Tench often feed close in to the bank.

3. *Size*: In general terms the pit, reservoir, estate lake or whatever, needs to be big rather than small, and deep rather than shallow: big, deep waters produce big, deep tench. Is it not logical to suppose that the more difficult the tench are to locate, the better their chance of reaching outsize proportions? So the more water that is available, and the more that is inaccessible to the majority of anglers, the better the chance the tench has of avoiding capture and of growing bigger as a result. An animal or a fish which is constantly afraid to eat isn't going to grow to its full potential.

4. *Other Fish and Stock Density*: Another feature shared by most of the waters which consistently produce big tench is the stock they contain not just of tench but of other species as well. This is very important. Eels in vast numbers are, it seems, a boon. Why this is so I am not too sure, although eels are reputed to consume plenty of spawn and the young of other species. Tench are certain to be affected too, so it could be that eels provide some sort of population control, a mutually advantageous situation because the number of tench present must not outstrip the water's food supply – in fact it is infinitely better if there is a surfeit of available food: if the tench have to expend too much energy, and therefore calories, in the search for a meal, obviously those calories cannot be utilized for growing. A given body of water can only yield a certain amount of natural food, and in some years it will be less than others: too much competition for that available food, and the tench are bound not to reach optimum size.

The presence of pike is also a good sign – although not in such numbers as to decimate the adult tench population – because they, too, help to control the population. The pike's effect is different from that of the eel, however: eels may help to control the numbers of little fish, but pike need a larger meal and are known to eat adult fish, even quite big ones. Tench that have grown up in a water containing pike know all about the danger these predators pose: thus as long as they remain fit agile and fast-swimming, they have little to fear; but once they become sickly, old or infirm, the pike is ready to take advantage (it isn't in his best interest to work too hard for his meals, either). So pike help to keep the remaining tench fit and healthy by eating those that are not. The ancient myth that the tench is a doctor fish, and because of this the pike won't eat him, is nonsense, however romantic the notion may be.

Carp and tench appear to live harmoniously enough together, although in a water where carp predominate tench may prove very difficult to catch; and in another water where tench predominate, the reverse may well be true. I can think of one water where this certainly was the case. This water, a pit near Staines in Middlesex, contained about twenty carp between 10lb and 15lb. My friends and I were the first anglers to use sweetcorn there – and everyone knows how much carp like that bait – but to my knowledge only one carp was hooked in eight summers. Among my friends who fished the water in those days were Bob Buteux, Bill Quinlan, Clive Diedrich and Kevin Clifford, none of whom can be considered 'slow' when it comes to carp fishing, all of them having caught a great many big ones; but they didn't hook one carp between them during all those years spent fishing for tench at that pit! More by luck than intent I in fact hooked the only one, and it was one of the 'biggies'; but it slipped the hook just as the landing net was about to lift it out.

During this period the water contained scores of tench and we all caught plenty of these to start with; but even when they had wised up to our baits and methods and returns decreased, we still didn't catch any carp! Furthermore, a couple of years later my son and his friends were the first anglers to use boilies on this water and a similar pattern transpired – plenty of tench caught, but no carp – even though we all know how effective boilies are for carp.

IDENTIFYING THE FEEDING AREAS

It is no secret that waters like these – large, clear, with a relatively low stock density and a surfeit of available natural food – may prove difficult to succeed on, and pinpointing the feeding areas is often the key. This may sound obvious, but it is an important criterion which is often overlooked; thus some anglers begin the process of location correctly by learning of a water that produces the sought-after species, but then seem to lose their way: either they appear to think that all the fish are bunched together and that, no matter what the conditions, a known hot-spot is the only place worth fishing; or that the tench are distributed evenly throughout the water, rather like currants in a cake. Both these observations are well off the mark.

It is true, of course, that in any water there will be hot-spots and that these are more likely to produce a catch; but not all the time: hot-spots can, and do, lose their reliability for any number of reasons – for example, fishing pressure alone may cause the fish to leave a favourite haunt. Then shallow, snaggy areas are likely to contain more feeding tench in May and June, near spawning time, than at other times of the year. The reasons for fish to be in a given place vary from day to day, and sometimes even from minute to minute: bear in mind that it only takes a relatively short time for the fish to swim from one end of the lake to the other.

I have always been intrigued by the idea of 'reading water'. Only a few anglers seem really skilled in this most refined facet of fishing, which I suppose is perfectly understandable. Water is a constantly changing medium and a certain 'feel' for its make-up and condition is required: its temperature, the speed of currents – large, so-called 'still-waters' do have quite powerful currents – wind strength, direction of drift, opacity,

oxygen content, and a hundred-and-one other things that combine to make big-fish lies.

Tench Feeding Habits: What to Look For

At Spawning
Although the location of big fish, even when you can't actually see them, is all-important, it is usually not as difficult as it would first appear. A good rule of thumb is that tench feed most where they frequent most. For example, in early summer when most tench carry out their spawning ritual, a likely spawning area is also a likely feeding area, so a shallow, sheltered stretch of water may be considered with optimism: to survive and hatch, the tench's spawn requires a water temperature approaching 70°F, and obviously this is more likely to occur in a sheltered shallow. And if tree roots (willow roots appear particularly suitable) and weedbeds are in the vicinity, so much the better because the spawn adheres to these, and the various underwater entanglements offer the newly hatched fry a measure of sanctuary from predators. Big bags of heavyweight tench can be caught from places like this at the appropriate times – although I am never entirely happy fishing deliberately for spawny fish.

Nomadic Behaviour
As summer progresses the shoals tend to disperse and the tench become more nomadic in their behaviour. I clearly remember an incident which illustrates how quickly they can travel. One day Bill Quinlan caught a particularly distinctive tench: for its size, 4lb 12oz, it had enormous fins and tail; its tummy was a brilliant shade of orange, unlike any other tench we had seen from that water, and as if to confirm identification, it also possessed a black mark on its right shoulder. This fish was so unusual that immediately after returning it, Bill walked round the lake to describe it to me. Almost as soon as he entered my swim I hooked a fish, and when it was landed Bill could hardly believe his own eyes: there were the big fins and tail, and so too was the orange tummy. 'If that tench weighs 4lb 12oz and has a black mark on its right shoulder, I've

just put it back!' he exclaimed. It was the same fish, It had beaten Bill from his swim to mine, a distance round the shoreline of some 150yds (140m). Incidentally, the bait in both cases was sweetcorn.

Tench Patrol Routes

Although tench often use gullies and channels in the lake bed as their patrol routes, when away from the margins they are more likely to feed on the sides of ridges and/or bars. This is where the more luxuriant weedbeds are to be found, and it is no coincidence that nature's own baiting-up programme is centred here. The water's currents are appreciably slowed by weedbeds, hence food that was being borne along is deposited, and floating titbits are filtered out by the fronds that reach up to the very surface. Crustacea and other 'live' food for the tench all frequent these places as well and, of course, the fish know this; and since our quarry must also feel relatively secure whilst close to such a natural haven, it is no wonder that this is where fish are most likely to be found.

To learn the wandering tench's patrol route in a large body of water could be considered a daunting task. However, in addition to plumbing and then charting the contours of a water's bed (of which more later), there is another aspect of tench behaviour that can help: their habit of 'rolling' at the surface.

Rolling Tench

Tench roll in diverse ways, but most commonly in a bodyroll with the dorsal fin breaking the surface first, followed by the tail which as it descends it will sometimes smack on the surface. However, tench may also roll in such a stealthy and silent manner that if you're not looking at almost the exact spot – and only then if there is little wind to ruffle the surface – the roll is likely to remain unnoticed, even if you are observing within a few yards. At the other extreme tench will leap, just like carp. However, it's not too important to know *how* tench roll, only that they do, because a rolling tench is usually a feeding tench, and finding where they feed is the ultimate aim of location.

Watch out for the Bubbles!

Look for bubbles whilst searching for feeding tench, too, because tench can and do bubble over all types of material on the lake bed. It has often been suggested that gaseous mud must be present in the area for tench to bubble, but this is not true. And although 'reading' carp bubbles can often indicate the size of the fish making them, this doesn't hold true for tench where the size of bubbles sent up doesn't in any way signify whether they are made by a 2lb fish or one four times that weight. Nor do I go along with the theory that *all* bubbles made by tench are small, those so-called 'needle bubbles' as christened by the legendary Fred J. Taylor. Tench do send up needle bubbles, but not to the exclusion of bigger ones; and in my experience it is impossible to differentiate, with any degree of certainty, between bubbles caused by tench and those made by other species, such as those sometimes sent up by carp. I have watched tench feeding on the fringe of a weedbed send up frothy bubbles, each patch covering the size of a saucer, yet on the other side of this same weedbed were tench making little bursts with only three or four bubbles in each. In my opinion, like rolling, it is not too important to know how or why tench bubble, only to recognize that they do, and even more so, to make use of the fact.

EXPLOITING NATURAL FEATURES

When nomadic tench are the target of a campaign, certain features of a water may be used to ambush them. These might include islands, underwater bars and promontories, all of which have the effect of funnelling travelling fish through certain areas. Some waters, especially those dug for aggregates, have more underwater features than an upturned egg tray and are impossible to map, and trying to predict patrol routes on a water with a bottom like this is just too complicated. When faced with such a situation you have no choice but to look for evidence of where tench are or to rely on your instinct or 'sixth sense'. The latter is more reliable than some might imagine; we all have this instinct to some extent latent within us, and by exercising it the better it may be developed.

Another pit I fished extensively for tench was much easier to read – although perhaps it wasn't so obvious because other anglers hadn't noted the prospects. This fishery can best be described as two lakes which are joined together by a channel; this isn't narrow, being about 140yds (128m) wide, but any fish travelling from one body of water to the other has to pass through it. Bill Quinlan and I recognized the channel's promise, and with help from Ron Chant constructed two comfortable places on an 'arm' of the shore from where to fish (there wasn't enough room for three pitches). Work began early in the close season because we wanted to allow as much time as possible for the fish to get over the disturbance and for the grass and plants to re-establish themselves. Before we started work, the area was covered in an evil-smelling black ooze and was sometimes completely under water; we anglers did not like it like that, but the mosquito population considered it paradise!

Ron and I toiled away carrying gravel in wheelbarrows from another part of the lake, and managed to transform the end of the arm into a com-

fortable and secluded fishing spot. Bill directed operations from the comfort of the pub! I even went to the extra trouble of building a narrow landing stage, so that hooked fish would not have to be brought into shallow water to be netted. Later this platform, just two scaffold-boards wide, proved invaluable, preventing hooked fish from kiting down behind the arm to our left. Where necessary we even planted rushes, irises and a couple of bushes, the latter providing additional cover, shade from the sun, and shelter from the wind.

We went to a lot of trouble but it was well worth the effort: Bill, Ron and I, together with more of our friends, caught more tench and, what is more, bigger tench from these swims than had ever been caught from the pit before.

CHARTING UNDERWATER FEATURES

The underwater landscape, of gravel pits especially, can be remarkably varied. There may be gentle inclines, bars with sides as steep as the white cliffs of Dover, shallow depressions and gullies or chasm-like drop-offs. Trying to make sense of it is often all but impossible – but nevertheless still try, because time spent charting the lake bed's contours is never wasted, and the more you find out, the better you should be able to predict tench movements. Having said that, in practice this doesn't always work – well, not for me – and it is your old ally, the subconscious, that is generally most helpful. Thus you don't really recognize from the underwater features, where the tench should be; but then something clicks in the subconscious, and that is where you want to fish. Of course you are not right every time, but you are right often enough to know there is more to it than just chance.

Those who have the use of a boat fitted with state-of-the-art sonar, especially with side-scanning capabilities are to be envied because this is the most accurate way of charting a lake bed yet available. It will not only show the underwater contours, but depth (in feet and/or metres), the composition of the bottom (hard or soft), as well

Bill Quinlan takes advantage of a 'new swim'.

as differentiating between small and larger fish present.

Otherwise you must rely on plumbing by rod and line for underwater charting – by no means ideal, but the only viable alternative. The set-up is simple, the two major components being a large pike float and a 4oz bomb. I use an old beachcaster for throwing the rig out, on the butt of which is a white mark, one foot up from the reel. After casting and tightening to the lead, the float can be allowed to surface; by pulling in the line one foot at a time using the white mark, the depth can be quite accurately ascertained.

You don't, of course, only allow the float to surface once per cast. Wind the float down to the lead and retrieve 10ft (3m) of line, again using the white marker as a guide, before allowing it to resurface. Make each cast progressively right to left, and thus you will obtain a fairly good idea of the bed's contours in front of you. Pay special attention to any areas that demand it, and if in doubt, keep plumbing; a relatively small feature, especially one situated on an otherwise flat area, can prove most attractive to tench, and you don't want to miss it.

By dragging the lead on the bottom and using a slow retrieve it is also possible to formulate some conclusions as to the consistency of the lake bed. A lack of resistance will indicate firm silt or sand, steady increased pressure means mud or soft silt, and there is absolutely no mistaking the bumpity-bump of gravel. Weed feels the same as when retrieving leger tackle across it: resistance builds up until the tackle comes free, then gradually builds again, comes free, and so on. The more you practise this technique the more you will glean from it.

Charting Canals

When tench are sought in canals, the far bank drop-off is generally considered the number-one holding area. Fish close to an overhanging bush or tree or some other feature – rushes and permanently moored boats are examples – and fish the bait as close to the feature as possible; for this task the pole is best. Plumb the depth accurately, and by studying the far bankside vegetation, note

Checking the lake bed with a hollow bamboo pole.

the exact spot. This is where you must fish and deposit any groundbait or free offerings. Absolute precision is vital if you want the full reward the swim probably has to offer. Aim to keep hookbait and groundbait within at least a 6in (15cm) radius.

Charting Estate Lakes

Most estate lakes are quite old, over a hundred years, and have beds mainly covered in silty detritus. Just how deep and/or extensive the soft layer is will be determined by various factors; thus lakes fed by streams, and those in wooded surroundings, will have more than waters that are not. A good place to fish is a hard area in an otherwise soft-bottomed lake, or where the detritus is firmer or less deep. As we have seen, establishing the location of such areas takes much time and effort from the bank, but all the estate lakes I fish are equipped with a boat and then it is much easier; an oar simply thrust down to the bottom will tell you much about the bed's make-up. Much better still, however, is a long bamboo pole: this is easier to wield, it will penetrate deeper and, furthermore, the contents of its hollow end will provide samples of the detritus. Again, much can be learnt from such exercises. You wouldn't for example, expect to catch much when fishing your bait in deep, stinking, almost liquid mud. A much better bet would be an inch or two of mud over firmly packed silt. But as we have said perhaps even more reliable would be hard patches: these may be of gravel, sand, rock or even large stones, in fact anywhere the bottom is of firmer character.

BOAT SAFETY

Safety is of paramount importance and must be the first consideration of every angler who takes to a boat. It is a sad but undeniable fact that each year there are tragic boating accidents in which anglers lose their lives, and many more than most people know about; nor do they all necessarily involve inexperienced and/or foolhardy anglers. For example, a couple of years ago on the placid waters of Queenford lagoon, one of Britain's top big-fish men, Andy Mundy, fell from his boat whilst occupied in the simple task of baiting his swim. A friend saw what happened and rushed to the spot, but arrived too late to save him.

Again, my long-time friend Kevin Clifford considers himself fortunate to have escaped with his life after a similar incident at a reservoir. A strong swimmer, he did not panic when suddenly pitched into the water. The boat disappeared, so Kevin struck out powerfully for the not-too-distant shore – yet if another friend had not dived in to help, he believes he would have drowned. Kevin admits he made mistakes: first, he was not wearing a life preserver; second, he did not remove sufficient of his clothes before attempting to swim to safety – the pockets of his Barbour jacket filled with water and acted as effective drogues; third, he did not appreciate how rapidly his strength would drain – the time lapse between the first signs of tiredness and complete exhaustion was surprisingly short.

Yet two more of my friends met their deaths last year as the result of a boating incident. It was a warm spring day when some of the members of the Savay syndicate foregathered for a working party at the lake. On a return trip from one of the islands the boat, with four anglers aboard, suddenly became waterlogged and sank. Two managed to struggle ashore, very sadly the others, Clive Rigby and Keith Sellick, perished.

Such incidents could be avoided by wearing a life-preserver. It isn't necessary to wear a bright orange life-jacket, although there is nothing wrong with these. Probably the best type of design is a 'Crew Saver', worn unobtrusively around the neck like a scarf; if the wearer ends up in the water, the Crew Saver inflates automatically and keeps the victim's head above water, even if he or she is unconscious or, indeed, can't swim. Being a strong swimmer, my own choice is a buoyancy aid, the type that resembles a bodywarmer or waistcoat; it

Kevin Clifford considers himself very fortunate to have survived a boating accident. This fabulous brace weigh 9lb 10oz and 8lb 2oz respectively.

In happier times – Clive Rigby with a cracking 7½lb'er.

has pockets, and is thin enough to wear under outer clothing. It is *not* suitable for non-swimmers, however. For further essential safety advice and survival techniques, see *Freshwater Fishing* by Hugh Falkus and Fred Buller (Macdonald & Jane's, 1975).

THE SEASONS AND TENCH BEHAVIOUR

Midsummer

Although tench are considered to be fish of warm summer days, this is an over-simplification. Around June time, the conditions don't seem too important since plenty of tench are generally being caught even when it is cold and wet, probably because whatever the weather (within reason) the water temperature is rising at this time of year. Furthermore, spawn is building up in most of the females and this means they have to eat more. As summer progresses, however, changes take place.

Late Summer

Once the water temperature has reached its summer norm and fish have completed their nuptuals, it takes something extra to get the tench to feed avidly again. It must also be taken into account that most natural food occurs later in midsummer; in fact there may actually be a surfeit. It is therefore no wonder that tench fishing can be difficult around, say, August. But all is not lost!

Tench are lovers of, and more active in warm water, so as long as the water temperature doesn't go too high, say over 70°F(21°C) you have a better chance of catching them. More than one reliable authority has proposed 68°F (20°C) as the optimum feeding temperature for tench. This is a reasonably accurate assessment in my experience, and it seems that the closer the water temperature comes to this figure, the better the tench will feed. This will apply whether the temperature is coming from below or above the optimum, and helps us better to predict under what conditions our quarry will feed best.

The water in gravel pits does not often reach 68°F (20°C), so the hotter the weather, and the longer that it has been enjoyed, the better our chances of tench at any given time, day or night. On the other hand, the temperature in shallow lakes regularly surpasses the optimum given temperature, and may stay above it for days on end. On such waters at times like these, it becomes almost impossible to catch tench at any time other than dawn, when the water is at its coolest. There are likely to be other influencing factors at work too, but trying to evaluate all the possible effects on feeding – such as the water's differing oxygen content (which in turn depends on the time of day, the strength and direction of the wind, and how much and what kind of water plants are present) and varying light levels – is enough to give one a coronary. Anyway, I think temperature is the most important, so will leave it there.

September

Fishing in the month of September is usually very good, in spite of what some tench-angling authors say. Admittedly, it is not as prolific as the easier times of early summer, but it is still good enough to make tench fishing very worthwhile. If you don't believe me, take another look at the latest Top 50 list: no fewer than five fish out of the top ten, including Gordon Beavan's record, were taken in September. Perhaps 'usual' tench tactics have to be abandoned to catch these September specimens regularly, but so what?

Winter Tench

Despite not fishing intentionally for winter tench, quite a few have been taken accidentally when after other species; estate lakes, pits and rivers have all produced, and fish have come both during the day and at night. These winter tench are exceedingly beautiful. They are not lank or flabby, in fact they look in the peak of condition, and therefore I find it difficult to believe that tench hibernate in anything like the strict sense of the word. Many (all?) of our native species become less active in cooler water, and hence require less food. And I don't doubt that at times when the water temperature is cooling most rapidly, tench

may become torpid for a time. As they become acclimatized to the cold conditions, however, I believe they, like other species, begin to feed once more. My biggest winter tench weighed 5lb 14oz and came from the River Kennet, and my heaviest stillwater winter specimen was caught from a gravel pit: it weighed 5lb 10oz and came at 10pm one frosty Christmas Eve!

Relating to winter tench fishing, it has been shown that cyprinids – and tench are cyprinids – can go for long periods without apparent sustenance in cold water, the statistics quoted being in excess of thirty days in water with a temperature around 40°F (4.4°C). As an example of this, let me relate this true tale: one of my friends, a keen pike angler, used to catch livebaits on the day before a pike trip, and put them in a bucket which he would hang on a hook inside the garage door overnight. One such late season trip was called off, and the livebaits in their buckets were forgotten. Not until a week or so before the following season, when my friend was readying his tackle for the new campaign, were the livebaits re-discovered. And do you know what, they were still alive! They were roach (another cyprinid), and had survived for more than two months in a bucket of pond water without any further food. Moreover my friend is a truthful person, and not one to exaggerate.

FESTENTE LENTE

The undoubted drawback to good pioneering location is that there is always somebody watching and waiting to take advantage of your hard-worked-for gains. There is no solution to this problem, so proceed with circumspection: give nothing away; don't make your new swims too obvious; fish at times when nobody can see what you are catching; and don't talk too much in the pub. To some anglers catching fish is all that matters; to others, who deserve the utmost respect, there is more to it than that. To my mind, locating fish by your own efforts, and being the first to catch them, is an achievement well worth the name.

4 TACKLE

It is extremely difficult for those who have taken up fishing in the past few years to realize how radically specialized tackle has changed. Just twenty-five years ago there was precious little in the way of purposely designed tackle, apart from a few rods. Necessary items that were considered not viable, for any reason, by the tackle barons had to be modified or home-made, or you went without. Initially it was Richard Walker who did more than anyone to rectify this situation, by designing and making sound tackle and then demonstrating that it worked satisfactorily and successfully. He died from cancer in 1985, and was surely the leading big-fish angler of this century. His angling was scientific and revolutionary, and in his classic book *Still Water Angling* (Macgibbon & Kee 1953) he told us:

> The importance of using good tackle which is right for the job is very great. It is no good knowing where the fish are and what bait they will take if you cannot reach them with your tackle: it is useless to hook a fish if you have no hope of landing it. A great many of the fish I have seen caught would not have been taken without the right tackle in some cases specially made.

Despite this sound advice the tackle trade as a whole was slow to catch on. To be fair, the major tackle manufacturers could not justify the costs of design and development at a time when the potential market was so tiny as compared to the size of the market today, and it was left to the smaller, more progressive tackle businesses to exploit the gap. Front-runners among these companies were B. James & Son of Ealing, West London, who produced, among other equipment, specialist rods and landing nets based on Dick Walker's designs.

But the situation really improved when certain far-seeing individuals produced a wide range of well designed tackle, of good quality and at reasonable prices. Eventually this policy resulted in the happy situation that all anglers take for granted today, in which just about every conceivable taste is catered for with a wide range of tackle readily available.

This chapter will cover the latest tackle used in my most recent forays after specimen tench.

RODS

The modern carbon-fibre rod, like those made from boron, Kevlar and other various composites, casts further and more accurately, picks up line quicker, and is essentially stronger, lighter and more durable than anything that has preceded it. Even so, the adaptability of such materials does not guarantee that one single design will answer all situations and circumstances – far from it. Therefore, unless you are rich enough to afford a rod to suit every purpose or contingency, a compromise must be reached. But this need not mean that you have to sacrifice efficiency. Any new rod should be assessed carefully, making sure that it is adequate for the job in hand and, wherever possible, ensuring that it will handle other situations, should the need arise. Versatility is the key word.

The rods I prefer all have in common a soft, progressive action, because a pliable rod is an important asset when playing big fish. The very good reason for this is difficult to explain, but Henry Sullivan Thomas writing over a century ago in his book *The Rod in India* (W. Thacker & Co, 1873) summed it up succinctly and expertly:

The rush [of a big fish] is so sudden and so violent that the hand, be it ever so light, cannot answer to it sufficiently quickly. And with a stiff rod the mischief is done in the very first tug. Whereas if you have a pliable rod it yields instantly to the tug, it yields before you have felt the tug down at the other end of the rod in your hand, and the first thing you are aware of is the noise of the revolving check winch. If you have a stiff rod you will require to strengthen your tackle, that is, you will be at a disadvantage of not being able to fish so fine.

It is friction you get rid of in a pliable rod; or, so to speak more correctly, you minimize uncontrollable friction, and have a greater command of the friction which you can control and utilize. The friction caused by two or three turns around a capstan or about a belaying pin amounts almost to a deadlock, and so, in a less degree, the friction caused by a single right-angle is considerable. The latter is about the friction caused by the line at the point of a stiff rod. In a pliable rod the point yields quickly, reduces the angle, and so reduces the friction, 'til you raise the point and renew and increase the friction at your discretion.

Leger Rods

The first of the rods made from 'new generation' materials I owned were 11ft boron rods made by Silstar, and these were superb. As bought they have big, clumsy-looking rings and I don't like the large-diameter handles, but neither of these features prevents the catching of tench. I changed the rings and handles on mine, but if I am honest the 'improvements' are mainly cosmetic.

The borons proved eminently suitable for long-range legering and for those occasions when stronger lines have to be employed. For example, where snags and/or dense weedbeds are encountered, lines of 6lb to 8lb are readily manageable, and in desperate circumstances I have got away

with using even stronger lines. These rods have never let me down, landing tench to over 8lb, plus a number of big carp as a very welcome bonus.

For those wanting to leger for big tench, the best rod to look for nowadays would be one such as the Drennan 12ft Specialist. This does all that the former rods did and more, besides being lighter and not requiring any modifications. This particular rod was designed primarily for legering for big tench (and big bream) at range in stillwaters, but it works admirably in many a diverse situation. It will handle bombs or feeders from the very smallest up to at least 2oz, will cast long distances accurately, and is excellent for picking up line and hitting bites at this long range. Furthermore it inspires confidence because of the seemingly effortless control when playing and landing big fish.

The Specialist's specification – and this is what you might look for in a legering rod, for best results – includes IM6 carbon-fibre construction, full twin-leg Fuji rings throughout, a 24in (71cm) full-length cork handle, and universal reel fittings. The stated test curve is 1¼lb although it has plenty of reserve power in the butt so not only will it deal adequately with big tench, but carp up to 20lb plus as well. The ideal range of reel-line breaking strains would be 3lb to 8lb though, again, I've gone even stronger.

In addition to long-range legering, this style of rod can be used for legering when swingtipping isn't a viable option. This is because first, on waters containing just a very few big tench, where a single bite is an event, it's just not worth the effort of 'sitting' on the rods for hour upon hour. Because the moment your concentration wavers, as undoubtedly it will, you can be sure that it will coincide with the only bite of the day. Secondly, inclement conditions such as gale-force winds will prevent the tip's messages being interpreted accurately, or even noticed. Some anglers will watch tips for far too long; then when conditions have improved and others are catching, they are still out of action recovering from the ordeal.

In my opinion the swingtip is the best all-round method of bite detection when legering for tench, and despite many trials I have yet to find

A pair of Kamasan 'Intertips', together with Shimano Baitrunners, ready for action. The rod-pod is by Solar Tackle.

a swingtip rod which will cover all scenarios. However, these same trials have suggested that just two particular types of rod will cover all but the most exceptional circumstances.

The first would be in the style of another Drennan rod, one called the Legermaster. To describe this particular example, which might be considered a stereotype for this sort of fishing: it is 11ft long and designed to be used in conjunction with a full range of screw-in swingtips (or quivertips). It is extremely versatile: sensitive enough to handle light reel lines down to 3lb bs and even finer hooklinks, whilst also able to cope with big fish on lines as heavy as 9lb bs. It is constructed from 96 per cent carbon, and will fish everything from light link-legers up to bombs and feeders of more than 1oz.

I personally use the Legermaster for most of my swingtipping, simply because I am generally indulging in this sort of fishing on gravel pits, where this rod excels. Being of smaller diameter, it casts further and is less affected by wind, important attributes on the exposed banks of large gravel pits. It is also most responsive, yet picks up line rapidly on the strike. Its reserves of power in the bottom half enable it to handle even quite big carp, too, so a model such as this is advisable in waters where these might prove a problem!

The other rod recommended for swingtipping work would be one such as the Intertip from the Kamasan company. This is characterized by aluminium oxide-lined rings for optimum life, the tip ring being threaded to accept screw-in tips. At 10ft long the swingtip is that much closer, making it easier to spot and 'read' those smaller indications. Its light 'forward' action makes it ideal for handling lines right down to 2lb bs. This type is the perfect general-purpose legering rod for the often shy-biting tench of estate lakes and ponds. However, it will also handle hard-fighting fish should the need arise.

Float-fishing Rods

When float fishing for long periods, and especially at long range, the sort of rod to look for would be along the lines of the 12ft 9in tench float rod from Drennan. Though sensitive enough in the tip for perfect float control, this is a stepped-up float rod which will handle the biggest, hardest-fighting tench with ease. Its extra power action comes in 'high up' in the middle joint, and this sort of design helps enormously with control of fish around marginal weed. The designer intended this rod to be fished in a pair of rod rests with the rod tip just under the surface drift, and this makes it ideal for the long-range lift method described in Chapter 6. It can, of course, be used to good effect when fishing other methods; however, when, for example, it is necessary to hold the rod for long periods, there are better rods.

Nowadays there are also 14ft rods which are very good for this and for general work. My current favourite is Drennan's IM9 14ft float rod, which in my opinion is the very latest in rod-making technology; even with a reel fitted it is difficult to believe you are holding a 14ft rod, and this style of rod should impress even those anglers who have traditionally been against rods of 14ft and over because they were top-heavy. That bit of extra length makes float control, and fishing deeper swims so much easier.

The main features of this particular rod are described here, as the stereotype for a very successful design: the blank is hollow throughout and boasts more of a through action, but it still provides for a crisp strike while offering some cushioning when fishing at close range. To keep the weight down, single-leg Fuji silicon carbide rings are used throughout, including the two butt rings. There are certainly enough of them, and this makes the problem of the line sticking to the rod almost a thing of the past, even in a wet climate. This point is important because, as tenchmen have recognized for years, float fishing for tench is often best in that tranquil, misty, damp half-light shortly after dawn: thus the 14ft rod may be the means of avoiding the sheer frustration, not to mention loss of temper, of lines which stick, as those on lesser rods were always prone to do at the critical moment.

As any of my rods, the fourteen-footer has to withstand a certain level of abuse, such as handling heavier lines than the designer intended. Only a few days ago I tested it seriously: I was fishing the near bank drop-off, hoping for some late season tench to photograph for this book – only it wasn't a tench that picked up the Richworth midi-boilie offering, but a near-20lb carp! Fortunately I'd taken the precaution of rigging up 6lb line for just this eventuality.

Alternatively you might look for a rod such as the Kamasan 12ft float rod. This rod has a three-piece blank constructed from 96 per cent graphite, fitted with an abbreviated duplon handle and aluminium oxide-lined rings throughout. It is recommended for use with 2lb to 3lb reel lines, but I rarely use it with lines less than 4lb to 5lb.

One final tip: the lead in an ordinary pencil when applied to the male spigot of a carbon rod will prevent the joint jamming.

The Intertip and Baitrunner combination is put to the test by a seven-pounder. The angler is Keith Griffin.

REELS

Centre-pin reels seem to be enjoying something of a renaissance recently, but quite frankly, I can't understand why, especially on stillwaters. I don't deny the undoubted aesthetic qualities of the centre-pin in skilled hands: however, if total efficiency is desired, then only reels of the fixed-spool type are really worth considering. Nevertheless, if it pleases you to fish with a centre-pin, do so; there is still more to fishing than just catching fish.

There was a time when all big-fish men relied on Mitchell reels and I was no exception. Even today, the even line-laying capabilities and width of their spools have not been equalled by any other company. The disadvantages of such reels were the unreliable line-roller, together with a clutch that needed continual adjustment, and the fact that it was prone to tangles. There were also reels such as ABU's early Cardinal 54 and 55 models, with superb line-roller and clutch, and excellent engineering altogether. However, these have been overtaken by reels with a baitrunner feature, a refinement which has proved a great boon in some styles of fishing.

The baitrunner allows a fish to take line without leaving the bailarm open, which does away with a major source of tangles. By pushing the baitrunner lever forward the gearing of the reel is disengaged. However, the tension provided can still be adjusted and preset to counteract, for example, drift on a large lake, or the flow of a river. You may also select a certain level of resistance to a taking fish, when bolt-rigging for example. Returning to 'normal' mode is achieved quite simply by turning the reel handle forwards or, if you prefer, you can switch the lever backwards manually to re-engage the gearing.

The gears are the heart of any fixed-spool reel and those in the new baitrunners have proved totally dependable. In a design such as the Shimano Baitrunner they are mounted in three stainless ball races, which are smooth-running and free from any threat of corrosion. The Baitrunner clutch holds its setting and is silky in operation, and the line-roller really works, and keeps on working.

Baitrunners such as the Shimano come in various guises, and each model is produced in several different sizes. The middle-of-the-road version has proved 100 per cent reliable and ideal for tench, not discounting other species of course. However, the new models available now have push-on spools, and these are not the only improvement, when compared to earlier models. The spools themselves have undergone dramatic development, being wider, tapered and with much improved line-lay, thus providing the means of longer and more accurate casting. Another important item, the line-roller, has also been improved: it is now manufactured from silicon carbide, a ceramic with a very low coefficient of friction, thus lessening to a significant degree the potential for line damage in this critical area. Finally, clutch adjustment is far easier to accomplish, now the knob is at the back of the reel, especially when a fish is 'on'. So, all in all,

the new models are much improved – although the handle is still too big and clumsy, and the anti-reverse lever remains in the same awkward-to-get-to place.

LINES AND HOOKS

The most important items of tackle, whatever the quarry, are lines and hooks. A skilful angler can cope successfully with the liabilities imposed by poor rods and reels, but he must employ the very best lines and hooks if he is to enjoy consistent success.

Monofilament

There are certain properties that affect monofilament lines, the six most important being:

1. *Knot strength*: This is generally lower on matt lines and highest on hard glossy line. Different types of knot suit different types of line, but the best knots, such as the grinner (also known as the uni-knot), the palomar and the overturn whipping knot, are good in most (all?) types of line. A tiny drop of very thin super-glue applied after the line is tied will penetrate the coils, sealing the whole knot very firmly in place as well as making it water-resistant. Use the pointed end of a cocktail stick to apply the minimum amount of glue; any excess will penetrate the hooklink, spoiling its flexibility.

2 *Abrasion resistance*: Often related to knot strength, you don't want a line that becomes roughed up too easily or which loses a high proportion of its strength as a result of the slightest damage.

3 *Optimum stretch*: A nice degree of elasticity is required: too much can prove a handicap, particularly when distance fishing, and too little is a recipe for sudden breakages.

4 *Shelf life*: Inexplicably, some lines do not keep well, deteriorating very quickly and losing much of their strength after just a few months. If you are about to re-use a line after a gap of two to three months, it is always best to pull-test it properly on a spring balance. (*Don't* use your best fish-weighing balance to do this, because a

'One of the very finest of big-fish anglers' – John Everard with one of his many nine-pounders.

snapping line lets the balance jolt back, thus possibly ruining its accuracy in the process.)

5 *Suppleness*: This helps both distance and accuracy when casting, avoids tangles and even aids bait presentation. Some perfectly good lines seem springy at first but just need gently stretching before fishing. Others have a tendency to coil and/or twist, and may be best avoided.

6 *Strength*: This is the most important property; however, it is the breaking strain × the diameter ratio which is the key. Some lines are not the diameter they claim to be, and the situation is further confused by the English tradition of under-rating the breaking strain.

Of the many monofilament lines available, my own choice of reel line for most situations would have to have the qualities of Drennan's Specimen Plus: good knot strength, it is abrasion-resistant, not too stretchy, supple, it has a satin matt surface of pleasing colour (copper brown), and above all, it is very reliable, being accurately and consistently rated. Available on 100m, 200m, 600m or 1,000m spools, this tough and highly durable line is fast-sinking, super-strong and very economical: it is therefore ideal for big-fish angling.

This past summer (1995) I was persuaded to try Kamasan's reel line. At first I was reluctant,

mainly because it is not available on bulk spools, but finally I did give it a try and the line is all it was promised to be, with good knot strength, very abrasion-resistant, a reasonable amount of stretch, and reliable. It is available in a wide range of breaking strains from 1½lb to 12lb, and its neutral grey colour makes it an ideal choice in clear water.

There are also 'resin-impregnated' lines, the first being introduced in around 1992–3. This type of line is supposed to be more resistant to abrasion than others, and moreover is packed in an ultra-violet screened bag, this allegedly keeps out 60 per cent of harmful rays as well as dust and dirt. It is very light in colour, and is generally available on 100m and 200m spools.

Further excellent monofilaments are Maxima, Bayer, Damyl, and also Brent which is cheap and reliable. I have included these other makes because a line that suits my style of fishing may not suit yours, or vice versa. There is also Berkley's Big Game line, which Kevin Clifford described in *Big Fish World* magazine:

Terry Eustace is now the British distributor for Berkley Big Game line and there is no doubt that it has some exceptional qualities.

My own tests clearly demonstrate the abrasion-resistant qualities of Berkley Big Game line. The other line I used for comparison I have been fishing with for the past couple of seasons and has given no cause for complaint. A weight was fastened to the end of the line and this was pulled over the edge of a piece of glass for a measured distance. These are the results:

NUMBER OF LIFTS BEFORE THE LINE BROKE		
	Very Popular 12lb Line	12lb Berkley Big Game Line
1st test	14	24
2nd test	7	31
3rd test	13	44
4th test	5	37
5th test	17	8
6th test	13	28

Interestingly, I also tried the same test using a couple of well known braids in 12lb breaking strain. They could only manage two or three lifts before breaking, and this really does bring into question their claimed abrasion resistant qualities as far as I am concerned.

When Terry first showed me a spool of the Berkley Big Game line I was deterred by its colour, or lack of it, because it is white, but try this simple test. Tie a length of Berkley, along with a couple of lengths of line which are coloured dark brown or green (which most lines are nowadays), to a lead and let it settle on, or near, the bed of the lake. You will discover that the Berkeley is almost invisible compared to the darker coloured lines, which stand out like a sore thumb.

If you are intending to fish any of those lakes in France, which are full of snags and boulders, then the Berkley Big Game line is an absolute must. It will definitely reduce losses. I am using the 12lb for barbel fishing near some snags, where I have lost a fair per-

centage of the fish I have hooked in the past. I am full of confidence that the Berkley Big Game line will cut those losses down dramatically. Finally, Terry has discovered that the Berkley Big Game line does not perform well when the bloodknot is used, which, although I have used it a great deal myself, I acknowledge is not a particularly good knot.

The Berkley Big Game line is available in breaking strains 10lb, 12lb, 15lb and 20lb, in green as well as in the original white. All heavier breaking strains are available in white only.

Since Kevin's comments first appeared in print, this brand has become very popular and is now available in several colours in a wide range of breaking strains.

Early trials with a new monofilament I have only just obtained from the USA seem very promising. It is made in Japan for the American Du Pont company, and is called Magna Thin. This line is fine for the given breaking strain, and combines the advantages of low diameter with high wet strength, It has an extremely smooth finish, is extra limp and flexible, and has a surprising amount of elasticity for such a thin line. This advanced formulation combines excellent knot-strength and low 'memory', and provides easy handling and good castability.

Magna Thin comes in three colours, crystal clear, moss green and aqua fluorescent: clear is available from 2lb to 130lb, the other two restricted to between 4lb and 30lb. I have just one 250yd spool of 8lb clear, and this consistently stands a pull of 7lb, knotted and wet, without breaking.

Where or when it is essential to use the finest line available, you can perhaps do no better than Drennan's Double Strength (which isn't pre-stretched). However, it is important to appreciate that super-thin lines such as Double Strength and Magna Thin are completely different from ordinary monofilament, and you must learn to choose line by diameter and not by breaking strain. There are three very important reasons for this:

1. Line damage has a far greater effect on thin line than on thick of the same breaking strain.
2. Being thinner, 5lb Double Strength at 0.007in will be far less forgiving than 5lb standard at 0.009in when a bad knot is tied.
3. Lines are traditionally under-rated, so the standard 5lb line will probably break at about 6lb, whereas Double Strength is accurately rated and will normally break at the stated strain.

Therefore instead of your old 5lb line, use 10lb Double Strength which is still the same 0.009in diameter, or if you want to fish both finer and stronger, use 7lb Double Strength at 0.008in.

Another unique feature of Double Strength line is that it is a resin-bonded and impregnated co-polyamide material: that is, it is not nylon. This gives it its surface sheen, and minimizes water absorption. All nylon monofilaments are hygroscopic and many lose up to 20 per cent of their dry breaking strain after immersion in water for just a couple of hours. Drennan Double Strength retains a remarkable 94 per cent of its dry strength even after seven hours' immersion.

However, like all other small-diameter lines, the slightest nick will seriously affect its strength, and I find Double Strength is also likely to break when subjected to sudden shocks. Furthermore, if the tackle is unduly strained – such as when pulling out of weed or snags – any line is liable to lose a proportion of its inherent strength. The implication, then, is clear: when using Double Strength or another of the small-diameter lines, be constantly alert for any damage and employ the softest rods suitable for the task required. To reduce the chance of breakage still further, where possible it is advisable to make just the hooklink from the thin stuff; then the elasticity of the reel line, say Specimen Plus, will to some extent absorb most shocks, particularly if the hooklink is, as suggested, of a higher breaking strain than the reel line. As mentioned earlier, fishing Double Strength this way means you get the best of both worlds: a stronger, yet finer and more supple hooklink. Should the need arise to go even finer and you have no choice but to use a weaker hooklink than the reel line, employ a length of power-gum between the two as a shock absorber. Another alternative is Peter Brownlow's rig.

Some authorities recommend joining the super-thin lines to ordinary monofilament by means of a water knot or double grinner knot; however, I feel that this method could result in the harder line cutting through the softer, particularly during an extended battle with a big fish. Admittedly the risk is probably small, but I feel happier using a swivel or small ring at the junction between the lines, and either of these then doubles as a leger stop. And why take any unnecessary risk, however small?

Braids

In all but very exceptional circumstances, monofilament remains the best line for use on the reel. Sometimes however, especially with certain rigs, it is preferable to use a braided line for hooklinks because of its extreme limpness. Limpness, strength and small diameter are the three primary qualities we yearn for in the lines we use and especially for hooklinks. The days are long gone when all braided lines were of much greater diameter than monofilaments of comparable breaking strain. In fact nowadays the reverse is very often true. The very latest, new generation high-tec braids are very much thinner than monofilament – and very much higher in price, too, ten times as much, or even more at the time of writing!

High-Tec Braids

Are these super-braids worth the extra cost? In a word, yes, simply because of the three primary qualities of limpness, strength and small diameter; as well as which they are abrasion resistant, they tie well (so long as correct knots, and the necessary care, are employed), have almost zero stretch, don't lose a high proportion of their strength when wet, and are incredibly reliable. What more could be asked of a hooklink material? It certainly isn't smaller diameters still – in fact already some fishery owners are banning these braids because they *are* of such small diameter, fearing that they may cut into hard-fighting fishes' mouths.

Of course, fishery owners cannot be blamed for taking such a stance. The fish are the most important asset of any fishery, and their welfare must be everybody's first concern. I am not sure, however, that these braids are more likely to cut a fish than some other braids that have been around for a lot longer. I am referring to those which had some type of stronger, harder material wrapped around the central core. This has the effect of making them feel rough, and with the sawing motion that takes place during a fight, I can imagine that this is exactly what they do: saw!

At the time of writing there are at least six, all American, of these latest hi-tec braids available; because of the high price, I could only afford to buy two spools, one called Spiderwire, and the other Iron Thread. I chose 6lb test Iron Thread for tying very fine hooklinks. The makers, Fenwick, do not state the diameter; with a micrometer I found it was 0.004in, which obviously compares favourably with 7lb Double Strength at 0.008in. I especially like the smooth finish of Iron Thread and its colour, watery green. It is available in 6lb, 8lb, 14lb and 20lb test.

Spiderwire is made from an entirely new class of fibre called ultra-high-molecular-weight polyethylene, now known as Spectra: it is 30 per cent stronger than Kevlar and ten times stronger than steel, with only 2 to 3 per cent stretch compared to most monofilaments' 25 to 30 per cent. It is also said to have no 'memory'. It is ultra-violet and chemical-resistant, and has a long spool life. There are eleven strengths available in three colours, and in two of the diameters, 0.009in and 0.012in, there is a further, even more expensive, option: incorporating the most advance fibre technology, these two test diameters are made from the new Spectra 2000 fibre, claimed to be the smallest diameter with the highest break strength of any fishing line in the world: with Spectra 2000, the 0.009in diameter Spiderwire has a 30lb breaking strain, and the 0.012in diameter an astounding 50lb breaking strain. Berkley now claim their latest braid, Fireline, made from 100 per cent MicroDyneema, is the strongest.

This is the very latest fibre from the 'original inventors of gel spun technology'.

Carp Silk
The foregoing 'super-braids' are expensive, but there is another very good high-tec hooklink braid known as Carp Silk which in fact breaks new ground on several counts: it is the first line of this type in which the Dyneema strands – the stuff that provides the fantastic breaking strains – have been dyed. Previous attempts to colour Dyneema failed, so the forerunners of Carp Silk had to incorporate a proportion of white, which perhaps made the braid more conspicuous to the fish. Carp Silk, however, contains coloured Dyneema, either green or brown, and thus provides unobtrusive hooklinks. This is a significant advantage for anglers wanting to stay one step ahead of the fish … and the rest of the pack.

Carp Silk also has a unique weave structure: to get ultimate strength coupled with durability, more than one material needs to be combined, and the chosen manner of weaving will affect knot strength, abrasion resistance, and the tendency to fray when cut. In all three departments Carp Silk is a vast improvement on anything that preceded it; in fact its knot strength is so good that it will withstand simple-to-tie knots and the occasional unnoticed wind-knot, and the improved abrasion resistance is particularly valuable when a hooked fish dives into tough weed. That it doesn't fly apart when intentionally cut is also a real boon, saving much time, and temper, when tying rigs.

Carp Silk's new weave structure was developed for yet another important reason: conservation. Other braided hooklinks with a rougher finish tend to cut into the mouths of hard-fighting fish, whereas Carp Silk has caused no discernible damage to tench up to 7lb 14oz, carp up to 28lb, and impressively battling Wels catfish up to 24lb, caught by me on it recently.

This material also has a reasonable tendency to sink, so in effect it hugs the bottom thereby improving both presentation and inconspicuousness. Six different breaking strains are available – 7lb, 10lb, 12lb, 15lb, 18lb and 24lb – and one of its most attractive features is being supplied on 10m spools; this means a wide range can be purchased without upsetting either the bank manager or the spouse.

Finally the one-piece, transparent blister pack in which the spool of Carp Silk is packaged provides further advantages: you can see the colour and breaking strain through the pack, they are easily transportable, and tangling in transit is a thing of the past.

Cutting Braids
Don't use nail clippers or pincers to cut Carp Silk or any other high-tec braids. Even some scissors won't cut them, and the edge soon goes off those that do, I use a small pair of electrician's wire cutters of the best quality, and these have worked very well so far. I am told, however, that a product is marketed specially for the purpose called Braid Blades. Otherwise those modelling knives with break-off blades do the job well, but take every possible care because they are very sharp indeed: the slightest lapse in concentration when using one could end in a trip to the hospital for stitches. So please be careful.

One further word of warning: *never* try to break any high-tec braid with your teeth, fingers, hands, or any other part of the body: severe injury could easily result.

Making a Braid Sink
In the search for improved presentation, the hooklink material you choose – whether braid, superbraid, Carp Silk or even ordinary mono – must readily sink. A hooklink which doesn't hug the lake bed is more easily seen, and felt by the fish. To ensure your hooklink sinks like a stone just run it through a knob of ordinary linseed oil putty.

Loading Fixed-spool Reels
Whatever line you choose to load your fixed-spool reel with, it needs to be spooled properly. To do so, proceed as follows: lay the spool on the floor with the label facing upwards, and tie the line around the reel spool securely. Wind the reel handle ten times, and by lowering the rod top, check to see if twist has set in. If it has, turn the

spool over; if not, carry on, and fill the spool to the required level. For longish casts the spool must be filled to full capacity, that is, level with, or only slightly under, the spool's rim. If, however, extreme distances are not a feature of your fishing, load less line on the spool, say 0.060in (1½mm) below the rim; it is much more easily controlled when loaded thus.

Hooks
Many, if not most specialist anglers have come to rely on Japanese hooks, and Peter Drennan explains why:

In recent seasons there has been a complete hook revolution, with the latest Japanese manufacturing techniques providing British anglers with a new range of hooks of unparalleled strength and sharpness. Not only has their high-carbon steel proved totally superior to the standard European wire, but the Japanese have successfully designed and built machinery to manufacture to improved standards of accuracy. By this method hooks are made with ground and chemically etched needle-points which are sharper and more durable than the European cut point. Of equal benefit, much smaller low-profile barbs can also be produced.

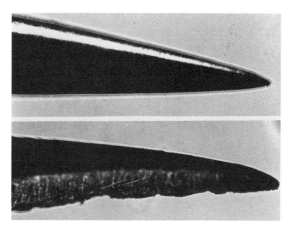

(Above) *The ground and chemically etched needle-point of a Drennan Carbon Match hook, magnified 100 times. (Below) The cut point of a similar match hook produced in Europe, also magnified 100 times.*

Following the standards set by Japanese suppliers, a full range of excellent hooks is now available in the UK.

The Starpoint Hook

The newer patterns of hook are especially exciting. One such design, the Starpoint, is in many ways revolutionary, because of its unique anti-eject bend, the point being more or less in line with the eye, a feature encouraging the belief that the new hook would behave in much the same way as the renowned bent-hook, and practice bore out the theory. In fact it works even better and has the advantage of inflicting no discernible damage to the fish. Not that I've ever experienced any noticeable extra damage caused by bent-hooks; however, there is rarely 'smoke without fire' so I've given up the bent-hook rig. Jim Gibbinson's 'line-aligner' works as well, if not better, anyway, and is described in Chapter 6.

The increased effectiveness of this pattern is due largely to the saving in weight compared to a similar gaped bent-hook, which improves bait presentation. Also, its much easier penetration must have considerable bearing on its effectiveness. Its point is designed on the principle well understood by the makers of swords and bayonets: the micro-engineered flutes hold the flesh apart, thereby reducing friction and so easing and aiding penetration. Therefore, this, coupled with a chemically etched needle-point, means that much less force is needed to achieve penetration than an equivalent-sized hook with a conventional point.

There are three variations of this type of hook available at the time of writing: Microbarb, Continental and Barbless. The Continental version is made from heavier wire and is particularly suitable where 'bullying' tactics have to be resorted to, for example close to snags and/or dense weed, and particularly where there is a chance of hooking carp. The standard-gauge wire Microbarb design, though, is probably strong enough for almost any tench fishing situation.

Barbless Hooks

The new barbless Starpoint, also constructed from the standard gauge wire, is an exceptionally useful pattern. Many commercial fisheries, and some club waters, have banned barbed hooks, again in the interests of the fishes' welfare. On such waters, and indeed for those anglers who prefer to use barbless hooks, the new design offers a better hook-hold than do ordinary barbless hooks; in other words, there is less chance of a fish slipping them during the fight. This extra-secure hook-holding capability is achieved by a small, onion-shaped bulge in the wire immediately below the micro-engineered flutes. Though I rarely lost fish due to them slipping ordinary barbless hooks, I have never had it happen on this new design.

The Continental design is available in sizes 1 to 8, both other versions in sizes 4 to 14.

The Continental Boilie Hook

Newly launched for the 1995–96 season is a stronger version of one of the most popular hooks on the market, the Drennan Boilie Hook. This brand-new pattern is known as the Continental Boilie Hook and is constructed from heavy gauge, super high-carbon wire, with the needle-sharp point of the hook slightly in-turned. They are of primary importance wherever ultimate strength is required, and are simply the standard Boilie Hook given even greater holding power and strength.

They are impressively packaged, too: each hook is individually clipped inside its holding box, thus preventing unnecessary damage to the point and also minimizing the risk of accidental losses, especially when tying up in poor light conditions when boxes can be dropped and the hooks lost. Incorporated in the transparent lid of the box is a small magnifying glass which gives the angler the opportunity to check for damage. This, of course, should be done prior to use, and at the very least after every fish caught. They are available in sizes 1, 2, 4, 6, and 8, and should be in every big-fish angler's tackle bag.

High-Tech Hooks

Kamatsu were the first high-tech hooks I encountered. Their chemically contrived sharpness soon became famous and everyone seemed to be using them. Nowadays they are known as Kamasan, and although the name is different, the quality remains the same: first class. The 980 pattern I use proves totally reliable, and likewise the barbless version. Both are available in sizes 2 to 20.

Other Kamasan patterns I use frequently are B983, B987, and B790. The former is a wide-gaped, round-bend hook, ideal for side-hooking boilies. The two others are chosen because, where possible, I like to match the colour of the hook with that of the bait. For example, the B790, being gold-coloured matches sweetcorn.

Spade-End Hooks

Other reliable hooks are available of the spade-end variety, the type I prefer. Similar in all other respects, a spade-end will not weigh as much as its eyed counterpart, which must significantly improve presentation.

Spade-ends have the undeserved reputation of cutting through line. In more than thirty years of using hooks of this type, never once have I had the remotest suspicion that a fish had been lost because the spade-end had cut the line. Perhaps I have just been lucky or, more likely, have taken the trouble to learn how to tie knots correctly. I asked Peter Drennan why he doesn't market more of the larger sizes of his popular specimen hooks with an optional spade-end, and his reply was that the vast majority of big-fish anglers don't want them. I wonder why?!

Rust Prevention

To avoid any chance of rust attacking hooks, smear the inside of the plastic box with a neutral, odourless grease such as Vaseline. This has the added advantage that if the opened box is dropped, at least some of the hooks will remain stuck inside.

Ready-Tied Hooks

Not so very long ago I would never have considered using ready-tied hooks. However, the recent vast improvement in quality and my rapidly failing eyesight made me think again. Not that I could ever tie very small hooks to fine hooklinks particularly neatly, and certainly not to the

standard of some of the commercial ready-tied hooks.

When feeder fishing, using maggot on the hook, my first choice is either a size 14 Carbon Feeder or a size 16 Carbon Chub, from the hook to nylon range. I nearly always use the former when hitting 'twitch-bites' is proving even more difficult than usual: this pattern's combination of a wide gape and curved point will reduce the number of missed bites, because when it is used in conjunction with heavy feeders, many more fish will hook themselves. The size 16 Carbon Chub is perfect for that most difficult situation of fine line and delicate single maggot presentation, which produces more than the odd big tench.

With the ever-increasing need for improved presentation, particularly when float fishing, more and more anglers are looking not only at the quality of the hook, but also to the line onto which they are tied. The finer the line, the better the presentation, and suppliers quickly realized that with a superb range of hooks it was but a logical progression to marry the two together and so provide a pre-tied, good quality hook to good quality line. To fulfil this need, Drennan now offer hooks tied direct to Double Strength, and these are amongst the best, with four popular patterns available, all with a proven track-record.

I cannot over-emphasize the importance of inspecting and testing every hook before use. You cannot be too particular or too careful when it comes to hooks and/or lines, not discounting every other part of your tackle.

KNOTS

To get the best from high quality hooks and lines, anglers must learn to tie good knots. Knots for anglers are specialized mainly because of the fine, slippery nature of their lines; conventional knots that are perfectly adequate for string or thick cord, only cause monofilament to slip, and super-braid to cut itself. The knots that follow are well proven for the purposes for which they are recommended. Note that it doesn't follow that a good knot for mono will also be good for braid, and vice versa. Moreover, for ultimate strength and reliability, mono may very well demand more turns than will be needed for braid, even when the same knot is suitable for both materials. This is another good reason why I very rarely, if ever, tie two dissimilar lines together: it is preferable to tie-in a swivel, or small ring, between lines of differing breaking strain and/or different materials. I know it means two knots instead of one, but two well tied good knots are better than one that is unreliable. It is always when the biggest fish is being fought that a weak knot fails.

It is also very difficult to learn to tie new knots from diagrams. Therefore, if at all possible, get an experienced angler to demonstrate any knot with which you are unfamiliar.

Before describing the knots I use in detail, here are a few tips that improve reliability:

1. Always moisten a knot before tightening, and make sure all knots are tightened carefully.
2. There is absolutely no point in 'making do' with a badly tied knot: if you're not happy with it, discard it and start again. Even now, I still find that on the odd occasion I'll have to tie the same knot three or four times before being happy with it. It doesn't matter how many times it takes to get it right, but it does matter to get it right. As a general rule, if it looks right it is right, and if it looks wrong it needs retying.
3. In most cases don't trim the ends of the knot too close. Allow a little leeway and you won't end up with a lost fish and a tiny 'pigtail' of curly line.

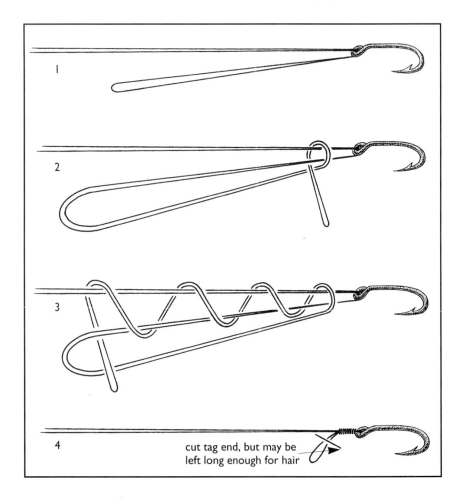

cut tag end, but may be
left long enough for hair

Double-line grinner knot.

4. Another virtue is patience. Practice tying knots, as with anything, makes perfect. It is well worth spending some time practising tying knots at home before using them out on the bank.

5. Always use a tiny drop of very thin super glue on a knot. This prevents it slipping, helps to protect it from damage, and also from water. To some extent all lines – and some more than others, especially monofilaments – are susceptible to absorption, and as a result lose much of their inherent strength. Therefore it makes sense to prevent as much water absorption as possible, especially at arguably the line's weakest point: the knot.

6. Pull-test every knot. This doesn't mean pulling to the line's limit, or even close to the limit, a practice which will only weaken the knot or line, or both. Just pull sufficiently hard to ensure nothing has seriously weakened the junction. How hard to pull depends on the strength and type of line.

7. Some lines, especially the latest generation super-braids, have recommended knots explained on the spool, or on an accompanying leaflet. In such cases follow the manufacturers' advice: they should know their product best. Using the wrong choice of knot will seriously weaken the line.

8. Whenever possible, tie knots at home, it is so much easier.

The Grinner, or Uni-Knot

The grinner, called the uni-knot by Americans, is the number one knot for eyed hooks and swivels. There are three versions, these being the single grinner, the double-line grinner, and the double grinner. The single grinner is the simplest and the one usually depicted in diagrams. The double-line grinner is the same knot, but the line is first 'doubled' before tying. The double grinner is used to tie two pieces of line together, usually of differing breaking strains, and less frequently of different materials; it really consists of two knots, a single grinner in each piece of line.

All three grinner knots are suitable for both monofilament and braids, but to get maximum strength and reliability, the number of turns varies depending on which material is being tied. My own tests indicate seven turns is best for monofilament, and three or four for most braids. The makers of Spiderwire recommend the double-line grinner with six turns as being one of the strongest knots they have found for this super-braid.

There are five stages of tying the knot, and as it is the most often used, I have chosen to describe the double-line grinner: this used in conjunction with the diagrams should enable you to tie it. (This procedure will apply for all the knots mentioned.)

1. Double the line 12in (30cm) from the end and pass 6in (15cm) of the doubled line through the swivel or hook eye.

2. Make a large loop leaving a long tail, then pinch the loop together with the other side of the doubled line.

3. Take the long tail and pass it neatly through the loop and round the other pinched part of the doubled line, for the required number of times.

4. Moisten the knot and tighten gently by pulling the tail.

5. Finally tighten the knot to the eye by pulling on the main line, and trim off. If all's well, add super-glue.

The Palomar Knot

This is probably the easiest knot to use with super-braids, suitable for swivels or eyed hooks. In fact because the grinner, in my opinion, is a better option I don't use it, but some swear by it, which is why it appears here.

1. Double the line 10in (25cm) from the end, and pass the doubled end three times through the hook's eye.

2. Make a single, loose overhand knot using the doubled end and the remaining doubled line the other side of the hook.

3. Open the doubled end to form a loop and pass this loop over the hook (or swivel).

4. Pull on the doubled line the other side of the overhand knot to draw the knot tight. Check, trim, and add super-glue.

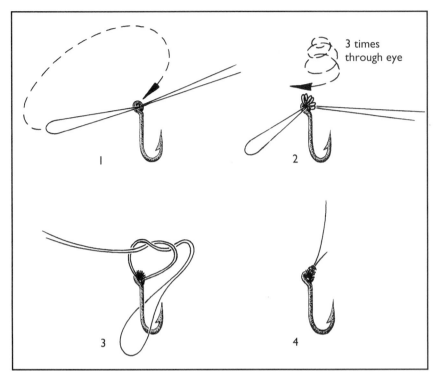

Palomar knot.

3 times
through eye

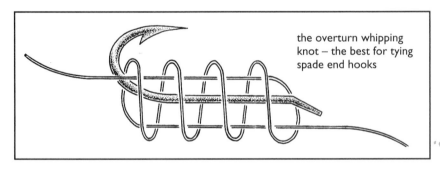

Overturn whipping knot.

the overturn whipping
knot – the best for tying
spade end hooks

The Overturn Whipping Knot

This is by far the most superior knot for tying spade-end hooks; in fact it is so good that it is my first choice for eyed hooks, too, and I only resort to the grinner when a particular rig dictates it. It takes just seconds for the experienced hand to tie, but it is difficult to explain. Nevertheless here goes!

1. Make a loop in the end of the line, ensuring the tag end is at the back. Pinch the bottom of the loop together with the hook shank between the index finger and thumb of the left hand, with the hook bend downwards.

2. Keeping the loop tensioned by the first two fingers of the right hand, rotate the left side of the loop over the shank. Make ten neat coils, accomplished by right-hand movements which are difficult to explain.

3. Whilst keeping the coils in place with the left middle finger, pull the tag end tight, but not too tight.

4. Pinch the coils with the right finger and thumb, and pull the main line just tight.

5. Inspect the knot. The 'straight' parts of the knot should be covered by the coils, and lie parallel to the shank.

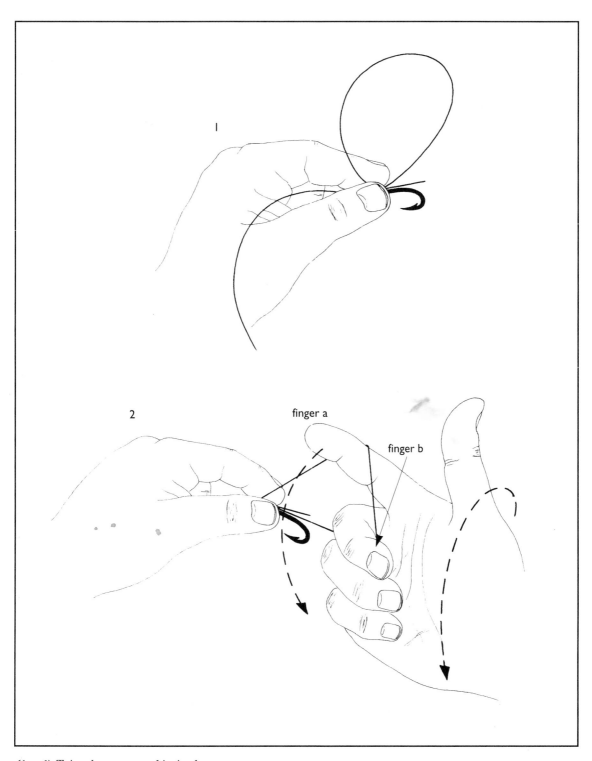

(1 to 6) Tying the overturn whipping knot.

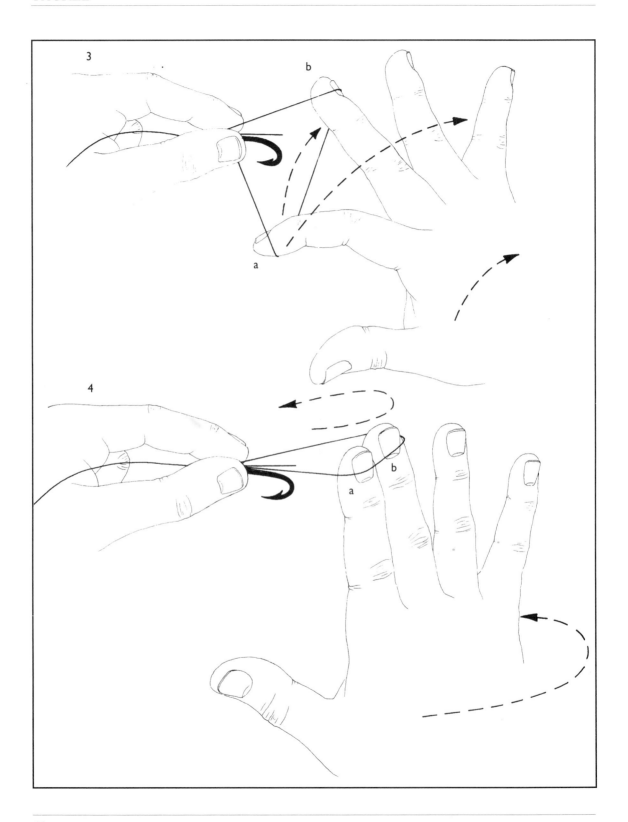

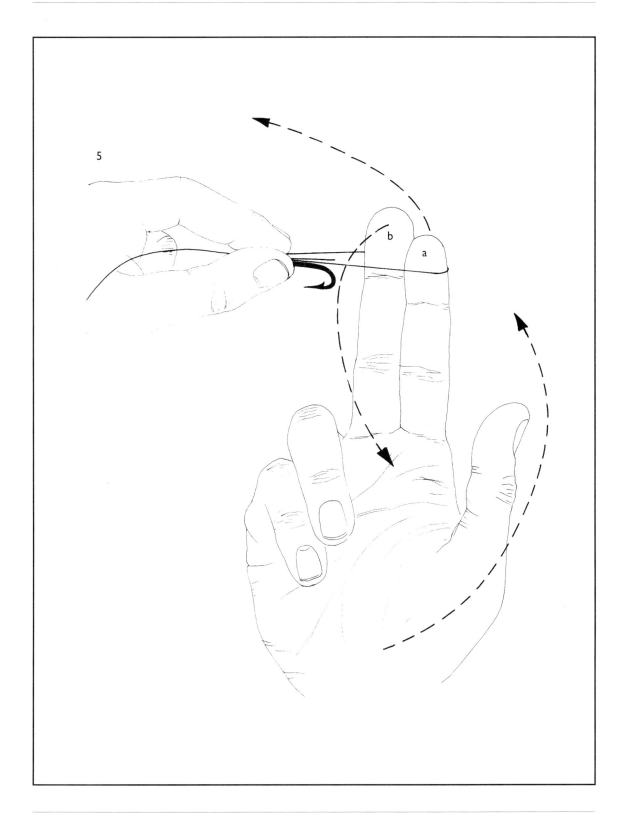

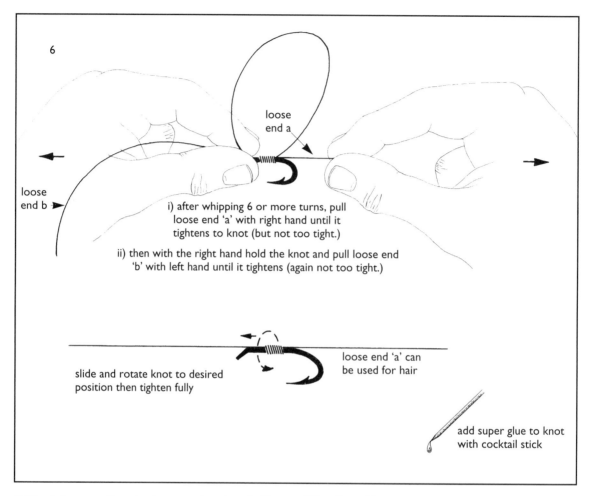

6

loose
end a

loose
end b

i) after whipping 6 or more turns, pull
loose end 'a' with right hand until it
tightens to knot (but not too tight.)

ii) then with the right hand hold the knot and pull loose end
'b' with left hand until it tightens (again not too tight.)

slide and rotate knot to desired
position then tighten fully

loose end 'a' can
be used for hair

add super glue to knot
with cocktail stick

6. To tighten, pull on both tag end and main line together. Ensure the knot is adjusted for perfect positioning before tightening fully. Trim the tag end, and stabilize with super-glue. NOTE: If not trimmed, the tag end can be fashioned into the hair, and is a very successful variation of the hair-rig.

The line should come off the front of the spade for optimum presentation, and off the back for increased strength. The actual number of turns, or coils, is dependent on the line being used and the size of the hook. For 3lb Double Strength to a size 12, at least twelve turns may be necessary; for monofilaments over 6lb to larger hooks, and for super-braids, eight turns is plenty.

The Stop Knot

The stop knot is used for a variety of purposes, but most frequently in two ways: to stop sliding floats, and as a marker to aid accurate casting. The position of this knot is adjustable by sliding it up or down, but don't forget to wet the reel line first otherwise damage will certainly result. It is simple to tie:

1. Take a 6in (15cm) length of line (or power gum) and bend it double forming a loop.
2. Lay this alongside and pinch together with the reel line.
3. Take one of the tag ends and wind it four times round both the reel line and the other tag end, pass it through the loop and tighten, pulling both tag ends.
4. Slide into the required position.

LEGER STOPS

These tiny yet vitally important items need to be readily adjustable, capable of standing severe shock without slipping, and they must not cut into the line. If the leger stop were to slip, the only certain result would be a frayed line easily leading to lost fish. A simple yet effective leger stop which satisfies every criterion can be made easily: a ½in (1.3cm) long piece of cocktail stick is plugged into two ¼in (0.6cm) long pieces of suitable diameter tube (I use the black insulation from ordinary domestic 13-amp cable). When wet the wood swells, ensuring a very tight fit. For absolute security, turn the line round the wooden peg two or three times, before pushing on the second piece of tube.

An excellent new design of leger stop is now available over the counter for those who haven't the time or inclination to make their own. This consists of the conventional principle of a small piece of plastic tube plugged by a tapered plastic peg. However, the peg has the line passing through it, which ensures that the stop is centred about the line (instead of being biased to one side, as in ordinary designs). This is yet another small but important step towards improved presentation.

Whatever type of adjustable leger stop is used, a small length of silicon rubber tube on the line above it, will help it to absorb shocks without slipping. This same dodge will help protect the knot from damage when using a tied-in leger stop, such as a swivel or small ring.

If a stop is required above the bomb or feeder to restrict the length of free travel, a firmly fixed leger stop is *not* required or desirable; it is much better to use a power-gum stop knot of suitable unobtrusive colour, tied on the reel line. A power-gum stop knot will provide the necessary resistance for the purpose, but will readily slip up or down the reel line for easy adjustment. Furthermore, and most importantly, the fact that it will slip prevents a lost fish becoming tethered should it break away.

SWIMFEEDERS

There are so many well designed and well manufactured swimfeeders available these days that it would be impossible to cover them all. Suffice it to say, for tench fishing I rarely use anything but maggots in feeders, and so two basic types, Feederlinks and blockends, cover most situations. On the rare occasion that it does become necessary to feed cereal or other groundbaits, I resort to open-ended cage feeders. I have a wide range of all these feeders, in all available sizes, and I also

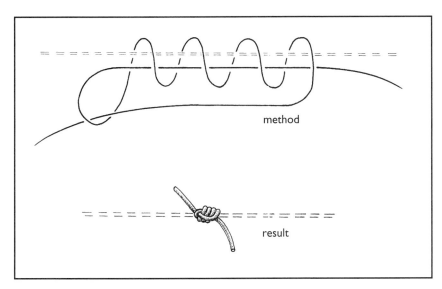

method

result

Stop knot.

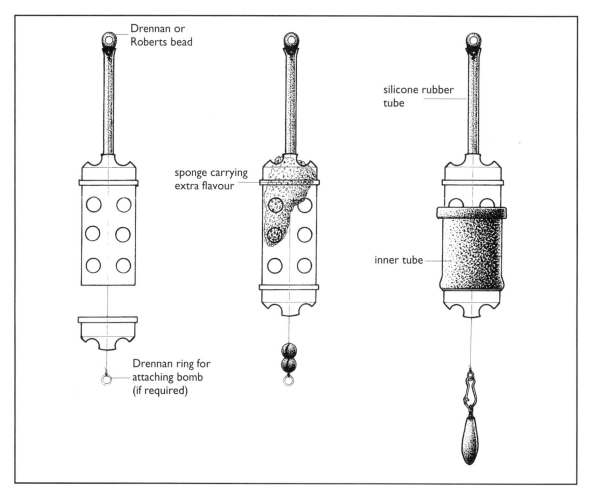

Drennan or
Roberts bead

sponge carrying
extra flavour

silicone rubber
tube

inner tube

Drennan ring for
attaching bomb
(if required)

Swim feeder modifications.

carry extra clip-on or saddle weights so as many contingencies as possible can be covered.

Preventing Problems

Invariably I will use the feeder on a sliding link in place of a bomb, because I want to keep drop-back bites to an absolute minimum. Used thus, some feeders have a nasty habit of tangling, although this annoyance can be considerably reduced by a simple modification: just cover the link with a suitable length of silicon rubber tubing (the tube is kept in position by locating it on the swivel or bead).

Also, caps on Feederlinks and other blockends have a nasty tendency to come misplaced, but the remedy for this is simply to invert the feeder, that is, have the cap at the bottom; then gravity ensures that it can't come off accidentally. Another remedy for this problem entails making the link from power gum. Undoubtedly this works very well too, but the snag is that the gum has to be stretched when loading the feeder, making filling more awkward, besides taking longer, you don't want to be wasting precious seconds when the fish are feeding avidly.

On very hot days, maggots are at their liveliest and escape the feeder almost before it is cast. To prevent this, at least some of the holes need blocking up. A suitable length of bicycle inner tube, black for preference, over the feeder is a simple yet effective method: you roll the tube back exposing exactly the number of holes required. Another way is to use PVA tape, keeping it in position by a couple of rubber bands; though more fiddly this is perhaps better, because it ensures that the feeder deposits all its contents in the swim. The disadvantage with the PVA method is that it has to be repeated for each cast, again wasting precious time, whereas the inner tube can be left on indefinitely.

Using Flavours and Weights

Recently I have been experimenting by adding either a piece of sponge soaked in flavours, natural or synthetic, or commercial feed-inducing rig tablets, to my blockend feeders. This tactic ensures that there is a food flavour leak-off and scented trail to draw fish to the swim, without the risk of overfeeding. To counteract the buoyancy of the sponge, simply add extra weight to the feeder.

All commercial feeders come with some kind of weight attached to them, clipped to the side, inside, or hanging from the bottom. Both the size and the position of this weight can be altered in seconds. Small clip-on weights and larger saddle weights are available, with little projections that clip into the holes on the feeder body; by adding or subtracting these, exactly the right weight can be achieved.

Don't Overfeed!

When large, perhaps solitary fish are feeding, it is very easy to overfeed, and once bait is put in, it can't be taken out again. So it is imperative to try to introduce the exact amount of bait required, and certainly not risk overfeeding – it is better to err on the mean side. Using small scissors, carefully cut back the feeder so that it holds the required amount of bait; a feeder holding just a dozen or so maggots will ensure a regular if meagre supply of bait to the swim. Even large feeders

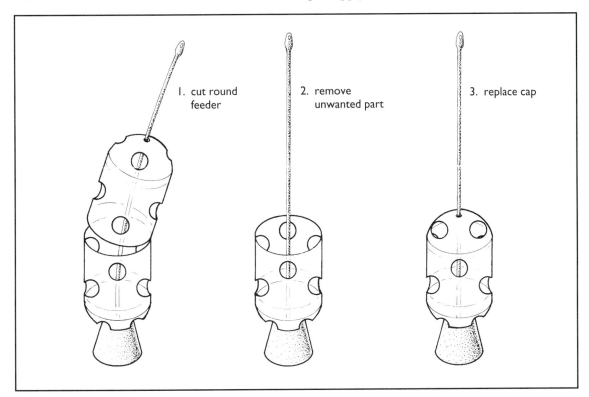

1. cut round feeder

2. remove unwanted part

3. replace cap

Simple feeder modification to hold less bait.

can be cut right back if a heavy weight is still required. They can be cut down to any size, even to the point where there is only just enough plastic to hold on the end caps, making the feeder little more than a link-leger with an added feed compartment.

The Importance of Link Length

Altering the length of the link from your feeder can make a dramatic difference to your catch rate. A feeder attached to a long link will undoubtedly attract more bites than one attached to a short link. The answer is to experiment until just the right combination is achieved.

In that excellent publication *Improve Your Coarse Fishing*, editor Kevin Wilmot summed up feeder fishing thus:

> Think of all the alterations you often have to make to your float tackle to keep in touch with fish during a session. Treat feeder fishing the same by making changes to the size, type and weight of your feeder, the way it is attached to your line and the length of the link. Your results can only improve.

This summary invokes only one criticism, in that it implies swim-feeders are only of use when legering. Nothing could be further from the truth: float-plus-feeder combinations can prove particularly deadly in the right situations, and will be examined in further detail in Chapter 6.

FLOATS

Tench anglers are now splendidly catered for when it comes to floats, and there is really only space enough here to mention a tiny fraction. Remember, though, that the float remains the most sensitive practical method of bite detection yet devised, and suitable for use in a wide range of conditions. There are tench about, and big ones too, that are almost impossible to catch any other way, so it would be a foolish tench angler indeed who dismissed float fishing without sufficient thought.

The float I once used mostly for tench fishing was homemade, to an early original Bill Quinlan design. Bill's float permitted the lift method to be employed at long range. Some anglers still consider long-range lift-method fishing to be impractical even impossible, and I suppose that to some extent this is understandable; however, Bill's float showed it could be done, and very effectively. (*See* Chapters 6 and 7 for further details.)

Today, Bill's floats have taken their place in my collection of angling memorabilia, having been superseded by modern patterns. The new floats are superior in every way. Besides, spending countless hours 'burning the midnight oil' making tackle that might or might not work, is time better spent fishing. The following tale should illustrate what I mean: every Monday after work, Bill and Bob Buteux would foregather in the latter's garden shed making Bill's lift floats. After weeks of trials and subsequent failures, the design was at last perfected, and those first successful models worked, in a bath, exactly as intended. Bob spent the next few evenings painting and varnishing them. The following weekend arrived and Bill was impatient to try them out. Disaster! Every single one sank! Bob's smart paint and varnish job had ruined the lot!

As I have said, there is no need to go to such lengths now because viable alternatives are readily available over the counter. In fact they are more robust, easier to see, accurately manufactured and more versatile. The range of patterns is vast, let alone naming all the available options, so I will restrict my remarks to the type described as Crystal Missiles. These floats are available in a wide range of sizes, they cast accurately over large distances and have the facility for interchanging tips. This latter feature is very convenient, and having the right tip to suit the prevailing conditions of wind, background, light and so on makes seeing the float that much easier. Furthermore there are also lights known as Mini-Nightlights which fit these floats for after-dark fishing.

The first hour or two of darkness can provide good sport, and because Mini-Nightlights are so much brighter, they are easier on the eyes than beta-lights: you must be able to see night floats

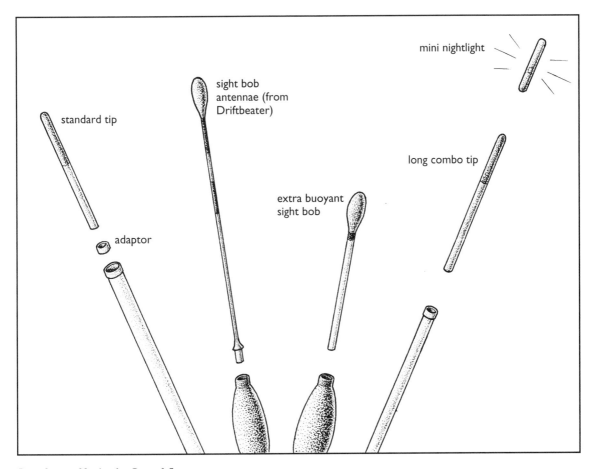

mini nightlight

sight bob
antennae (from
Driftbeater)

standard tip

long combo tip

extra buoyant
sight bob

adaptor

Interchangeable tips for Crystal floats.

clearly, unless you want a blinding headache. Nevertheless you should still avoid looking directly at the float, and should keep it somewhere to the side of your field of vision; positioned like this you will see it more clearly and avoid eye-strain, too. Mini-nightlights do tend to wear the socket in the float however, so I keep floats just for the purpose. And by using float attachments it's only a matter of seconds to change floats. Moreover included in the packets of interchangeable tips are small plastic adaptors which allow the smaller diameter tips to be fitted into the larger-sized float stems. These also tend to cause wear, so it is better to superglue them on the base of suitable tips.

Whether necessary or not, I always fish the above floats 'slider fashion', because then if con-ditions dictate that much deeper water should be fished, I won't have to waste time changing the whole set-up.

SWINGTIPS

Over the years I have spent a lot of time wrestling with the problem of bite detection when legering for tench, and have discovered that one of the most sensitive of bite indicators is a small dough-bobbin suspended on the line in front of the rod. However, there are several reasons why I dislike dough-bobbins (*see* Chapter 6), and swingtips have proved a reliable and very successful compromise. Although lacking some of the bobbin's sensitivity, they retain the advantage of being

A swingtip indicated the bite from the author's first 8lb'er.

positioned in the right place, at the front of the rod, so there is no question of a taking fish being alarmed because of friction through the rod rings.

Originally I thought that the longer the swingtips, the more sensitive they would be, but this just isn't true. The maximum length that retains sufficient sensitivity and does not prove too difficult to cast with, is about 18in (46cm). My favourite type are 17in (43cm) long and are made from tubular carbon-fibre to keep weight, and hence resistance, to a minimum.

The swingtip's hinge is a suitable diameter, 1½in (3½cm) length of silicon rubber tubing. Two narrow bands also cut from this tubing are used to connect a Mini-Nightlight to each swingtip. This method is preferable to more permanent fixings, because the Mini-Nightlights need removing at dawn to decrease weight and thereby resistance.

I have several kinds of swingtips, some home made and some made commercially. The lengths vary between 8 and 18in (20 and 46cm) long, and some are thicker than others; the thicker ones are easier to see, and the thinner ones less affected by wind. Invariably I fish a pair of rods armed with identical swingtips so as to be able to compare one to the other; thus making any small movement that one might give, much easier to read and therefore dealt with more quickly. Tench can, and do often give very small indications of a bite, and sometimes a small indication is all they *will* give; so those anglers who say they prefer to wait for a small bite to develop, will wait a very long time on some of the waters I've fished!

FURTHER BITE INDICATION

When float fishing and swingtipping is impractical, I resort to Solar's multi-functional Quiver-Loc system, used in conjunction with an electronic audible bite alarm (buzzer), for bite detection. This sort of system comes with three different arm types which can be switched in seconds, the choice of arm being governed by the fishing situation and method. As a guide, the stiff

Solar Tackle's Quiver-Loc system; set up here in 'balanced lead' fashion.

fibreglass arm, or quiver, is ideally suited to closer-range fishing or in gentle weather conditions; though in the latter case I'd prefer a swingtip. The stainless steel arm, using its adjustable weight, can be critically balanced to counteract sub-surface drift. The third arm is a flexible, fast-recovery quiver, in effect trying to drag the bomb, or feeder, back towards the rod. This enables a critically balanced lead situation to be set up, in other words a self-hooking rig, which is difficult for fish to deal with. All the arms are equipped with heads of different translucent colours, and they are hollow to accept beta-lights or Mini-Nightlights; the latter being much easier to see, of course.

BUZZERS

The Optonic bite indicator is probably the most popular buzzer available, and is particularly suitable when fishing for shy-biting fish, as tench can be. Its lack of resistance to a taking fish is well known: a single human hair drawn across the line wheel is sufficient to start one 'singing'. My own Optonic heads were 'tuned' before this practice was unfortunately frowned on; for reliability

Delkim conversions have proved better, and Bamford louder. Personally I don't need loud buzzers to wake me up because I rarely sleep and fish for tench at the same time; nevertheless they are needed so they can be heard over a gale force wind, for example, as it whistles through the trees. And under such conditions the stove is likely to be roaring in the bivvy, too!

It is advisable to obtain a couple of extras to complement the Optonic system. First, the 'vee' which locates the rod is of too shallow an angle, and as a result strong winds or a fast-moving fish can dislodge the rod from its perch. A pair of screw-on extensions, christened 'carp ears' by Carp Society president, Roger Smith will solve this problem. Optonics are fixed to buzzer-bars, or what have you, by means of a plastic screw whose thread is prone to being stripped. An alternative stainless-steel screw is now available and much more durable – besides making it more difficult for a thief to make off with your costly Optonics!

If by any chance you retain that silly plastic bolt, purchase a key that fits its head. Without this it proves virtually impossible to loosen the bolt with cold and wet fingers, and it must be removed to replace spent batteries. Replacements are available, good quality stainless-steel ones, with coin-slotted heads.

I also own a set of Steve Neville buzzers which although they provide more resistance to a taking fish than Optonics, do have significant advantages; they have never let me down since buying them more than five years ago. Condensation never affects them, no matter how hard or long it has rained, or how long they have been out in the elements. And, compared to Optonics, their battery life is remarkable, a full year at the very least.

ROD-REST SYSTEMS

Bank-Sticks

Bank-sticks are, arguably, the most abused item of an angler's kit, and so need to be sturdy and tough without being too heavy or too bulky. Stainless steel is, without doubt, the best material to make them from, but it is quite difficult to machine and, consequently, components made from it will not be cheap. On the other hand, it is virtually indestructible so that bank-sticks made from it will last a lifetime and are therefore not so expensive as would first appear.

Two pairs of bank-sticks, each pair of different length, will suffice for all but exceptional circumstances. Mine are 17in (43cm) extending to 32in (80cm), and 32in (80cm) extending to 50in (125cm). The shorter pair is made from ⅜in (9mm) diameter stainless-steel tube and the latter from ½in (13mm) diameter. Both are pointed and have stainless rod centres which, of course, are the extensions. These, too, are pointed so they can be utilized independently of their outer tubes, providing a greater measure of versatility. Twin buzzer-bars screw into both the front and back bank-sticks of each pair. Excellent, commercially made, stainless-steel products similar to those described are now widely available.

On some venues it can be extremely difficult to get bank-sticks (and brolly poles) into the ground. Where this is the case, a nylon-faced mallet is an indispensable item.

Buzzers are always fished in situ *when legering. This is Ron Chant's set-up.*

Rod Pods

There are some waters, particularly gravel pits and concrete-sided reservoirs, where it is impossible to drive in bank-sticks. Here a rod pod is the answer.

The best rod pod I have ever used is made entirely from high-quality stainless steel by Solar Tackle and is sturdy and very hard-wearing. The well thought-out design ensures that setting-up is easy, and it remains stable whatever the weather and however uneven the terrain. When not in use it folds down into a plastic tube 24 in (60cm) long and 2in (50mm) in diameter.

Buzzers

Whichever type of rod-rest is in use, either bank-stick or rod pod, buzzers are fitted to the front buzzer-bar and non-slip butt holders to the rear. There are two main reasons for the buzzers always being *in situ*, whether audible bite detection is required or not: first, the buzzer head is eminently suitable for holding the rod as, of course, it was designed to, so there is no need to carry further rod-rests; and second, should conditions change, dictating the use of a buzzer, it is already in position thereby maximizing fishing time.

Ideally, buzzer-bars should have a provision for adjusting width so, for example, swingtips can be positioned close together, making it easier to watch both simultaneously.

LANDING NETS

It really is a matter of personal preference whether you use a round or triangular-shaped landing net; my choice is the triangular type. To obtain the features I consider necessary in a landing net – light weight coupled with strength, and no loose pieces to lose – I designed and made my own. It has 32in (80cm) arms which spring into a strong spreader; this was machined, out of the solid, from aircraft-quality duralumin, and is permanently fixed to the 6ft 6in (2m) long handle. Arms and handle are tubular carbon-fibre, salvaged from old rods.

Knotted meshes and nets are now illegal, so use one of the knotless micromeshes; these are

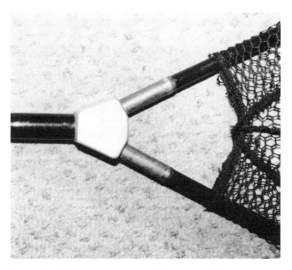

Spreader-block arrangement of the author's home-made landing-net.

kinder because they do not remove the scales from fish such as roach, neither do they split fins and/or tails as knotted meshes were always prone to do. Furthermore, it is rare for terminal tackle to get tangled in micromesh: the last thing you want to be doing is wrestling with a tangle (perhaps in the dark), especially when the fish are avidly feeding.

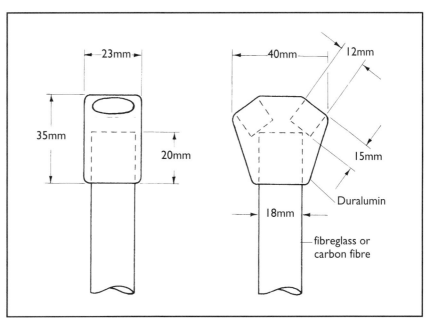

Landing net spreader-block.

LEGER WEIGHTS

Relatively recent legislation forbids anglers to use lead weights in sizes No 8 to 1oz inclusively; however, this restriction should prove no disadvantage, as excellent alternatives are now available. Some non-toxic weights have an unsatisfactory shine, but this disappears with wear and tear, and soaking them in vinegar overnight will remove it – then all the weights need is a swill under the cold water tap before being placed in your tackle box.

Some interchangeable link-legers (for example, Drennan) need no such treatment, and have the advantage that the supplied link may be extended by stretching, thus providing versatile presentation. They don't tangle, and the link-to-bomb connection is threaded so the weights can be interchanged without breaking down the tackle. These link-legers come on a card in five different weights.

To reach feeding fish, especially on large, heavily fished pits and reservoirs, it is now more necessary than ever to cast prodigious distances. After a long and perhaps difficult cast, and after a fruitless wait, it is frustrating, to say the least, to find the end-rig has been tangled round the lead all the time. The incidence of tangles increases with the length and difficulty of the cast, especially when braided hooklinks are employed. However, there are now leger weights on the market specifically designed to obviate this particular problem; several firms supply them.

When bolt-rigging for tench, I usually use the 'in-line' type of anti-tangle weights. These are designed to maximize self-hooking, their cunning shape ensuring that there is very little likelihood of the lead coming to rest in any position other than the one intended. Maximum resistance to a taking fish is therefore almost guaranteed, besides which the lead won't shift at an inopportune moment, when even a slight movement could scare the fish.

WEIGHING SCALES

For your own peace of mind weighing scales must be accurate, reliable and easy to read, and they must cover a suitable range. For example, it is hopeless attempting to weigh, say, a 2lb roach to within a dram or two on a balance that weighs up to 30lb in 2oz divisions.

Although certain well known dial balances come well recommended and are reasonably accurate and reliable, some models can be confusing to read. On these, the pointer travels more than one complete revolution round the dial and a colour change, seen through an aperture in the face, signifies this. However, unless one is very careful, and even then, mistakes can happen, and

Drennan link-legers, Kasaman hooks, together with home-made leger links and leger stops.

that is why I don't rely on this type even though many successful big-fish men do.

My own 'everyday' balances are manufactured from tubular brass; they will last a lifetime as long as they are properly cared for, and I have them checked regularly at a Weights & Measures centre for accuracy. For tench fishing, the model that registers weight up to 11lb in 2oz divisions is ideal – although forever the optimist, I carry a 20lb version as well!

I also take with me when I'm fishing, kept in the car inside its own leather case, a very expensive, super-accurate dial balance. This is only used for very special fish, or when I am called out to witness and verify a particular specimen, and its accuracy and reliability make it well worth the cost. This is also regularly checked, and the maximum error found so far was about ½oz (14g).

To get an accurate reading from a spring balance, suspend it from something stable such as a suitable tree branch. If this is not possible, use a landing-net handle or a bank-stick held steady by a couple of colleagues for the same purpose; either of these methods is usually more accurate than a hand-held reading. And if accuracy is your aim, as of course it must be, always suspend the balance by its handle, *never* by gripping its sides.

KEEPNETS, KEEPSACKS AND TUNNELS

Under no circumstances should a keepnet be used for retaining powerful specimen fish: they are quite unsuitable for the purpose. They are also now unnecessary, since keepsacks and tunnels are ideal for retaining tench and other specimen fish, and excellent examples are available from all good tackle outlets.

The very best in keepsack design incorporates the following features: first, a weighsling. In the interests of the fishes' welfare this is a big step forwards, because then there is no need to transfer a fish from weighsling to sack, thus obviating any risk involved in that manoeuvre. It also boasts a zip which comes part-way down each side, making it easier and safer, when putting a fish in or taking it

out. This style of keepsack is made from fully permeable material, generally in either dark blue or dark green, and of course has no trouble in meeting NRA regulations for this type of fish retainer.

The recommended procedure for using such a keepsack is as follows:
1. Wet the sack thoroughly, hang it on the balance, and zero.
2. Place the unzipped and opened sack on the unhooking mat.
3. Place the fish carefully on its side into the sack, taking special care when closing the latter not to damage its fins and/or tail.
4. Weigh, using the handles provided.
5. Place the sack in a deep, shady margin, ensuring that the fish is upright and breathing strongly, and that the sack is well secured.

It is very important not to retain any fish for more than a minimum of time, and to be aware of its well-being. Also, retain only one fish per sack, as according to NRA regulations.

It may be prudent to quote here the National Rivers Authority's (NRA) latest regulations regarding fish retainers:

A – No person shall use a keepnet having a depth of less than 1.5m (5ft) when fully extended or having hoops less than 35cm (13¼in) external diameter or if rectangular of less than 35cm (13¼in) by 30cm (12in). The keepnet shall be constructed from a knotless material and the mesh shall not be smaller than 6mm (¼in) internal circumference or approximately 2mm (0.1in) internal diameter.

B – Keepsacks and keep tunnels may be used for the retention of fish, provided that not more than one fish is retained in a keepsack or keep tunnel at any one time. For the purpose of this byelaw:
(i) a keepsack shall have a minimum size of 90cm (35½in) by 120cm (47¼in), be constructed of dark coloured, soft, non-abrasive, permeable fabric with rounded corners.
(ii) a keep tunnel shall be constructed of a dark coloured, soft, non-abrasive, permeable fabric, supported by a rigid frame, incorporating knotless mesh at one or both ends. The length of any

The author and Bob Buteux (right) share a swim.

An estate lake tench for the author.

fish retained shall not exceed the length of the keep tunnel.

BIVOUACS (BIVVIES)

On some waters bivouacs have been banned, and having experienced the anti-social, loutish behaviour of some bivvy users, I understand the objection. Nevertheless if you are to spend a weekend at the waterside, a bivvy will make the stay that much more comfortable – although it will be at the expense of a certain amount of efficiency. For example, it takes much longer to move swims, and by the time you get there, somebody has often beaten you to it.

Many and varied are bivouacs now on the market, and most are quite good. Best of all are those

Square bait-boxes make excellent containers for sundries.

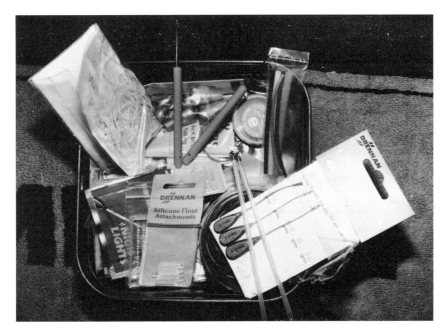

with a double skin and a sewn-in groundsheet, being waterproof and with no condensation problems, cool by day and warm in the colder hours.

BEDCHAIRS AND CHAIRS

The angler who spends more than the occasional night at the waterside would do well to invest in a well made, comfortable bedchair. This statement comes from experience of too many nights spent on cheap two-legged versions, and is made with some feeling – right in my lower back! The better ones are not cheap but are to be recommended. They come in various sizes; mine is the biggest, and with its built-in mattress, the most comfortable. Bedchairs with adjustable legs are also available, and can be set up quite level even on sloping terrain; a great boon.

It is also essential to acquire a comfortable chair from which to fish: the angler who is uncomfortable cannot concentrate on the job in hand, and consequently cannot possibly fish efficiently. Very low chairs are not recommended; one with a seat height between 14 and 16in (35 and 40cm) is about right: sitting at this height, the hand can be poised over the rod, or rods, ready for an instant

strike. In a new swim, make a few practice strikes before fishing; it wouldn't be the first time a big fish has been lost because the line tangled or a rod was smashed on an overhanging branch.

SUNDRIES

Other diverse, useful bits of gear can be found in my tackle bag, including scissors, sharp knife, catapults, pointed pliers, polarizing sunglasses, PVA tape, PVA string, disgorgers, artery forceps, baiting needles, boily drills, small screwdriver, various beads, rig books, and so on and so forth. Where and when some of these items are used will be discussed in the appropriate places.

Some means of primitive first aid is also important: a small tin of plasters and some paracetamol tablets (headaches at the waterside can become absolute misery) are essential and always carried; also a roll-on variety of insect repellent to prevent being eaten alive, and a tube of antiseptic ointment to ease the itching after you have!

Incidentally, allow me to share a valuable tip: if you apply the insect repellent to the inside of your bivvy, especially round the door, it keeps the mosquitoes out while you are asleep!

5 BAIT AND PRE-BAITING

Soon after becoming interested in hunting big fish it became obvious that experimentation with tench baits could revolutionize this branch of angling. At this time my friends and I were mostly after carp rather than tench. However, many more tench than carp were caught on the new baits we were constantly experimenting with, and over the years we gradually learned which of our baits carp would accept. As a by-product so to speak, our experiments also indicated which of our baits were particularly effective for tench. For example, I well remember the first time Clive Diedrich and I used trout-pellet paste at a carp lake in Surrey. The paste had been knocked up very hard to withstand vigorous long casting, and was used in lumps too big for any tench – or so we naively thought. On that first evening's trip we used trout-pellet paste on one rod, and cherry-flavoured paste on the other, and it was a real eye-opener: the cherry paste accounted for three carp, and no tench: the trout-pellet paste accounted for no less than five tench, and one was easily over 6lb – and this was in the days when a six-pounder still made headline news. Not that we reported it, or even 'counted' it, because at that period we were carpmen first, second and third, and any fish other than carp was just a minor distraction.

Then at Longfield, later becoming famous as Fox Pool, the tench greedily accepted almost every new bait we tried, including frozen pastry, cockles and sausage paste. The tackle used was 12lb line and size 4 hooks, and should have been enough to deter them; but it wasn't. Eventually we discovered a bait the tench didn't like, namely sultanas – but no Longfield carp were caught on them, either! Later still, at another water near Farnborough, Clive Deidrich and the late Malcolm Winkworth were trying out the then almost unknown bait, sweetcorn, for carp. After a week's pre-baiting they had started fishing with high hopes of success – and success they had, both beating their previous bests by quite a margin. But it was the number of tench caught that really surprised them.

USING BAITS EFFECTIVELY

It has been said that bait is not the most important aspect in the quest for big fish, and at times this may very well be true; but in many cases the use of the correct bait, or the use of the bait correctly, is absolutely crucial. How to select a particular bait, and how and when to use it is the crux of the whole matter, and only experience will help you with this complex problem. A bait's effectiveness varies according to many factors: these include different waters, different presentation, different times, different conditions, and its novelty value.

Different Waters
A successful bait on one water may be ineffective on another, and the veracity of this statement can be assessed from the following actual example. The southerly bank of one Colne Valley gravel pit is only separated from the northerly bank of a second by a small and narrow river, the Colne. In the former water, tench proved susceptible to a maggot bait, but in the second maggots proved useless because of the countless small perch and eels this pit contained. These were a real menace and did not give the tench time to get a look in; without doubt, if they could have been kept at bay, we could have caught the tench on maggots

Young Gary Stevens looks suitably pleased with his morning's work, caught on worms.

– but we didn't have enough time, or enough maggots, to prove the point: or so we initially thought!

Different Presentation

Crucially, it must be noted that it may not be the bait itself which provides the success, rather the way in which it is employed. The late Edward Ensom, who used the *nom-de-plume* 'Faddist' put it like this: 'Bait presentation may be of more importance than the bait itself.' Undoubtedly it very often is, and this point cannot be over-emphasized.

Different presentation eventually solved the problem in the second pit. A very short hooklink

in conjunction with a heavy bomb took the hook-bait quickly to the bottom, whilst catapulting maggots, being slower to sink, were employed to keep the perch occupied thus giving the tench time to find the bait hard on the bottom. This ruse worked quite well during daylight, but the eels foiled us as soon as the light began to fade.

Different Times

As a generalization, eels only feed in numbers at night, so if the second pit's nuisance fish had been restricted solely to eels, we could have fished any method confidently for tench with maggots during daylight hours only.

Different Conditions

On the other hand, if immature perch had been the only problem, the tench could perhaps have been caught whenever the water was coloured, for example, after heavy rain or during an algae bloom, as it would appear that perch rely on sight more than tench when feeding.

A Bait's Novelty Value

Where and when you are the first to use a bait which the tench are partial to, a great many fish can be caught. Furthermore, at least initially, you do not have to worry too much about presentation. A good new bait will be taken voraciously by the tench no matter how crude the tackle – although be warned, this happy situation will not last long. Tench are quick to learn, and you will soon appreciate the importance of staying one move ahead of them – and other anglers!

Take note where in the mouth each landed fish is hooked, because this can be the first sign that they are wising up to a particular bait. As a general rule, the nearer the hook is to the front of the mouth, the more cautiously they are feeding.

Types of Bait for Tench

Bait for tench can be loosely classified under two headings: individual or large baits on the one hand; and particle or small baits, also known as mass or scatter baits, on the other. Individual baits, as the name implies, are usually – though by no means always – quite a big mouthful.

Among these are worms, bread, luncheon meats, various pastes, mussels and the larger sized boilies. They are sometimes used when stalking, or perhaps when trying to deter lesser fish from taking a bait intended for their larger brethren. Particle baits are nearly always quite small, and some, such as hempseed for example, are minute. Included in the category are maggots, casters, sweetcorn, mini- and midi-boilies, black-eyed beans, tares, dari-seed, maple peas, buck-wheat, stewed wheat, and so on, and on – the list is endless. Fred J. Taylor and, a little later, Bill Quinlan and Rod Hutchinson, were among the pioneering anglers who demonstrated the effec-tiveness of particle baits.

There are baits that can be used in either of these forms. Large worms may be chopped up small, and paste is an obvious example; so is lun-cheon meat. This latter bait has accounted for countless big fish, some engulfing a piece almost as big as a matchbox, others being fooled when the meat has been diced into ⅛in (3mm) cubes. Boilies can also be made into any size you care to choose, although it is difficult to imagine cir-cumstances which would require you to go beyond, say, ¼in (6mm) through to ¾in (20mm) diameter. I say diameter, but boilies don't neces-sarily have to be spherical; in fact sometimes a distinct advantage can be gained by altering the shape, or apparent shape, of any bait where fish have become wary of its usual appearance. It could be that tench become so good at recogniz-ing how a particular bait behaves naturally in the water, that they can readily spot when this same bait is on the hook. But perhaps changing the shape and making it act differently confuses the fish. Counteracting the weight of the hook so its lack of buoyancy is neutralized, or partially bal-anced, also perhaps significantly alters the behaviour of the bait, and helps fool the fish into taking it.

SUCCESSFUL TENCH BAITS

Let us now look at a selection of successful tench baits in more detail. Those baits which perhaps can be termed 'traditional' will be considered first, followed by more modern baits.

Worms

Jim Gibbinson in his book *Tench* (Beekay, 1990) considers the gilt-tail worm to be the best tench bait of all. I don't know that I've ever seen a gilt-tail worm, let alone put one on the hook; but what I *do* know is that the worms I get from my garden, the enormous dark red ones I call lob-worms, are a great tench bait. Another, smaller, red-coloured worm, which I think is the redworm proper, is also good. The worm that is practical-ly useless, for tench at least, is the one with wide yellow rings around the body called, I'm told, a brandling.

Lobworms are one of my favourite tench baits, for three main reasons: they are very successful, they are readily available at any time of the year, and they are absolutely free to anyone who can be bothered to collect and to keep them. On a mild, damp night lobworms can be collected from any suitable local lawn. Time your activities careful-ly and it is an easy task, provided you can put up with a bit of backache – a small price to pay. By the light from a not-too-bright torch, check the chosen lawn regularly, say every half hour or so; the aim is to wait until the worms are fully emerged from their burrows, and then simply pick them up and put them into a suitable recep-tacle. Too late and they will have returned underground; too early and only part of the worm will be visible, making collection difficult. Sand first rubbed into your fingers will enable you to grip them more easily. Any vibration, however, such as a false footfall, will send a worm back underground with amazing alacrity. To forestall this disappearing act, the collector has to move rapidly to grab a worm if it is lying half in, half out of its burrow. Inevitably many will be gripped too tightly or broken when being extract-ed, and these damaged worms will soon die; if kept, they will ruin the whole supply, so discard them.

It seems to me that an enterprising parent might encourage his children's competitive and hunting instincts by arranging worm-catching contests in the garden; deductions made from any prize money offered for each crushed or broken worm!

Worms can be kept indefinitely in compost. The ideal medium is a mixture of leafmould, shredded newspapers, corrugated cardboard and grass cuttings, which needs to be kept cool and damp; not wet! The mixture is placed in a suitable receptacle with small holes in the bottom for drainage, and sited in a cool, shady corner of the garden. Mine is kept behind the shed. From time to time, used teabags and dry porridge oats are added to my wormery as extra food for the inhabitants, but this shouldn't be strictly necessary. One word of warning: don't add milk products because after a while they smell, besides attracting mice and other rodents. In wintertime cover the wormery with loose-weave sacks to protect from frost. Check over the contents regularly, replenish as and when needed, not forgetting to remove any casualties, and throughout the year you will always have worms at your disposal.

If, for any reason, it is not practical for you to have a wormery of your own there are other sources. When still in my teens, worms were always available from the local sewage farm, although I doubt whether anglers would be allowed access today if, indeed, they could face the prospect. A keen gardener's compost heap may provide a ready supply, as long as compost-making chemicals have not been added. But farm dung-heaps are probably the other most reliable source of worms.

Hooking Worms
Worms only need hooking once. In fact it would appear from experience that there is no advantage whatsoever to be gained by impaling them more than once, and this holds true whether a whole lobworm, a 1in (2.5cm) section, or a smaller worm is used. However, there is great advantage in using worms in conjunction with some other bait. For example, maggot and a lobworm tail can be an effective combination, as can worm and breadflake. The first 7lb-plus tench that I heard of coming from a water in my vicinity was caught on a lobworm injected with air by

way of a hypodermic needle to make it buoyant (Lee Kitchen being the fortunate angler). Personally I find this method distasteful, and achieve a similar presentation by employing buoyant materials to balance the worm: breadcrust, cork and rigfoam will each do the job. Fishing 'balanced worm' has proved itself many, many times.

For no apparently logical reason, lobworms are more successful if mounted on the hook more than one at a time: three appears to be the most successful number. Perhaps presented in this way the fish mistake them for some other live food that figures in their diet; though just what resembles three large lobworms all entwined together is a mystery. However, this theory could explain the savage bites experienced when using worms in this way. Maybe the fish grabs the bait with such ferocity because it is trying to kill whatever it resembles – and those who know what this bait looks like could hardly blame them!

Bread
If ever I had to go tench fishing without a slice or two of bread in my tackle bag I would feel less than totally confident, so highly do I rate bread as bait. Nothing is more versatile, and even with the marvels of modern bait technology, breadflake is still unique in its consistency. When used in thick weed, flake settles on, rather than sinking into the weed, thereby remaining more visible to the fish. Furthermore, after being in the water for more than a few minutes flake becomes very wispy, and it is easy to visualize just how difficult it must be for the fish to mouth it without pricking itself on the hook. If one considers these two factors alone, is it any wonder flake is such a good bait?

In the past a fresh uncut 'sandwich tin' loaf was used for my flake, but even by looking very closely before buying, there was no guarantee as to whether the crumb would be any good for flake or not. Nowadays the major supermarkets' medium- or thick-sliced wrapped loaves are fairly consistent, no matter where in the country they are purchased, and are therefore preferred. These loaves can be readily flavoured, too. As soon as you get one home, open both ends of the

Bob Buteux swears by breadflake – and who would argue with his results?

wrapping carefully, and by way of an atomizer spray, introduce a flavour and/or sweetener at each end; then close up the wrapping, put the whole loaf in a polythene bag and place in the freezer. As the bread thaws when it is removed from the freezer, the flavour is drawn evenly through the loaf. Flavours that have proved successful include cream, blue cheese, evaporated milk/ice cream and salmon supreme. Flavoured bread has accounted for many tench and is a particularly successful ploy where tench have become wary of ordinarily flake. Coloured breadflake is also worth trying.

Similarly, breadcrust is a very successful tench bait – in fact I have experienced days when nothing but crust has worked. And there have been other days when switching between crust and other baits has kept the fish coming. Almost any uncut loaf is suitable, although a 'tin' loaf is preferred since crust from this type of loaf is tough

and never burnt. As mentioned earlier, crust is also a good medium for balancing other less buoyant baits – and not only larger baits: a single maggot on a size 14 hook balanced with a chip of crust has proved its worth over and over again. This works particularly well when tench are feeding over fine silt.

Good old-fashioned breadpaste seems to be neglected these days. This is a pity, for it is a versatile bait in its own right, and when used with the hair-rig it can be knocked up stiff. Breadpaste is made from the crumb from an unwrapped loaf three or four days old, and preferably, with the water from the actual venue. If there is no alternative but to use tap water, let this stand for at least twenty-four hours to allow the purifying chemicals it contains to evaporate. It is as well to remember that fish can detect much smaller concentrations of flavour than can humans, so the chlorine in tap water might alarm them. For the same reason, cleanliness is essential, not only when making breadpaste but when preparing any bait. Be sure your hands are clean and free from the taint of soap, tobacco and so on, and that all cloths, work surfaces, utensils and receptacles are unsullied.

My own experiments with flavoured breadpaste began with such simple expedients as custard and blancmange powders, in addition to the better known honey and cheese. With such a variety of flavours available today, both natural and synthetic, the scope for experimentation in the art of flavouring all sorts of baits is limitless.

Mussels

To collect freshwater mussels ideally you need the use of a boat: mine is a small lightweight dinghy with built-in buoyancy tanks. The underwater feature to look for is a shallow bar or shelf, and if it has adjacent silt deposits, so much the better. If you can reach the mussels by hand, enough for a session are soon collected. A strong landing net will scoop up those in deeper water, but this method is more awkward and consequently will take much longer.

Unless you understand how to look after mussels (feeding them is a real problem, and a

Bob Carter has caught many of his big tench on mussels.

constant supply of fresh water is a must), gather only sufficient for your current needs. A knife with a serrated blade is ideal for opening the shells: just enter the blade in the slit and nick each end of the hinge. They will then open easily and you can cut out the orange 'foot' which is the bait. I know this may be considered a lot of trouble, but it can be worthwhile. My friends and I have used freshwater mussels extensively on certain waters, and this bait has accounted for many tench, including specimens over 8lb.

On one gravel pit, mussel proved encouraging in the early season. However, big bites soon became a thing of the past and we moved on to other baits. But Bill Quinlan, who really enjoys his sleep, took to using them at night, reasoning that he was unlikely to be disturbed if he did so! One night whilst putting this theory to the test, he awoke in the early hours and noticed the odd tench 'rolling' over his baits. Confident of getting a bite he sat by his rods, awaiting the run he felt was sure to come. But it didn't. His buzzer 'bleeped' briefly a couple of times and then the tench stopped rolling; when they did, Bill returned to his slumber. Come the dawn, on retrieving his baits to re-cast for the morning session, he discovered the mussel hookbaits had been chewed - 'They looked as though they had

been through a mangle!'. What the night before had been a mussel 'foot' of about 1in (25mm) across was now 5 to 6in (125 to 150mm) of stringy sinew!

Twitching tench again? We never discovered the answer to this question, but whatever fish chewed those mussels they must have done so with their teeth, and why they didn't either hook themselves or run off with the bait remains a mystery.

Luncheon Meat

Luncheon meat is another effective and versatile bait for tench; it may, of course, be fished in either 'individual' or 'particle' mode, and is an offering which again, they will accept when other baits are refused. It is equally effective on both estate lakes and pits, though for some unknown reason I've not yet used it on reservoirs.

In most tench situations ¼in (6mm) cubes are about the right size, and it may be that when more than one such piece is mounted on the hook together it alters the apparent shape of the bait and so disguises the fact that it is made up of cubes. Every hookbait made up in this fashion has its own unique shape and therefore acts in its own particular way in the water, a circumstance which may just fool an especially wily tench.

My son, Tony has demonstrated that luncheon meat may also be used with great effect for tench in strips, say ¾ × ¼ × ¹⁄₁₆in (20 × 6 × 1mm). He considers that used like this it is likely to flutter enticingly, perhaps emulating a pop-up bait, rather than staying 'nailed' to the bottom. Other predicted advantages are: the new shape may also hook a particularly wily fish; the hook point can be left more exposed to encourage self-hooking; and the weight of the hook may be neutralized with or without resorting to cork or rig-foam.

A further variation is luncheon meat paste, another successful ploy especially where tench have become wary of little pink cubes.

Luncheon meat should really be considered as rather more than just a single bait. Obviously different brands are not made to the same formula, and from time to time manufacturers will also change their recipe for one reason or another. Therefore, if you find a brand that works particularly well, buy as much of that batch as you can afford before the recipe is changed or the brand can no longer be obtained.

Luncheon meat bait does have one major problem: nuisance fish love it!

Sausage

In diverse waters, tench love a paste made from sausage meat, and pork always seems more productive than beef. To make an effective sausage paste is simplicity itself: add either dry breadcrumbs or fine sausage rusk until the meat is no longer sticky; about 5oz (142g) breadcrumbs to 1lb (450g) of meat is about right. Beware, though, because the paste will continue to harden long after it is first knocked up, and cold conditions will harden it even more. Also bear in mind that the more dry ingredients you add, the more you will compromise the paste's attractive sausage smell; although this may be countered by adding a few drops of synthetic sausage flavour to the finished paste.

If you plan to mount the sausage paste on the hook rather than on a hair-rig, you must pick out all the pieces of gristle in the intended hookbait; a tiresome task but well worth the effort, because a piece of gristle can effectively prevent hook penetration. There is no need to go to this trouble for free offerings or if the paste is to be mounted on the hair-rig, and the latter is by far the best procedure because it means that harder baits can be employed without the above anxiety. (Special versions of the hair-rig for paste and seed baits are described later.)

Maggots

I suspect more tench have been caught on maggots than on any other single bait. However, maggots have one serious disadvantage: all the 'genuine' nuisance species love them, too, especially those slimy little horrors, bootlace eels. Immature perch are possibly the number two menace, and seem slow to learn that a hook baited with maggot will keep extracting them from the water with monotonous regularity. Roach and rudd are equal third in the nuisance stakes. Nevertheless, the tench angler who never uses a maggot hookbait is at a distinct disadvantage, because there are times when this bait will outfish any other. Besides, if you give presentation and so on enough thought, maggots can be used in ways that deter unwanted fish without putting off the tench unduly.

Most tench fishermen when fishing maggot use them legering. There is no denying that this can be an extremely successful ploy, and when used in conjunction with a swimfeeder especially so; however, on a new water, perhaps where tench have not been fished for before, or on another water where they have become wary of the splash from a swimfeeder, float-fished maggot can be devastating.

Maggots can be coloured and/or flavoured to increase their attractiveness to fish. This is not a new idea: the match fishing fraternity have been doing it for years, although it took some time for specimen anglers to catch on. Perhaps this was because it used to be recommended that colour and suchlike was best introduced via the maggot's food, and the big-fish man did not want the bother of breeding his own maggots, which would have been his only alternative if he wanted to control the colour of his own bait. Nowadays, however, things are much simpler, with

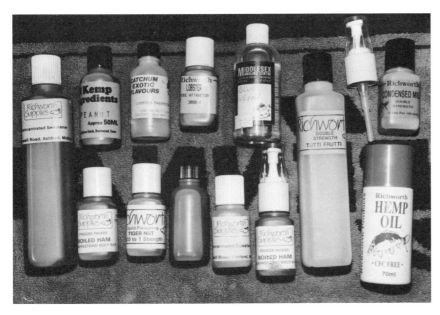

All these flavours, and more, have been used to flavour maggots on which the author has caught tench.

modern flavours and dyes widely and readily available which can simply be added to the maggot as bought – an exciting and profitable prospect. Furthermore there is now no need to employ older, more dangerous dyes such as the red dye, chrysodine, used extensively in the past but which is now known to be probably carcinogenic (cancer causing).

Fishing a large reservoir in the late 1970s. I first became involved in experiments with flavoured maggots. Fished in conjunction with a swimfeeder, these proved a much more effective and selective tench bait than identical tactics with unflavoured maggots. Even when they were fished side-by-side, nine times out of ten the flavoured bait was taken by tench in preference to the unflavoured type.

As the word inevitably spread about the results of these trials, several respected anglers expressed doubts that the success was in fact due to flavoured maggots. It was argued that as maggots constantly exude ammonia, this powerful solvent would neutralize any attempt at flavouring. This may sound very plausible in theory, but in practice, flavoured maggots did the trick then, and they continue to account for many big fish caught each year, fish that I am certain would not have been caught on unflavoured maggots.

Keeping Maggots Fresh

During extended summer fishing trips, Thermos flasks are a boon in helping to keep maggots and casters fresh. Ice-cubes will undoubtedly revert to water after a relatively short period, even if they are kept in a large flask and this is kept in the shade. Nevertheless, the resulting ice-cold water is invaluable in keeping the maggot container cool: the bowl containing the maggots floats in the bowl holding the water.

Another ploy is to scoop out a depression in the soil in a cool shady place, just big enough for the bait bucket. In such places, the temperature of the soil remains constantly moderate and will do the same for the bait. However, make sure that the holes in the lid of the bait-bucket – and lidded buckets are best for the purpose – are not masked, because without a good supply of oxygen, maggots will soon suffocate. Also, riddle the maggots regularly, at least once every twenty-four hours, changing the medium, preferably bran or sausage rusk, in which they are kept.

Casters can be kept fresh for quite long periods in a previously cooled Thermos flask. To cool it I used to put the uncorked flask into the freezer for a while, and have never experienced any problems. Recently, however, I've been told that this can cause the vacuum element to shatter, so now

I first cool them in the fridge before putting them into the freezer – inside a cardboard box, just in case!

Small bait boxes are fine for holding small quantities of hookbait such as worms, sweetcorn, luncheon meat and so on, and small portions of hookbait maggots. But don't fill bait boxes to the brim with maggots, because standard maggots, pinkies and squats don't store too well this way. And even if the bait survives, it becomes hot and smelly and will shrink in size. Give live hookbaits plenty of room by selecting a container twice as big as you think you need. Given air, maggots will stay fresh, smell less of ammonia and will not dehydrate, all reasons which led me to use washing-up bowls for keeping maggots.

Casters

I haven't used casters as much as I might, probably because they are so expensive in the vast quantities you feel you need to buy. And even though most good tackle shops now 'turn' their own casters, they can sometimes be difficult to obtain unless ordered in advance, particularly early in the season and especially at weekends. It would be a major mistake, though, to underestimate the effectiveness of casters; especially where lightish lines can be employed, they are one of the best, if not the best tench bait of all.

Turning Casters

Fish prefer fresh casters of good quality, and the only way to guarantee supplies is to turn your own: it will save money, and after a bit of practice, it is relatively easy. I took the following procedure from *Coarse Angling* magazine:

1. Always riddle the maggots through a sieve to remove unwanted rubbish such as old skins or stale sawdust, rusk and so on.
2. Place the cleaned maggots in a large container, without the lid, and add an equal amount of freshly sieved sawdust.
3. Lightly dampen the sawdust with water. The maggots will absorb the moisture, swell up and then turn into big casters.
4. Try and store maggots in a cool place, a garage floor or an old fridge set at about 50°F (10°C).
5. In order to speed up the process, once the maggots have started to turn to casters, move them to a slightly warmer environment, although do not allow them to overheat as this will result in deformed, spongy specimens.
6. Sieve off the casters as frequently as necessary.
7. Allow the casters to darken to a golden orange colour before you bag them, or they will end up spongy.
8. Store in a rolled-up plastic bag, and keep in a fridge at approximately 35°F (1.7°C).
9. Open up the bags daily to give the casters air. They are still alive, and doing this will help to keep them fresh.
10. Never try and hurry the maggots into turning by 'forcing' them with extra heat; it just doesn't work.

Sweetcorn

The lengths to which some anglers went to keep sweetcorn's effectiveness a closely guarded secret now seem far-fetched, not to say ridiculous. But at the time, those with early knowledge of the sweetcorn secret, and having experienced just how effective a bait corn was, did everything to try and keep it quiet: not striking a bite if a stranger was near in case the corn remained on the hook and was seen; only baiting up at night so that the bright yellow flash as a catapult's load was sent on its way could not be seen; a groundsheet spread so that any loose grains could be readily picked up before being found by someone not in the know – believe me, many and varied were the 'strokes' pulled to keep corn secret. Eventually, however, the word inevitably got out and life was made easier for all except the tench (and carp).

Sweetcorn is readily available in supermarkets. The 12oz (340g) tins seem most popular, but a considerable saving may be made when buying large quantities, by ordering the much larger cans intended for the catering trade. Sweetcorn may

Sweetcorn accounted for these three fine estate lake specimens. The anglers being Peter Drennan, famed chef Ramonde Blanc, and his son Sebastian.

be used straight from the can, but I prefer not to take cans onto fisheries: they are unsightly, and potentially dangerous to stock animals and wildlife, and if you don't take them you can't leave them behind. Corn is best transferred to another container, but keep the juice as well because it helps to keep the corn moist and flavoursome. And don't worry if the corn goes sticky and slightly sour because tench prefer it like this. Don't ever waste the juice; just mix it in with your groundbait.

On some fisheries sweetcorn was shovelled in by the bucketload before it worked, yet fish in other waters responded to the 'corn treatment' immediately. Why the difference I have no idea. Corn's effectiveness has the reputation for being short-lived, but I refute this; however, tench may give no more than small indications when feeding on this bait (*also see* Chapter 6), and you will have to come to terms with this.

Eventually, of course, sweetcorn's effectiveness will decline; but it can be given a new lease of life, again with the use of flavours, sweeteners and colourings: the following method works well for our group. (Because of its firmness and its less inherent flavour (to me), Iceland's frozen sweetcorn is probably more suitable for flavouring.)

Ingredients
1lb (450g) sweetcorn
lemon flavour
Banana flavour
Richworth clear sweetener
black syrup

Method
Cover the corn with water; then with, for example, an eye-dropper, add 2 drops of lemon flavour, 8 drops of banana flavour, and 5ml of the sweetener.

Bring to the boil and simmer for 3 minutes. Drain off the water. Cover with fresh water, add 8 drops of banana flavour and 5ml of sweetener. Again, bring to the boil and simmer for 3 minutes.

Drain off the water, put in a container, and whilst still hot, add 1 tablespoon of black syrup. Stir this and allow to cool. When the corn has cooled, each grain will have a very sweet coating which the tench adore. There are other successful variations: strawberry-flavoured corn, sweetened and dyed red, is another good example. The permutations are limitless. And if you don't want to go to the trouble of flavouring corn yourself there is an alternative, because some canned sweetcorn is now available in various flavours and colours.

Almost twenty years ago, sweetcorn accounted for my first 7lb-plus tench, and it still accounts for many of this size and bigger ones that I catch each season.

Trout Pellet

Although it has been suggested that various additives can improve trout pellet as a bait, I have found no need for them – hardly surprising since pellet has been specifically developed as a nutritious, balanced fish food. There are two main ways to use pellet as bait: for paste, just mix with a minimum of boiling water until the required consistency is achieved; and to use as a boiled bait the following procedure remains the easiest I know:

Use a coffee grinder to reduce the pellets to a powder, and mix with raw eggs to form a stiff paste. Roll into balls – ⅜ to ½in (10 to 15mm) diameter is about right in most instances – and drop into boiling water for about half a minute; do not put too many balls in together or the water will go off the boil. Boiling gives the bait a tough leathery skin, which has several advantages: it defeats the attentions of small fish, it means the bait can be cast or catapulted further without it breaking up, and it lasts longer when submerged. This latter consideration depends on how stiff the original paste was, and for how long it was boiled. The principal disadvantages are that boiling baits inevitably burns off some of their inherent flavour, and the tough skin lessens the flavour leak-off. If trout pellets are first drilled they can be fished directly on the hook, but they will last only a few minutes in the water before breaking down; just how long they last depends on factors such as water temperature and the attentions of small fish.

Trout pellet is one of the best 'instant' baits: that is, the fish seem to recognize it immediately as food, without any pre-baiting. I caught my first six-pounder on it the very first time I used it, from water where I'm quite certain trout pellet had never been used before.

Cockles

Cockles need no preparation, they can be readily fished in any number of ways, and tench love them. So why don't more tench anglers use them? Thirty years have passed since I learned of cockles for tench from Frank Guttfield's book In Search of Big Fish (EMAP, 1964), but they are still just as effective. In fact a friend of mine uses them almost exclusively for tench, and he catches more than his fair share of whackers!

Seed Baits

Hempseed

I buy hempseed in half-hundredweight sacks; in my opinion the small packs of pre-cooked hempseed as sold in tackle shops are not cost-effective. As a rule-of-thumb, a gallon of hemp is perhaps sufficient for a complete day's tench fishing in early, and towards mid-summer, and half that amount as the fishing inevitably slows down as the water cools. But I never travel without plenty of back-up stocks; on the day the fish are really responding to it, the last thing you want to do is run out of hemp.

Preparing quantities of hempseed on the stove at home is easy but it does create a lot of condensation, and certain members of the household, may find the aroma obnoxious. The usual method of hempseed preparation is to bring it to the boil and then simmer it in a large saucepan or metal bucket containing sufficient water.

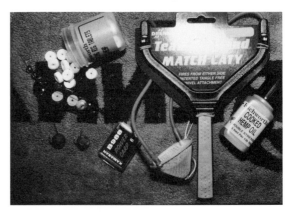

A well-designed catapult is an essential item in the tench fisher's kit.

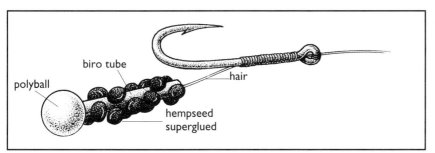

Seed rig.

However, it is quicker and better to prepare it in a pressure cooker, because you get less smell and condensation. After learning how much quicker and easier it is to prepare hemp in an electric boiler, I just had to get one of my own. Eventually an almost unused boiler turned up at a local car-boot sale, costing me the princely sum of £2. Hempseed is now prepared, up to 10lb (4.5kg) dry weight at a time, out in my workshop, free from any hassle.

Whatever the chosen cooking method, pre-soak the hemp overnight in clean cold water, as this will reduce the cooking time considerably. Hemp is ready when the seed starts to split and shows the white kernel.

Although I don't know of a flavour that improves the attractive qualities of hemp, nevertheless I add a few drops of concentrated sweetener. Also a pinch or two of bicarbonate of soda added to the cooking water will turn the seed several shades darker, a ploy that might keep the fish looking, and hence in the swim that little bit longer. And our sweetened, dark-coloured hempseed is a little different from everybody else's.

When away from home it isn't easy to prepare hemp without the expenditure of too much attention and too much time. However, Bill Quinlan discovered a straightforward solution: fill a Thermos flask three-quarters full with hempseed, plus any additions of sweetener and bicarbonate of soda, then top it up with almost boiling water. Three or four hours later the hempseed is just right, split and showing the white interior. When on a trip of a few day's duration, the hemp can be cooking in the flask(s) while you are sleeping; a valuable time-saver.

Besides being one of the best big-fish attractors, hempseed is a successful hookbait in its own right, although I suspect that the difficulty of impaling it on a big strong hook deters many anglers. They need not feel this way, however, because there are simple and effective ways to overcome the problem; the following examples are suitable for hempseed and other seeds.

An uncomplicated method entails simply drilling through the seeds and then threading them on a round-bend hook (tight corners will split too many seeds). Seeds may be super-glued directly to the shank of the hook, or to a short piece of plastic tube or bead on a hair-rig. But perhaps the most versatile method involves using a certain product called 'Bogey'.

Bogey This is a sticky, jelly-like substance which enables the angler to create solid seed hookbaits of any shape and from any seed, which may be used on the bottom or popped up. Bogey also provides the means of making hookbaits which are proof against small fish in seconds and without breaking down. In fact the permutations are endless. The one important principle is that the seeds and so on must be perfectly dry, otherwise they will not adhere. Just use a hair-dryer on a handful and keep them separately in a bag or bait box until you need them. If you run out on the bank, put some seeds in a suitable container, and use your car's heater to dry them. Here is how to use Bogey:

1. With moistened forefinger and thumb, pinch the required amount of Bogey from the pot.
2. Either mould into the desired shape or around a cork ball, depending on whether you require a pop-up or not.

3. Turn slowly in the dried seeds until it is covered.

4. Press the seeds carefully into position.

5. Repeat as necessary to fill in any gaps, though powdered flavours/attractors may be employed with added advantage.

The result is a particle hookbait that will last almost indefinitely in water. Baits can be made to any size, shape or form. Popped-up or on the bottom, and balls of seed soaked in a flavour of your choice are well worth trying. Bogey can also be used for bonding rig-putty to hookshanks.

Black-eyed Beans

Some time ago, black-eyed beans cooked in tomato soup were recommended to me as a brilliant tench bait. On a water where they haven't been used before, or where the tench have had time to forget them, tomato-flavoured black-eyes are certainly a very good bet.

Soak the beans overnight, then cook for twenty minutes in double-strength tomato soup powder (that is, use half the amount of water mentioned in the packet's instructions). When sufficiently cooled, pour the whole lot into a bait bucket and use like this – and if you have to bait up by catapult it is a messy business, especially if the wind is blowing towards you! But well worth it, I caught my first ever 5lb-plus male tench on black-eyes and plenty more since.

Canned baked beans may prove a ready-made substitute for the above.

Groats

Groats (crushed grain) are used principally as groundbait, and I have not yet tried them as hookbaits. They are simple to prepare and use, and the tench love them – but so do carp and bream! Put, say, two big handfuls of groats into a bait bucket, then add a large can of evaporated milk. Measure out 10ml of bait flavour and add this to a pint of clean, cold water. Add the flavoured water, a little at a time, until the groats won't absorb any more. When they have swollen by absorbing the liquid, the mixture can be pressed into loose balls for feeding. Once on the bottom the milk disperses through the water, attracting fish to the area.

Modern Specials

Early specials were usually made with a pet-meat base, and although they were originally intended for carp, these baits turned up some really huge tench. When he was developing bait for carp, Fred Wilton thought a little more deeply about the subject and, working on the theory that all animals need a balanced diet, originated the ideas behind baits that are now termed 'high protein' (HP) or, more correctly, high nutritional value (HNV). This book could be filled with typical recipes and not cover even a fraction, so I will limit my remarks to a few successful ones. Some basic principles apply to the baits which follow, and to avoid unnecessary repetition, will be stated now.

To achieve consistent results, measure all the ingredients very carefully. An ordinary set of kitchen scales will do for the dry ingredients, but for the concentrated flavours and sweeteners you will need special measuring cups or spoons; even better are spray caps, because each bottle can be fitted with its own, thus preventing one flavour being contaminated by another; each squirt from a commercial spray cap generally delivers 1ml. An eye-dropper is adequate for adding flavours drop by drop.

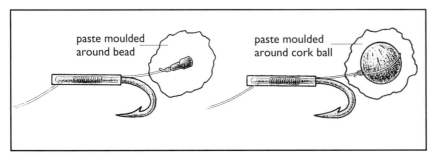

paste moulded around bead

paste moulded around cork ball

Paste rigs.

Take two bowls, mixing the dry ingredients in one and the wet ingredients in the other. Add the wet ingredients to the dry (not the other way round!) a little at a time to control consistency, which needs to be stiffer than might first be supposed. The resulting paste can be used, of course, as bait, and it is as well to remember that paste disseminates its flavour faster than boilies. These days I use Richworth boilies, and only make my own either when fishing a hard-fished water, or when I require a different-shaped bait from the universal spherical boily. Mine are cube-shaped and made thus: make the paste as above, and roll into pancakes ¼in (6mm) thick; then with a sharp knife, cut into ¼in (6mm) cubes before boiling. This ploy has proved very successful, but it has disadvantages: cubes won't catapult as far as balls do, and wind plays havoc when trying to bait 'tightly' with a catapult. Neither of these drawbacks matters much in practice because tench very often feed close in, so accurate feeding is relatively straightforward. At longer distances I usually revert to spherical boilies.

Always make your bait to the same standard weight; the dry ingredients of my mix equal 16oz (450g). This way, it is easy to determine how much concentrated flavour and/or sweetener to use to maintain consistency; 5–10ml per pound dry weight is recommended for both sweetener and a standard flavour, and 3–5ml per pound dry weight for the more concentrated range. When I do go to the trouble to make bait, I make several dry mixes and keep each in a polythene bag until required. It is so much quicker to take a ready-made mix out of the bait cupboard which then only needs the liquids added.

Incidentally, all my bait ingredients are kept in a locked metal box which is rat-proof, mice- and pet-proof, and finally childproof!

The advent of the hair-rig was the keen paste-user's panacea. No longer was there the risk of the hook not being able to be struck free because the paste had hardened in the water, nor was there any chance of any hard particles in the paste masking the hook. Fixing paste to the hair is simplicity itself once you know the trick: this is to tie

You are never sure what is going to be served when Fred J Taylor does the cooking on the bank...

...On this occasion – freshly baked bread!

a bead, or a cork ball if you want a pop-up, to the end of the hair and mould the paste around that.

Sodium Caseinate Paste

Sodium caseinate is a milk derivative and an excellent binder, and these qualities make it almost unbeatable as a basis for any number of paste baits. Again, because of the limitless range of possible ingredients, flavours and additives, I will give just one example. This particular recipe was first used for river fishing, but recently I've used it for some wily tench, and very effective it proved to be:

Ingredients
7oz (200g) sodium caseinate
6oz (170g) ground hemp
3oz (85g) Casilan (available from chemists)
5ml sweetener

Depending on the purpose for which it is required, the desired consistency may be controlled and achieved by the amount of water added. For example, hookbaits obviously don't want to break down too quickly, so hookbait paste is made quite stiff, adding beaten egg when extra-long hookbait life is needed. On the other hand, it is imperative that groundbait should attract and stimulate without overfeeding, so paste for this purpose must break down quickly; therefore it should be knocked up very dry – it should only stay together long enough to be thrown in, ideally breaking up as it hits the surface or very shortly afterwards.

Fishmeal Paste

This is very easy-to-prepare paste which at the time of writing has been most effective. It is made from equal amounts of Richworth 'Fish Meal Mix' and '50/50 Mix' and ground hemp. As groundbait or for pre-baiting just add water; to stiffen up for hookbait, add either wheat gluten or egg albumen as well.

Boilies

As already stated, for the most part I have long given up the tedium of making my own boilies,

and use Richworth ones almost exclusively. Company director Bob Baker tells us; 'The formula for these was developed by the Leatherhead Food Research Association. The preservatives used are commonly found in food for human consumption, and are not harmful to fish or the environment'. My own choice for the majority of my tench fishing is the midi-boily size. To deter nuisance fish, though, I often used bigger ones as hookbaits, sometimes two at a time. Using a sinking boily balanced by a pop-up is a particularly successful ploy, and remember that negative buoyancy may also be achieved by combining polyballs, rig-foam, cork and suchlike with ordinary sinking boilies.

Midi-Boilies

Why midi-boilies are not more popular with anglers is a mystery, since almost every fish in our waters loves them. Furthermore, even a very big fish won't need to eat many large boilies before becoming satiated, but that same fish will need to

Boilies accounted for this magnificent 8lb 12oz female for the author.

The scope for experimentation is limitless.

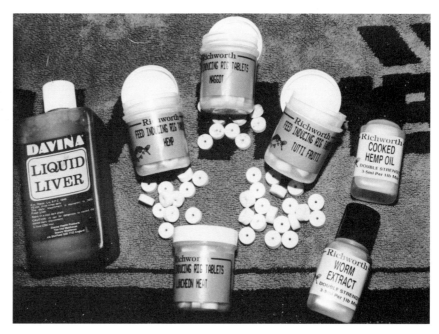

eat many more of the midi variety before it reaches the same state. And it is obvious that the more baits a given fish picks up, the more chance there is of it picking up the one attached to the hook. In other words, the longer our fish spends feeding, the greater the chance you have of catching it. Another thing to bear in mind is, the more baits it eats before being caught, the longer it will take the fish to connect that particular bait with danger; in other words, the bait's effective lifespan will be prolonged.

Commercial midi-boilies are, at last, now available in bulk packs, so helping to keep down the cost. Two new flavours – 'White Seed Mix' and 'Pink Seed Mix' – have been added to the more established favourites such as 'Tutti-Frutti'. 'Luncheon Meat', 'Cheese' and 'Strawberry Cream'.

Frozen Boilies

Commercial frozen boilies have been so successful over the years they hardly need any introduction. They contain no preservatives, are frozen as soon as they are made, and keep for long periods in an ordinary domestic freezer. I now use them for one specific purpose: where a unique flavour/sweetener combination in the boily is considered necessary.

Unflavoured boilies, called neutrals, are best for the purpose and they must be frozen to get 100 per cent flavour penetration; they are easily flavoured and/or sweetened to your own requirements. For example, on a heavily fished water one can produce a unique bait perhaps by combining several flavours, that would be difficult for anybody else 'outside' to copy. Simply spray the chosen flavour(s)/sweetener into a resealable plastic bag, and as the boilies thaw out, the flavour is drawn into them. This procedure works better than might at first be expected due to the fact that freezing dehydrates them and, as they thaw, they absorb any moisture in the bag.

As a general guide, weigh out 1lb (450g) of frozen boilies, introduce ten squirts of the chosen standard strength flavour (three to four squirts of a more condensed sort) by means of a spray cap, and shake the bag well to ensure that all the baits are covered. Clear sweetener is added in the same way. The bait will be ready in about four hours left at room temperature, but is better if it can be left overnight. Lately I've been experimenting with other flavours, namely 'Cream' and 'Maple', 'Ester Strawberry' and 'Ester Bunspice', and early results are encouraging.

Food is cooked in the van whenever possible.

Of course, you don't have to keep to the flavours mentioned; the choice is yours, and the opportunities are limitless. Don't be tempted to overdo the flavour, however: too much, and the bait will repel rather than attract, and the same applies to the use of sweeteners. Besides, overdoing the flavouring/sweetening could perhaps harm fish (though hookbaits will stand a certain amount of over-flavouring because they are not actually eaten). If in doubt, the supplier will be only too happy to advise. When a bait begins to lose its effectiveness, you can sometimes bestow a new lease of life on it by changing the colour: orange through to pale yellow seems a good bet for tench.

For use in conjunction with boilies, feed-inducing rig tablets are now available; in a swim-feeder these dissolve soon after casting and rapidly disseminate their flavour. The range includes 'Aniseed', 'Cornish Cream', 'Tutti Frutti', 'Vanilla' and 'Waspgrub'. I am also currently experimenting with other products such as bird-food enhancer, worm extract and hemp oil, the last two having been formulated after a spectroscope analysis of the real thing.

A Boilie Campaign

When Bill Quinlan and I decided to give boilies a trial on a 'new' tench water, we knew we would need hundreds of them, and were thankful to be able to purchase the frozen, ready-to-use sort. At first their size – ⅝in (16mm) diameter – concerned us, because they had been developed and marketed with carp in mind, and we were afraid they would be too big for tench fishing. However, Bill was quick to point out that we had experienced plenty of 'tench problems' when we had been after carp, and on much bigger baits than those now under consideration.

Another plus factor for using larger-than-average size baits, we felt, was that maybe they would produce larger-than-average size tench! So a considerable stock of frozen boilies was obtained. Which flavour to use did not occupy our thoughts for too long since we had no previous experience to rely on. We therefore selected four flavours: 'Peach', 'Honey', 'Salmon' and 'Ham'. The first two are yellow and we thought might be the most conspicuous to the tench; the latter two are red, and Bill and I chose these for exactly the opposite reason – we feel that sometimes the more carefully feeding fish pick up something their more avaricious brethren have missed, and that occasionally this ploy may just fool the very largest fish.

To keep the baits fresh whilst at the lake we each purchased two 3½-pint (2-litre) thermos flasks, each one filled to capacity with a separate

*Accurately adding water to the groundbait mix (*above left*) .*

*Another 8lb'er for son Tony (*above*).*

Bob Buteux and the author hold a 6lb'er apiece; caught when such sized tench were still considered enormous.

Sunrise over Wilstone Reservoir.

Mick Brown shows how to remove a hook using artery forceps (left).

Portrait of a big tench (below).

Renowned wildlife film-maker, Hugh Miles, tench fishing 'Hugh's Hole'.

A brace of 'biggies' for Bob Carter.

All these are excellent tench baits.

This kind of container keeps tackle sundries nice and dry.

The author shares a boat with Newall White for Blenheim tench action (below).

Blenheim Palace Lake.

John Everard's 10lb 6oz specimen caught margin float fishing.

Dawn caught 9lb'er for Janet Jackson.

Bill Quinlan's best so far – 9lb 7oz.

An immaculate female tench for Bob James.

Renowned chef, Ramonde Blanc, looks on whilst Peter Drennan drags their tench swim.

Peter Jackson certainly qualified for an 'Early Breakfast' with this 9lb 3oz specimen.

Bernard Cribbins using every scrap of available cover whilst margin fishing.

Golden tench – 'beautiful, more yellow than golden'.

flavour straight from the freezer. Kept like this, the boilies remained fresh throughout the week spent at the lake – and will do so even in the height of summer, so long as the flasks remain in the shade. I generally keep mine under the bed-chair wrapped in an old towel, and only take enough bait out of the flask for immediate requirements.

On arrival at the tench lake for that first 'boilie sortie' Bill and I, as usual, used two rods each. One was to be baited with a boilie, the other with one of our conventional baits – sweetcorn or maggots – so we could compare the effectiveness of each bait. Bite detection was by swingtips. I was the first to cast out, the bait being a salmon-flavoured boily – and before I'd filled the feeder with maggots on the other rod, a tench was doing its best to drag the first one in! Although it was not the monster fish we were after, weighing 4lb 10oz, it answered some of our doubts concerning bait size: it reassured us that the tench in this lake would indeed pick up baits of at least ⅝in (16mm) diameter, also that they would take boilies as food with a big, sailaway bite. And I am happy to report that this set of results was far from a 'one-off'.

As the seasons passed and the effectiveness of the baits began to wear off, we had to try different things, although in fact the really successful alterations amounted to just two. Thus on some days midi-boilies outscored the bigger version, and we had to ring the changes with flavours and sweeteners. For example, it was found that when results started tapering off on the salmon-flavoured baits, we could give them a new lease of life simply by adding sweetener. Flavours found to be particularly successful were 'Salmon', 'Honey' and 'Tutti Frutti'. The colour of the bait did not seem too important, although it was difficult to form a conclusion on this because there were so many variables.

PVA Stringer

As I have already emphasized, accurate baiting is a vital pre-requisite of successful tench angling, and when legering, especially at longish range, there are several ways to ensure that a few free-

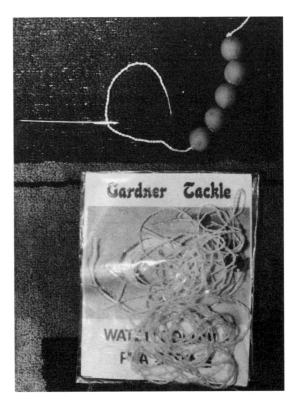

A stringer.

bies lie close to the hook. The easiest, however, is a PVA stringer, and it provides absolute precision. Up to ten baits, most usually boilies, can be threaded onto PVA string with a baiting needle; the PVA string is then tied to the hook and when cast out soon dissolves, leaving the free offerings adjacent to the hookbait.

Here is a simple method to do it. Push up to three boilies onto a baiting needle, fold the string and pull it through these baits; repeat until the required number of baits are in position. Tie a double-overhand knot in the string, and pull the boilies down to it. Cut the string leaving sufficient to tie to the hook, and cast out. Having given the PVA enough time to melt, say five minutes, I move the hookbait a few inches by pulling on the line. This is because I think a bait on the outside of the cluster is likely to be taken before one in the middle, and because this ploy, to my mind, helps maximize the chance of the hookbait being taken first.

PVA string is sometimes cabled (made up of several separate strands); by unravelling it you get more string for your money, and then if you stretch each single strand before using it, you get even greater value! An advanced version called 'Meltdown' has been hailed as the finest all-season stringer material yet available, guaranteed to dissolve right down to freezing point within five minutes, and in summer within seconds of casting.

PRE-BAITING AND GROUNDBAITING

I distinguish between pre-baiting and groundbaiting in this way: pre-baiting is the introduction of bait samples to the chosen pitch day after day and ideally at the same time, prior to actually fishing, the intended purpose being to accustom the fish to a particular bait, at a particular place and time. Groundbaiting is the introduction of bait samples and/or groundbait whilst actually fishing.

Pre-baiting

Over the years I have been involved in many pre-baiting schemes, and most have met with some measure of success, one or two spectacularly so. Invariably the most successful of these have involved tench.

Pre-baiting for big fish is not, and never has been, an easy option. It requires a great deal of planning, expense and downright hard work, and obviously takes time to get right. The right time to pre-bait for tench is during the close-season when the angler has the most free time available to him. Many recommend pre-baiting overnight during the season, in readiness for the following morning's tench fishing. Undoubtedly this works on occasions, but to my mind, it is far from the best plan. Any reasonable angler will tell you that the best time of the day to seek tench is early in the morning, so it hardly makes sense to chuck in bait intended for tench during the night.

I realize that bait introduced the previous evening may remain uneaten until the next

Pre-dawn – the correct time to pre-bait.

What a large appendage!

morning, for the tench to find when they begin their feeding patrol. But alternative fish species, as well as other animals such as diving birds and crustaceans, are bound to take advantage of this abundant food supply before the targeted quarry. For example, last winter I was pre-baiting for barbel. and was therefore introducing the bait at the best barbel feeding time: after dark. The margins were the chosen area, and by using a powerful torch I could check that the bait was ending up in exactly the intended position. However, after dropping in a handful of diced luncheon meat I was surprised and horrified to observe large crayfish – undoubtedly the American Signal variety – collect every piece of bait, before scuttling back to their burrows with it. And this happened not once, but on numerous occasions.

Moreover, of the bait that does survive uneaten overnight, some will undoubtedly be lost in deep silt or mud deposits, and underwater currents may also move it from its intended position. I realize that any tench feeding in the baited area will probably be aware of its presence, but why make them work any harder than they need, to find what you want them to feed on? (Note that this ploy may be used to your advantage when groundbaiting, when you want to keep fish in the area longer than they would otherwise stay.) We know, too, that a favoured tench feeding area is an incline, which may or may not culminate in an underwater bar or island. But how long do you think a bait will stay in such a position, particularly if the incline is steep? No, there is not much to be said for pre-baiting overnight for tench. It is far better to introduce feed at the time you expect the fish to feed, then not only can you feel confident that more tench will find it, but also that they will eat more of it! Remind yourself, pre-baiting is the introduction of bait, especially hookbait samples, to the chosen swim day after day, ideally at the same time, so the fish is used to finding a particular bait at a particular place and time. So of course when fishing proper commences, you use the same bait, in the same place and at the same time of the day.

Pre-baiting a Colne Valley Tench Pit

I well recall Bill Quinlan and I having stunning results after pre-baiting a Colne Valley tench pit in this way. We decided to give the tench the 'boily treatment' in late July, and every day for five days, 150 boilies went into just one swim which Bill and I could fish together; fishing

would commence of the sixth. (We were confident nobody else would be fishing the area because at this period it was covered in stinking black mud.) The baiting-up time was one hour before dawn, and there were good reasons for the timing: this particular pit has a large population of tufted ducks, and we knew from past experiences on adjacent lakes, just how much these birds loved boilies. By baiting whilst it was still dark there was less chance of the tufties seeing what was going on.

Other reasons for pre-baiting at that unearthly hour was that we could only fish short early-morning sessions before work, and we didn't want the tench to expect food at any other hour. Nor did we want to risk other anglers seeing what we were up to and reaping the rewards of our labours; at this time of day – or rather night! – they were safely tucked up in their bivvies.

'Being late summer fish – these were very big fish indeed.'

On the sixth day fishing commenced, and we succeeded far beyond our wildest dreams. Right from the start, and for the following five or six weeks, we caught plenty of tench, including big ones to over 8lb. And being late summer fish and therefore not carrying any spawn, these were very big fish indeed.

The following season, on the same water, the pre-baiting was once more carefully planned; though by this time news had spread of our successes the previous summer. Well, it is especially difficult to keep things quiet on a water where nobody is catching except you, particularly as sometimes we could only fish one rod each because of the frantic action! So we decided to bait two areas in case somebody else had designs on beating us to our first choice, namely the swim we had fished before.

For the reasons already given, we decided on the same time of day for the pre-baiting campaign. How many boilies to put in and how often were the questions that puzzled us, but eventually, after taking into account what we knew of the water and its inhabitants, the following procedure was planned and then carried out: two hundred ⅝in (16mm) diameter boilies were introduced every day from the middle of May, this number being systematically reduced until the week prior to the season, when the number was thirty per day in each swim; none at all were put in for the two days before we intended to begin fishing. And this time we planned a whole 'opening week' session!

Again, it worked like a charm. Several ninepounders were caught, including the lake record – and I firmly believe that, at the start of that season, almost all the big tench in the water were congregated in the baited area, so much so that the only anglers to catch more than the odd fish were in adjacent swims. To be honest, I'm not sure about the ethics of success on this scale; although every other club member had exactly the same chance to pre-bait as Bill and I had done. So all being equal, the equation is clear: determination, plus hard work and careful planning equals success.

Groundbait

Significantly, the numbers of quality tench caught by anglers using groundbait does not at first sight, seem to justify the faith many place in it. Although there are occasions when I do use groundbait, there are many more when I don't. Used without sufficient thought, groundbait is positively detrimental to your chances of success; yet there are certain occasions when its intelligent use will result in many more big fish being caught. Consider the purpose of groundbaiting carefully, and this will become clear. It has three main functions: to attract fish; to induce them to feed; and to keep them in the area. The ingredients for the groundbait mix should be chosen with these three functions uppermost in your mind.

Making Groundbait

My great friend, Bob Buteux, once went to considerable trouble to determine the best groundbait base for big tench. His trials indicated a base mix containing equal amounts of breadcrumb and sausage rusk, tench being partial to both; in fact, a successful hookbait is a paste knocked up from just these two ingredients. They can be obtained in bulk readily and at reasonable cost, crumb directly from a bakery and rusk from a butcher.

Unless you are using it for a particular purpose (such as when fishing 'The Method', *see* Chapter 6), groundbait should be of such a consistency that when mixed properly with water – and unless you are combining additives, use water from the actual venue – and squeezed together with the hand, it remains together just long enough for it to hit the surface. No more than just a very tiny proportion should then float; floating groundbait attracts ducks, seagulls and swans, which obviously won't improve your chances! Thus most of it should sink at once; although don't overdo the mixing to achieve this because over-mixed groundbait sinks like a stone and like a stone it stays together, perhaps scaring fish in the process – and those that aren't scared will soon become satiated by eating its big, stodgy lumps. It is therefore vital to get the consistency just right.

Bob Buteux in action.

Flavouring Groundbait

In so-called 'stillwaters' – and gravel pits are in this category, of course – there are currents nevertheless, and when strong winds are blowing, these may be quite powerful. The flavour from groundbait will be transmitted by the underwater currents to fish in other parts of the lake, and certain additives can make the message that much clearer. My favourites include canned evaporated milk, milk powder, potato powder and, latterly, water-soluble flavours, enhancers and sweeteners. The juices that baits have been cooked or kept in are also ideal for this purpose. For example, when canned sweetcorn is the bait, what could be better for carrying its scent than the juice from the can? Similarly, use the water in which a seed bait such as hemp has been cooked to flavour the groundbait used with it.

Keeping Tench in a Swim

To keep tench in the swim, once attracted there, may not be easy. However, the following three tips may help: firstly, don't introduce large lumps of groundbait, for the reasons given already. Besides once put in it can't be taken out again. Second, use maggots in the mix: some will burrow in the mud or hide in crevices in the gravel, and it will take the tench a long time to dig them all out. Third use something in the groundbait that is small and dark-coloured and has a strong smell that the tench are partial to. Casters and hempseed are obvious examples: being inconspicuous the tench will have trouble finding these baits, but the strong, attractive smell will keep them looking.

Placing Groundbait

Groundbait needs placing accurately. Using features such as weedbeds or reflections from the opposite bank can help, but a marker, or markers, in the actual swim is much better; clear plastic lemonade bottles tied by means of fine line to a heavy stone are ideal (these can be picked out in darkness with a torch). Fine line should be used in case a hooked fish tangles on it, although this rarely happens in practice. (Having said that, I bet it will, now!)

Dyeing Groundbait

Waterfowl, and especially the tufted duck, have very keen eyesight and seem wonderfully adept at spotting food lying on the bottom, whether they are flying over the water, paddling on the surface or diving beneath it. In the very clear water of gravel pits they won't have any trouble seeing, and finding, light-coloured groundbait, even in depths exceeding 10ft (3m), and can drive even the calmest of anglers almost crazy with their attentions. To reduce this particular frustration, match your groundbait's colour to the bottom on which it lies: weedy-green, and a gravelly-brown shading through to almost black, will cover most eventualities.

There is another good reason for dyeing groundbait: wary tench may have learned to recognize and avoid it in its uncamouflaged state.

No margin for error here!

Avoid Overfeeding Groundbait

By observing tench feeding in clear water I am now convinced they can easily be overfed by the introduction of too much cereal-type groundbait such as the crumb/sausage rusk combination mentioned. Some proprietary brands I have tried are less inclined to do this, but still have to be used sparingly. Moreover some very big tench I've observed lately seem to be solitary creatures, and even just a few thumbnail-sized balls of groundbait will soon overfeed in this situation: a ball the size of an orange thrown in at the start of a session, as so many tench anglers seem to do, will ensure that that tench is not caught on that day. It is a far better plan to put in just a little at the start, only increasing the quantity of feed when you are certain it is of benefit.

Judging the most effective feeding rate, whether loose feeding hookbait samples or using groundbait, is one of the most difficult, but most important things to get right. There are so many factors involved, some you are aware of, but a lot more you are not, which means you often have to rely heavily on your intuition. However, I do firmly believe that no groundbait at all is better than too much.

Fishing a Groundbaited Area

As expert match-fisherman and successful big-fish angler Alan Brown explains here, the technique to use when fishing a groundbaited area is this: 'Try to catch from the near side of the groundbait initially, progressively casting further throughout the baited area, hopefully taking fish as you go.' The reasoning behind this advice is that, should you cast to the far side first and then bring a hooked fish through the main feeding area, you will undoubtedly scare at least some of the confidently feeding fish already there. But a tench taken from the edge of the shoal can more probably be removed from the feeding area without alarming its brethren. An analogy can be drawn from the world of the wildfowler: if the leader of a skein of geese is shot, the remaining birds will scatter; but if the last one is picked off first, the chances are that the remaining birds will continue to fly in formation.

6 TECHNIQUES AND METHODS

Undoubtedly tench have the capacity to learn fairly quickly, perhaps more so than any other fish found in British waters. They seem to learn in a variety of ways, both from their own personal mistakes and from those made by their fellows. Furthermore, they must have a memory of sorts because they don't repeat many mistakes. For example, they will soon recognize the danger posed by a certain bait or rig they have been caught on before; and they may even become wary of certain areas of the lake from which they have been caught before. Certainly there are tench hotspots which consistently produce year after year, but the really 'hammered' swims do seem gradually to lose their reliability. However, given a year or two of neglect by anglers, and big tench will, most likely, once again be caught there.

Tench anglers should therefore be constantly alert, always on the lookout for new ideas or new baits, or thinking of new ways to adapt an existing idea or bait. Techniques for catching tench should be readily variable, and easy to adjust to a wide range of circumstances. This presupposes they should also be simple: complex float and leger rigs can take much time to perfect, time that can usually be better spent actually fishing – unless you are certain that a complex rig is the only way to success. In short, the tench angler with the adaptable approach is the consistently successful tench angler.

First, however, let us discuss the bite indications that can be expected from tench, because this facet of tench behaviour has great relevance to the particular techniques employed.

TENCH BITES

One lesson I have learned over and over again during my years spent hunting tench, is just how delicately they can, and do feed, and just how small are the resulting indications on the tackle, no matter how fine or well presented that may be. In my experience a tench soon becomes tackle shy, or rather, becomes wary of a particular bait on the tackle: after being caught, or nearly caught once or twice, or perhaps just seeing some of its fellows being caught on, say, sweetcorn, it soon learns to differentiate between free offerings and those on the tackle – and it can learn this astonishingly quickly.

The Problem of Twitchers

Once this stage is reached, tench feed differently, testing each grain before either eating it or, if it doesn't act correctly, rejecting it. This testing of the bait by the fish is, I think, one reason why the angler experiences those small bites some call 'twitchers'. Moreover tench must be able to do this testing very quickly indeed, for they would starve on a hard-fished water if it took more than just a second or two to test each grain. Just consider how many grains of corn there are in one tin, and how many maggots there are in a single pint!

Some anglers are more aware and are ready for this behaviour when it occurs, and by one method or another manage to catch the twitching tench. However, the tench in turn refine their own skill and become even better at testing their food for possible danger, thus giving even smaller indications to the angler (if they are discernible at all!) Remember, however, that their very existence depends on them being able to spot danger. This third stage in the tenches' feeding behaviour is extremely difficult for the angler to come to terms with; yet by changes to presentation, bite indication and tackle the angler can, albeit with some difficulty, stay one step in front of the tench. Some of these changes may be quite small and refined, others are anything but subtle! But, whatever benefit each provides, everything will eventually turn full circle, of this you can be certain.

I try to work on the premise that prevention is better than cure. Prolonging the period between each feeding stage, once the tench are 'on' to a bait, can only be to the angler's advantage. One way is to keep to a minimum the chucking in of free offerings identical to the hook bait; then the tench will have less to practice on, consequently taking longer to differentiate between the two (yet another reason for keeping groundbaiting to a minimum). Another ploy is to use something entirely different on the hook; for example a worm over sweetcorn groundbait works very well. Or you might try a combination bait such as maggot and corn. The most popular technique is to try to get the baited hook to act identically to the free offerings, and this works well. Equally effective is to make the baited hook behave quite differently from the free offerings. This may seem contradictory but in fact it is not: let me try to explain.

The advantage of having a hookbait behave exactly as a free offering is obvious: the fish can't tell one from the other. But it is impossible to get a baited hook to act exactly like a freeby, and it can equally be to the angler's advantage to get the bait to over-react. For example, a pop-up hookbait works so well because it balances the hook, and many would say that that alone was the secret of its effectiveness. I wouldn't disagree, but there is more to it than that. Let us say that a certain fish has picked up dozens, if not hundreds, of ½in (14mm) diameter boilies over the years. It has done this so many times that it knows instinctively exactly how much suction to exert to bring that size boilie to its lips. Then it comes across our ½in (14mm) pop-up; it exerts the correct amount of suction but, because of the additional and unexpected buoyancy, this one goes much further into the fish's mouth than it intended. The fish cannot reject the hook now (so long as the rig does its work properly), and so ends up on the bank.

It was Bill Quinlan who told me about the minute bites tench often gave at Southill Park. On many occasions when using sensitive float tackle the only discernible indication would be a ¼in (6mm) lift of the float – the type of bite that would

A twitch-bite produced this 5lb 12oz tench for Bill Quinlan to equal his then best.

not even have registered on ordinary leger tackle. Finicky bites at Southill became so notorious that this water was christened 'Twitchalot Pool'.

Over the years anglers have had to endure a lot of flack when discussing the small bite problem, being accused of making out that fishing is more difficult than it really is, to make themselves appear cleverer as a result. This is nonsense, and for example, my own purpose for discussing small bites is to help other anglers, or to get help myself. Other reasons suggested as to the cause of small bites include that they are the result of using coarse tackle, or too many free offerings, or both. This may very well be true in some cases, but not in mine. I've scaled right down to gossamer tackle where conditions have permitted, and put out no free offerings at all, but still the twitches have persisted. Other successful and well respected anglers confirm that tench are prone to giving small bites. Twitchers are a feature of tench fishing, and if only that undeniable fact were acknowledged, many more tench would be landed than are at present.

Dealing with Twitchers

In coming to terms with twitchers there are two broad lines of approach. In the first, the aim is to encourage the tench to give bigger bites. If this can be accomplished, so much the better, and although there are limits as to how far you can go in this direction, employing one or more of the following points may help:

1. Lighter tackle, especially finer and more flexible hooklinks and smaller hooks.
2. Longer tail, i.e. more line between hook and weight, and/or when fishing a paternoster, using a longer link from bomb to main line.
3. A new bait or a different version of the same bait.
4. A new rig, or method.
5. Twitching tench can be persuaded to run if the bait is pulled away from them.
6. A bolt-rig.

The second approach is probably better at putting more tench on the bank in the long term. In this, the aim is to use tackle and bite indication that allows twitches to be detected and

struck successfully; by some methods, the twitches can even be exaggerated. Always bear this in mind: it is vitally important how you set out to detect bites; by overlooking this vital aspect of tench fishing you will do yourself no favours at all. The angler who sets out his tackle solely in the expectation of big bites is unlikely to notice, let alone successfully strike, twitches should they occur. Conversely, a set-up to detect small bites should in no way interfere with the development of big sailaway bites. Therefore, although the aim behind most of the techniques, methods and rigs that follow is designed and developed specifically to sort out the small bite problem, it will in no way hinder a more boldly biting tench. The exceptions to this strategy are when certain conditions and/or situations dictate the use of bolt-type rigs.

FLOAT FISHING

Let me make it clear, float fishing is very much a second string to my bow, and swingtipping is by far my favourite method. Having said that, should a situation dictate a float to be the better option then of course I will use it, and in many particular circumstances it still can't be beaten. Remember, a float remains more sensitive than any leger rig yet invented. I don't pretend for one moment to be a good float fisherman, but strive to be proficient enough to make it count when the occasion warrants.

I still find magic on a still, summer morning, watching a float gliding serenely on the oily surface of some old estate lake; although most situations that would profit from the use of the float seem to occur on windswept gravel pits. Nevertheless, H.T. Sheringham's words remain immortal: 'A float, so pleasing in appearance, yet even more pleasing in disappearance' and will always conjure up wondrous visions in the mind's eye. Long may it remain so.

The Lift Method

Though the principle of the lift method has been understood for more than a hundred years, it was

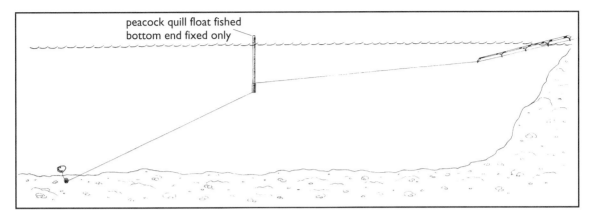

peacock quill float fished
bottom end fixed only

Fred J Taylor's lift-float set-up.

not until the late 1950s that it was popularized by the persistence of the legendary Fred J. Taylor. Fred recommends that the lift-method float should comprise a length of peacock quill attached to the bottom end only by a wide, tight-fitting band; it should be set overdepth, and all drawn gently taught until the float cocks. A good lift float should sink slowly under the weight of the single cocking shot and the bait; thus the shot will always be resting on the bottom providing the float shows. When a tench picks up the bait it inadvertently raises the shot as well, and as a

result the float 'lifts' in the water – hence the name. An immediate strike is essential. Two virtues of the lift method are obvious: it poses very little resistance to a taking fish, and it magnifies the bite.

On large and windswept waters the lift method as described above is of limited use, and won't work at all at distance. Nevertheless there are ways to adapt the method for use in strong, choppy conditions, and at long range – that is only limited by the quality of your eyesight. This is how my friends and I have adapted the lift method for

Fred J Taylor still fishing for the big ones.

large waters that invariably have uneven bottoms: the float to use is a long antenna type; this pattern makes for very easy bite detection at long range and in ripple. For improved visibility, colour is also important. Black stands out best against bright water, and vivid red, yellow or orange against dark backgrounds.

Changing floats when the light changes has always been tedious, but Drennan have cleverly got round the problem: they now supply interchangeable tips which fit a number of floats in the Crystal range, as well as other patterns. These floats are as light and buoyant as peacock quill, they are practically invisible to the fish, immer-

sion doesn't affect their buoyancy, and examples of a particular size are identical. This means that no fiddly shot adjustment is necessary when swapping whole floats, bodies, stems, or tips. Another valuable time-saver.

The variety of colours and lengths provided by the interchangeable tips means you no longer need to carry such a large selection of floats, and it also enables the perfect float to be assembled to suit the prevailing conditions without breaking down the tackle, even when that great little idea, the float attachment, isn't used. Extras such as 'Sight Bob Tips' are included in some packets, and not only do these provide a visual aid, but just as important,

Floats and interchangeable tips.

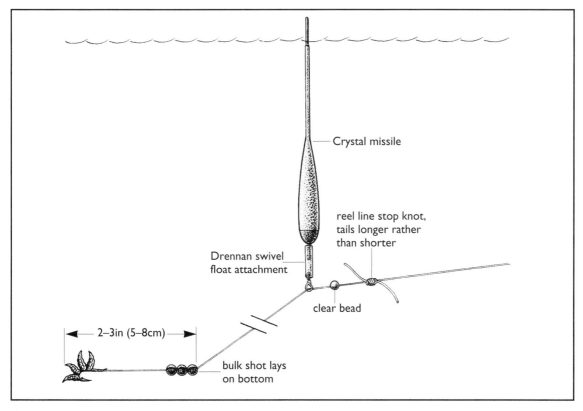

Crystal missile

reel line stop knot,
tails longer rather
than shorter

Drennan swivel
float attachment

clear bead

2–3in (5–8cm)

bulk shot lays
on bottom

Crystal missile lift-float set-up in use.

they allow adjustments against drift to be made quickly and easily. In really windswept conditions, the 'Long Sight Bob Antennas' can be removed from Driftbeaters and fitted too, enabling floats up to 17½in (44cm) long to be assembled. Such a float will allow the line to be buried well below the surface where it is far less affected by wind and drift, and that fine carbon stem remains stable even in

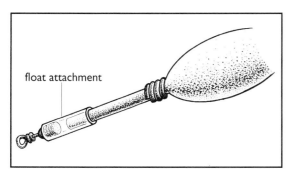

float attachment

Drennan swivel float attachment.

quite a heavy chop. The rod tip is also submerged for the same purpose. Of course, if there is no wind, the standard long antenna type works even better.

A sliding float arrangement employing a swivel-type float attachment is recommended whatever the depth being fished, because adjustments can be made quickly; it's just a matter of seconds to adjust the sliding stop-knot. Don't forget to wet the reel line first, though, with a drop of spittle, or it will certainly be damaged when moving a tight-fitting knot. Leave the knot tails at least 1in (25mm) long, then they will pass through the rod rings easily.

The float should be over-shotted so it will sink completely if the shot is not on the bottom. This load will depend on the size and combination of the float components selected, it will not alter so long as any changes subsequently carried out are made using parts of similar size (each similar-sized float is of exactly the same buoyancy). The bulk shot must be bunched close to the hook, say

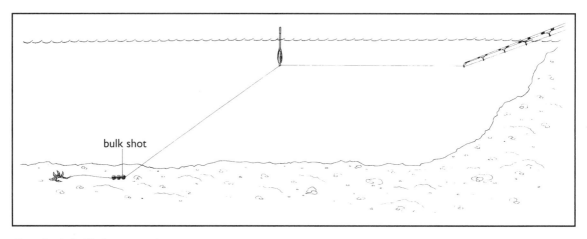

bulk shot

Crystal missile lift-float set-up in use.

within 3in (76mm); and this is important. Under no circumstances must the shot be dragged once on the bottom; the smallest piece of debris caught on the hook will ruin bait presentation. For this reason I don't mind if the bulk shot is heavier than it need be; even two swan shots doesn't provide too much resistance for a big tench, and is certainly less than moving a bite indicator back on the bank, thirty or more yards (27m) away.

Set the float well overdepth; this ensures that the line coming up to the float is kept clear of the tench's powerful fin movements. False float indications are distracting and frustrating, so try to keep them to a minimum. After casting, place the rod in its rests (ensuring the tip is submerged), then gently wind in the line until everything is drawn taught. The float is set correctly when the tip, and only the tip, shows; then as soon as a tench picks up the bait, inadvertently lifting the shot, the float rises like a Polaris missile being launched.

This version of the lift method can be used in any number of ways at the terminal end. Nowadays, more often than not, it is used in conjunction with one of the hair-rig variations described later in this chapter.

Float Leger

When the potential of pop-up baits was realized I tried fishing them in conjunction with the lift method, but it wasn't successful because too many false bites occurred. After further abortive experiments, the lift method was discarded and the float leger used instead. It is well known that the float leger is particularly effective when used with another buoyant bait, breadcrust, so I thought it a possible candidate for fishing pop-ups; and so it proved.

The float leger is set up in identical fashion to the lift method described above, with this exception: a sliding 1oz bomb is stopped a few inches from the hook. I think it was Ray Webb who said: 'When using a float leger in conjunction with a 1oz bomb, no matter how finicky the tench are feeding, or whatever manoeuvres they make, when they pick the bait up there is only one way the float can go and that's down.'

The float leger is not restricted to fishing pop-up baits, however; it is much more versatile than that, and in fact I am using it more and more. When small fish are proving very troublesome on ordinary float tactics, it is usually because they are taking the bait on the drop. So you need to get the bait through them and down to the bottom as quickly as possible, and a float leger often proves the answer. Throwing in very slow-sinking feed may help to keep these small fish occupied high up in the water.

One very effective variation is to swap the bomb for a feeder. This provides very accurate feeding in addition to delicate bite indication;

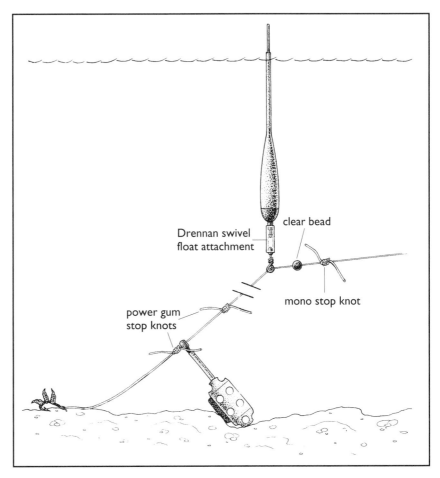

Crystal missile float-leger set-up.

clear bead

Drennan swivel
float attachment

mono stop knot

power gum
stop knots

used with maggots and casters it is particularly deadly.

Margin Float Fishing

Make no mistake about it, tench can and do feed so close to the bank that the angler often unwittingly ruins any chances he has of catching them before he even sits down. Fishing a rod length out, or even a half rod length, is very often much too far. You don't believe me? Let me tell you this: on an Oxfordshire gravel pit there is a pitch where bulrushes grow at the water's edge. Beyond the bulrush fringe the depth increases quite steeply, and many anglers note its potential. However, most of them fish too far out. My friends have proved on countless occasions that to catch tench all day long, your float must be within 12in (30cm) of the rushes. Two feet

(60cm) away and you might get two or three tench in a day; more than 3ft (90cm) away and you can forget it!

Selecting Bait

When float fishing for marginal feeding tench, especially where they can be seen, many valuable lessons may be learned. I've seen tench come in and mop up all my free offerings and leave just the hookbait. To all intents and purposes, the hookbait hasn't even been noticed; the float certainly hasn't moved. But I believe that not only have the tench noticed the hookbait, they have tested it, and found it wanting, and hence rejected it. And although I've seen this on numerous occasions, I still have no idea how they do it. But it underlines the problems of fishing for tench when you can't see what is going on. There is,

Margin caught male tench and the tackle used.

however, a ploy that often works when posed with such a situation, and that is to use a completely different hookbait from the free offerings. Worm over corn is good, and so is caster over maggot, or vice versa.

Keep Quiet!

Despite tench feeding close in in crystal-clear water, they are very often not to be seen when you are actually fishing for them, mainly because they are so easily spooked. Therefore, you must sit well back from the water's edge, keeping as low and still as possible. Should you have to move, keep movements slow and stealthy. You will, of course, wear sombre-coloured clothing and soft-soled shoes. Take advantage of every scrap of available cover, and if none exists, fabricate a screen; anything which helps to camouflage you and your movements will be beneficial. Noise will frighten them, and a screaming bite alarm is certain to drive them away; so if you are convinced that legering with buzzers for bite indication is the way to catch margin feeders in your lake, keep the volume turned down – just the light in the head will warn you of a bite, as long as you stay alert.

Planning and Strategy

Knowing when to feed the swim is difficult when you can't see what is happening beneath the surface, particularly if a solitary fish is sought. Therefore watch carefully and take careful note of any untoward happening. If the float moves but a hittable bite doesn't develop after a few minutes, you can be quite sure that any loose feed will have been cleared up. Most often though, the feed is cleared up without any discernible float movement. So watch for vortices, bubbles, small bits of debris rising to the surface, in fact anything untoward. Any information at all, no matter how small, is better than none.

If fish are in, or visiting the swim and you don't get a bite, keep ringing the changes: try altering the hooklink length; changing the hook size or pattern; a balanced bait or one 'nailed' to the bottom; a hair rig; a pop-up; a finer hooklink; a different float size or pattern; and so on and so forth. The options of what you can try are limited only by your imagination. And remember, what works one day might not do the trick the next. In fact, changing back and forth between two or three successful combinations in the same session often promotes continued action.

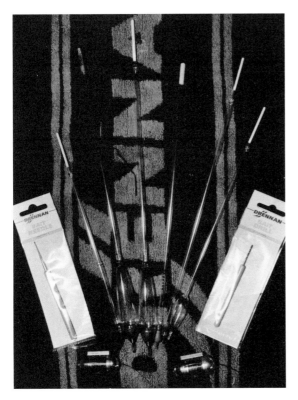

A few of the Crystal float options.

Odd Behaviour

I've seen tench behaving in a way that really is puzzling. Another friend, Pete Cranstoun, first brought it to my attention, although I've only witnessed it on one venue, a mature gravel pit. The tench in question were positioned mouth down on the bottom, body vertically upwards, and practically motionless apart from very slight fin movements. The ones we observed stayed like this in the same spot for hours, and despite manoeuvering baits to within a few millimetres of their mouths, a take was never forthcoming. They just ignored everything when behaving in this way. One day frustration got the better of me and I tossed a small pebble at one such fish, an absolute whacker. The pebble landed close enough to disturb it, but it just moved a few inches and then carried on as before. When I packed up a couple of hours later, it was still there. Another friend suggests they are simply sleeping tench. Maybe, but then you'd think they would

be seen more often. And why would they sleep in that vertical position? Surely tucked up horizontally in a weedbed would be a better and safer option. No, I think there is some other explanation, although nothing plausible comes to mind. Does anybody have any ideas?

Selecting Tackle

As mentioned elsewhere, floats with clear bodies of the crystal type are best for margin-feeding tench, fixed to the line with a link float attachment. This is a bottom-end-only arrangement, hence allowing rapid float change and depth adjustment. This float attachment also ensures a straighter, more direct line so less line needs picking up on the strike. Furthermore the float stays away from the line, collapses quickly and causes less disturbance on the strike. Should the float attachment need to be 'locked' in position, I prefer to use stop knots rather than shot. There is less chance of damaging ultra-fine lines and, just as important, stop knots are less noticeable to fish. I am convinced that many big tench, especially those that live in clear water, have learned to recognize suspended split shot, and for this reason I even cover any bulk shot with silicon rubber tube. This has the added advantage of being less likely to catch on weed and snags.

LEGERING

There are two distinct legering strategies: sensitive legering and bolt-rigs. In sensitive legering the aim is to see and deal with bites before the fish is alarmed; the bolt-rig's intended purpose is for the rig to pose considerable resistance against which the fish hook themselves.

Sensitive Legering

When fishing stillwaters it is probably true to say that, no matter how sensitive the leger method employed, float tackle, even when relatively crude, will be more sensitive. Why, then, is sensitive legering so popular? The answer can be summed up in one word: versatility. There are relatively few situations or swims where leger tackle can't be employed, yet there are many reasons for ineffectual float fishing. Legering is no less skillful; carefully thought out, it will pay dividends.

There are three main considerations in successful sensitive legering for tench:

1. Bite indicators should be mounted in the most sensitive place, i.e. in front of the rod; friction through the rod rings is therefore eliminated.

2. Rod(s) should be positioned close to hand, so that you can strike instantly without taking your eyes off the indicator.

3. Keep resistance to a minimum, and endeavour to build up resistance as gradually as possible.

Let's take these points one at a time.

Bite Indication

In stillwaters the most sensitive bite detection I know of is by watching the bow in the line between the rod tip and the water. But this can't be done if the line can't be seen, or if the wind is blowing it all over the place. Also, long spells of line-watching will lead to eyestrain, and maintaining concentration is difficult. Small dough-bobbins (¼in/6mm diameter are plenty big enough) suspended on the line in front of the rod can make things easier. However, dough-bobbins have disadvantages: wind plays havoc with them, rain washes them off, and torchlight is needed to illuminate them at night. This latter consideration poses more problems: possible battery failure, also positioning and fixing them accurately, besides which some anglers take exception to seeing the light.

Although the above factors are tedious, there are two, more significant objections to bobbins: the movement and noise associated with fixing them can, and does, disturb the fish; also fixing them takes time, and should a bite occur then, as it sometimes does, the angler is in no position to strike and therefore a chance is lost. So I consider dough-bobbins downright inefficient.

Swingtips offer the most efficient compromise I know. Although they lack some of the bobbin's sensitivity, the tips are in the right place: at the front of the rod. They offer other advantages, too: heavy weather hardly affects them – even if

'Swingtips offer the most efficient compromise'. Here, the lilies shield the swingtips from drift.

the wind is blowing furiously, they can be prevented from flailing around (*see* below) a chemical Nightlight or beta-light can be readily attached to provide after-dark visibility; and most important of all, they always remain in place, and even critical adjustments can be made without getting out of your chair.

Using Lights At night, even after a very short time indeed and especially if it is windy, your eyes can play tricks when watching beta-lights, and it is very difficult indeed to differentiate between real and imaginary bites. Quite a few headaches, literally, can be prevented by the simple expedient of obscuring the isotopes with something like a piece of board. I've made a gadget especially for the purpose, and it doubles up to hold a swingtip steady in strong winds. In no way does it hinder a bite.

Quite simply it resembles a right-angled rod-rest head, and could be used as such, but the head is 3in (7.6cm) deep. It is fashioned from sheet aluminium, and bolts to a bank-stick. This must be positioned accurately so the swingtip

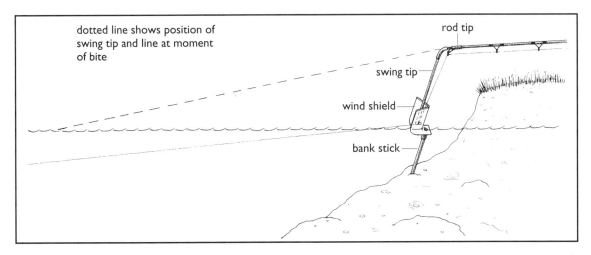

Swingtip shield.

drops directly into the slot, and once there it stays there, unless you or a fish move it! When a bite occurs the light comes into view, and you have a sure strike every time! Using this method, concentration need not be so intense; you generally notice the bite in time, as long as you are awake! Of course, this device is only resorted to when conditions dictate.

Audible Swingtips What is really needed is an audible swingtip. I've tried an Optonic buzzer mounted in front of the swingtip: in the event of a bite the Optonic gives out a 'beep' before the line loses contact with the roller. Admittedly it's only a short beep, but long enough to attract your attention, should concentration have wandered, before the bite is over. But fixing and setting the Optonic like this is fiddly and takes time, so is not a very good solution to the problem.

Setting the Swingtip Another important aspect is how the swingtip is set, because you need to be able to spot the slightest movement (providing weather conditions permit). It is a mistake to have the tip's lower end set high above the water, because then, the chances are that even a 1in (25mm) lift won't be noticed. But set the tip so it just touches the water, and a lift as small as

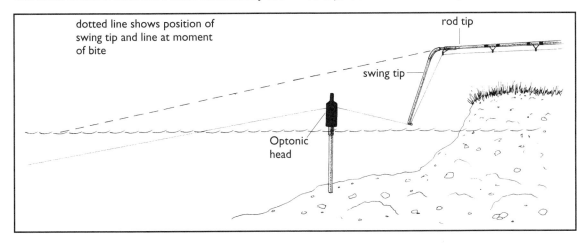

Optonic in front of swingtip set-up.

'All four landed weighed in excess of 7lb.'

morning was very hot and still and the tench were twitching. I had several bites, out of which four were 'nailed'. All four landed weighed in excess of 7lb and not once did the bite lift the tip out of the water. The bright yellow bands appeared darker when under the surface; however, as they emerged the colour change was dramatic and that is what I struck at. Concentration was, I admit, pretty intense, and couldn't be kept up for long, not by me anyway.

Fishing Two Rods There is more to be gained fishing two rods than just increasing your chances of a bite twofold. When using swingtips, for example, the movement of the tips can be compared one to the other, thereby making it easier to spot bites. The tips must be set close together so both can be watched simultaneously; then a sudden puff of wind is not so likely to get you striking at thin air. This brings to mind another advantage of swingtips over bite indicators set further down the rod: if the tip moves sideways rather than outwards, it is a line bite, that is, a fish has blundered into the line and not taken the bait. This happens much more often than first expected, and striking a 'liner' will only scare the fish. The more you use the tips, the better at interpreting their movements you become.

When fishing two rods simultaneously it is advisable to have the anti-reverse in the off position, or the bait runner on, that is so line can be taken freely; otherwise when a fish is being fought (or your back is turned for some other reason) there is the ever-present danger of the unattended rod being pulled in, particularly if carp are present. It is also a good idea to have audible bite indication as back-up; then should a big bite be forthcoming whilst your attention is diverted elsewhere, the buzzer will alert you. Reels must be set to allow line to be taken, again to preclude the chance of a lost rod. It soon becomes second nature to drop a finger on the spool when striking. This way I get the best of both worlds: small bites can be successfully dealt with, and there is no hindrance to a fish that takes off in a rush with

¼in (6mm) is easily discernible. This point cannot be over-emphasized, and when the tench are twitching it is absolutely vital for success. Let me repeat the example given in my book, *Catching Big Tench* (now out of print) – and in no way is this extraordinary:

It was a morning session, so the beta-lights (I now use chemical Nightlights) had already been removed from the tips, but the tight-fitting silicon rubber bands that had held the isotopes were still on. The bands, bright yellow for visibility, were positioned one adjacent to the tip-ring, the other ½in (15mm) higher, and the rodrests were set accurately so that the water level came precisely between the two yellow bands. The

the bait. What is a small bite? If the tip moves even the tiniest fraction and holds, I'll hit it!

Swingtips in Heavy Weather When the wind is strong it is advisable to sink the swingtips by varying degrees, depending on the strength of the wind, as this may prevent them flailing about. It is unlikely twitches will be seen, but it is still worthwhile keeping the tips on as long as possible for the effect they have on building resistance gradually. However, when the strength of the wind makes the tips a liability, take them off and resort to a more wind-resistant system, in conjunction with a buzzer of course.

My choice the Quiver-Loc system works like this: it has two conventional swinging-type arms, one in stainless with an adjustable weight and the other a stiff lightweight quivertip. Both are very sensitive, and will show any movement of the line. There is a further arm for a 'balanced lead' set-up, but as this is intended as a means of promoting self-hooking, it will be explained later in this chapter, under 'The Bolt-Rig'.

Detecting Small Bites It is important to use whenever possible a method of bite indication that permits the detection of very small bites – and there is at least one other good reason for this besides those already discussed. With experience, coupled with careful observation, one can often tell from how the indicator moves just what is happening below the surface. For example, not all twitch bites are from fish feeding warily, neither are they always given by confident fish. I only wish they were! And not all the indications are in fact bites at all; false bites can be caused by any number of reasons, including fish hitting the line (line bites), drifting weed, undertow and wind; therefore it is important to understand and interpret the indicator's message – and anybody can do this with practice.

Plainly, bites from wary fish will nearly always be more difficult to connect with than those from confidently feeding fish. Whether you can tell the difference between those types of bite with any degree of certainty or not, won't prevent you catching. However, if you can recognize when wary twitchers are the cause, you can make adjustments to the presentation, aiming to allay the fishes' suspicions. The ultimate alternative may be to resort to a bolt-rig. If, on the other hand, it is felt that twitches are from confident fish, it may be necessary to try an even more sensitive bite indicator. When I feel the latter is the case, so long as there is no wind, the rod tops are raised and the bow in the line between the bottom of the swingtip and the surface of the water is watched for bites. Either way, an accurate assessment from the movements of the bite indicator of what is happening below the surface can only lead to more fish being hooked.

Position

It follows that to connect with small bites you must strike as quickly as possible (note, however, that 'quickly' does not mean 'wildly'); therefore your fishing position, and the way the rods are set up, is vitally important, and time lost between noticing a tiny bite and striking will mean less fish on the bank. Even when tench are giving big pulls you don't want to give them time to realize they have made a mistake by delaying the strike, because if you do they may either drop the bait or reach some underwater refuge such as a weedbed or snag, where they might slip the hook or break the line. If a tench does get into a weedbed, don't pull too hard because if you do, the weed will pack tight to the fish, restricting its movements. Better to keep the fish on a barely tight line, and hold the rod high. This enables the fish to use its strength to break free from the weed and, consequently, you stand a much better chance of landing it.

Comfort must be considered essential, too. The angler who is not fishing comfortably is not fishing efficiently, because he will not be able to relax and therefore concentrate on the job in hand. For this reason a comfortable chair with a firm back-rest is recommended. The seat height should be such that one's hands, when at rest, are slightly above the rods. Then it's so much quicker to strike rather than if the hand has to be raised first.

The rods must be within easy reach; it never ceases to amaze me how many tench anglers

It is so much quicker to strike if the hand, when at rest, is above the rod(s).

overlook this obvious consideration. Because I strike with my right hand, my rods are set to that side, with the reels about in line with my knees; this means I have to bend slightly forwards to pick up a rod, therefore in an ideal position to execute a powerful strike, should the need arise such as when fishing at long range. The rods are set as close to my side as is possible without constantly knocking them, and they are angled in toward the tips so that both swingtips can be watched simultaneously. Fishing thus, I can strike quickly without taking my eyes off the swingtips. Soon it becomes second nature, so much so that often, nowadays, the bite is forgotten – the first thing I'm aware of is a bent rod in my hand!

Minimizing Resistance

As previously noted, it is important that bite detection offers minimal resistance. It is equally important that resistance is kept low at the 'business' end of the tackle. I experiment continually, but really the basics are simple, there being three primary considerations: heaviness of leger weight; strength and/or stiffness of line; end-rig employed. The first is straightforward: use the minimum weight you can get away with, unless of course you are using a bolt-rig. (I once considered bolt-rigs a liability when tench fishing, but have since learned my lesson.) Of course you may have to use more weight than normal if there is a strong undertow, or when casting in a side wind or against a headwind. What can easily be overlooked, however, is that when the wind comes from behind the reverse is often true. Incidentally, the speed a legerweight sinks can be slowed by the addition of cork or polystyrene balls, without losing accuracy or too much distance.

Line Choice The important aspect of line choice is to use the lowest possible breaking strain adequate for the job in hand. There are several advantages in this: the finer, therefore more supple line, especially the hooklink, allows a more natural bait presentation; it needs less weight to achieve the same casting distance, and wind and undertow affect it less. Furthermore, a taking fish must take some of the 'bend' out of the line, so the finer the line the less resistance there will be from the water to this straightening. So you can see how important it is to use the lightest, thinnest, most supple line obtainable, with reliability the overriding factor. I am not, however, recommending the use of gossamer tackle adjacent to weedbeds or snags – our quarry is the most important consideration, and leaving hooks in lost fish is totally unacceptable. What I am saying is, by carefully considering the job in hand, you might use finer line than other anglers in the same situation, which will certainly pay dividends.

High-Tech Braids The new high-tech braids offer exciting possibilities, particularly for hooklinks, because they are so supple. This suppleness is very important because tench, in common with most (perhaps all) fish, don't actually pick up an item of food, they suck it into their mouths from some distance away. Therefore the more flexible the hooklink, the more natural the presentation.

The Choice of End-Rig This is yet another aspect and can considerably affect resistance. For example, when fishing a soft-bottomed swim, the leger weight will sink into the mud or silt, and with the lead fitted directly on the line, the line will be drawn down into the muck as well. As a result, resistance will be increased in a number of

Rigs are better tied at home.

ways: the bomb's eye will be at least partially blocked, so preventing the line's free passage; the line will be drawn into several acute angles, one of which, where the line goes through the bomb's eye, will be particularly bad; and because line can pass through water more easily than through mud, friction will be increased. For these, and not discounting other considerations, the bomb is rarely fitted directly to the reel line (exceptions being, for example, anti-tangle and bolt-rigs). It is much better to employ a fixed paternoster rig or a link-leger, the latter sometimes called a running paternoster.

Fixed Paternoster and Link-Leger Rigs

I've not been able to convince myself, by comparing the two rigs in action side by side, of the fixed paternoster's advantage over the link-leger. However, many matchmen have extolled, over

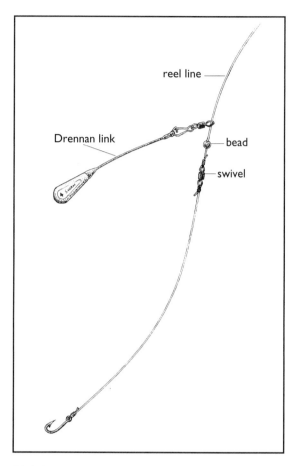

Link-leger rig.

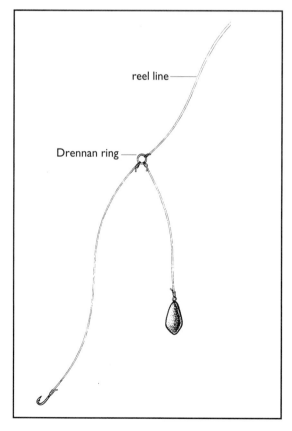

Fixed paternoster rig.

the years, the former's virtues and they are rarely far off the mark in their conclusions. However, drop-back bites are far more likely using the fixed paternoster, therefore I mostly prefer the link-leger when using swingtips.

Both these end-rigs are infinitely variable, sensitivity being mainly adjusted by altering either the length of hooklink or the bomb link, or both. When trying to induce bigger or more bites, the lengths are increased, the idea being to allay the fishes' wariness. (But bites are more difficult to hit successfully.) After taking the bait they can move off without feeling much in the way of resistance until, hopefully, it is too late. When using the fixed paternoster, my own choice is a starting length around 3ft (90cm) on the bomb and 18in (45cm) hooklink. For the link-leger both are

As already intimated, a leger-link buoyed up with cork or polystyrene ball(s) will help prevent the bomb sinking in bottom debris. It will also keep the link vertical, easing the passage of line through it. It does, however, have one major disadvantage: as a fish takes the bait the upper, buoyant end of the link moves as well, and this sudden unexpected movement will catch the fish's eye and may alarm it, the only sure result being an ejected bait and another missed chance. So, keep all parts of the end-rig as unobtrusive as possible.

The bomb may be replaced by a swimfeeder in both these rigs. Again, my own preference is the link-leger version.

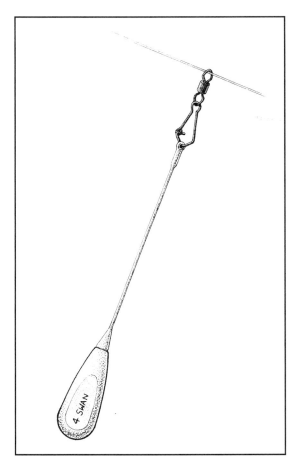

Drennan link-leger to swivel.

considerably shorter, the bomb link 2–6in (5–15cm) and 9in (23cm) hooklink, except in special circumstances. For example, when fishing on a soft muddy bottom or in dense Canadian pond weed, the length of the bomb link will be increased, though by how much depends on the depth of the mud or the height of the weed. I'll also use a shorter hooklink if twitch bites prove difficult to hit. Some consider that shortening the hooklink only exacerbates the problem, turning even more bites into twitches. Well, Bill and I don't think it does, and certainly not in every case. It may do on some waters, but whatever the truth of the matter, it pays to keep an open mind. Dogmatic belief, in any aspect of fishing, will only be at the expense of less fish on the bank in the long run.

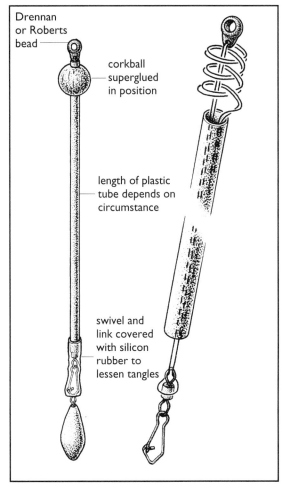

Drennan or Roberts bead

corkball superglued in position

length of plastic tube depends on circumstance

swivel and link covered with silicon rubber to lessen tangles

Leger link.

A bolt-rig fooled this 9lb 4oz tench for Pete Jackson.

The Drennan Link-Leger system is very versatile; rather than directly on the line I mount them on a link-swivel, and there is reason for this. The flexible link may be stretched, then when shortening the length, it is quicker to unclip the swivel rather than break the tackle down.

Making a Link A simple and quick-to-make link can be made thus: you need leger beads, fairly rigid plastic tube, link-swivels and some low breaking-strain line. In fact the line must be weaker than the chosen reel line so that if the link becomes snagged it fails before the reel line. A suitable length of line is doubled, and the doubled end is put through the swivel's eye to form a loop; pass the loop over the swivel, and pull tight. Next, pass both free ends of the line through the tube, then thread on a leger bead. Finally three or four half-hitches over the bead will hold the whole lot together. Stretch the line passing through the tube as the half-hitches are made; on release, everything pulls neatly together, leaving the link snag-free. A refinement is to tuck the ends into the tube, after clipping off the surplus. In fact the tying is quicker than the explanation!

Bolt-Rigs

Carp anglers evolved the bolt-rig on waters where the fish had become wise to the hair-rig, and as a result had once again resorted to their habit of sucking and blowing baits It was developed to counter this habit, the idea being to get the fish to prick itself on the hook; alarmed it would rush away, and then the hook would be driven home against the resistance provided by a heavy lead, and/or the line being clipped tightly to the rod. Yet another idea involves a degree of free movement, so the fish can get up some speed before the hook is driven home by the backstop hitting the lead. Hooks must be as sharp as one can get them, and of the finest wire that circumstances will allow.

Side-hooking Rig

Bill Quinlan and I collaborated on trials for self-hooking bolt-rigs for tench; they evolved as follows: in the first instance it was decided that the baits (boilies) would be mounted on the shank of the hook, with a hook that was generally larger than normal, the idea being for the fish to hook itself when the bait was in its mouth; in other words, the fish would find it more difficult to eject a bait with a hook sticking out of it, than if the hook were buried in the bait.

Almost immediately this side-hooking rig produced big, sailaway bites, but many of the tench came 'unstuck'. At first we thought the hooks being used weren't big enough, but increasing the hook size did not improve the bite-to-landed-fish

A side-hooked boilie.

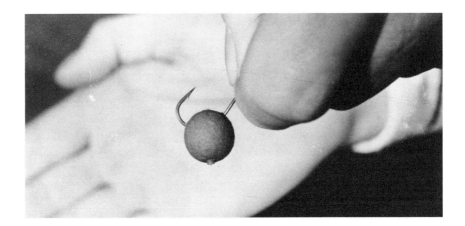

ratio. Subsequently we discovered that on the larger hooks especially, the boily was mounted completely on the hook's shank and was therefore able to swivel round (probably during casting), thereby effectively masking the hook's point. So we had to try a different pattern on this rig.

Bill had the answer in his hook box: low water salmon hooks which were shortened in the shank and solder-blobbed to our usual carp-fishing standard. In this particular pattern, the bend continues sufficiently up the shank, almost eliminating the boily-swivelling problem. In practice these hooks outfished any other pattern we tried on this rig, and when we used the last of them an alternative had to be found. Suffice to say, it has: Kamasan's B640, a spade-end, forged round-

bend hook, with a bronze finish. Another ploy, found to be successful when using a boily on a side-hooking rig, was that after the bait had been mounted, the part nearest to the hook point was sliced off, leaving the point even more prominent.

Wherever possible, always make up rigs and so on at home, for two simple reasons: it is much easier to work in comfortable surroundings, with everything to hand; and it saves much valuable time on the bank.

Bite Detection
When using any bolt-type rigs the best method of bite detection I've yet tried is Solar's Quiver-Loc system, developed principally by Martin 'Lucky' Locke. The system has been developed from, and incorporates earlier ideas, such as swingers and butt indicators. Basically it works like this: it has two conventional swinging type arms, one in stainless with an adjustable weight, and the other being a stiff lightweight version. Both of these cover the usual swinger type situations, and can be set up very sensitively. Where fish have become wise to this kind of set-up, the unique Quiver-Loc sleeve is engaged and the arm changed to the third in the set, this being a flexible fast-recovery quiver-type tip. Simply tension the line until the bomb is just – and only just – at the point of moving, and clip up the line. The lead is now delicately balanced, and the precise moment that the slack in the hook-link is taken up, the lead will be disturbed. Not having experienced this before, the fish often bolts with the hook already in its mouth.

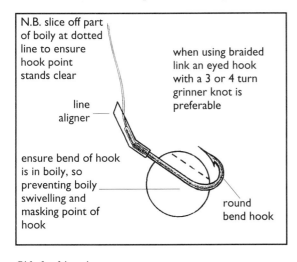

Side-hooking rig.

Of course, this system isn't restricted to use with bolt-rigs. If for any reason I can't use swingtips, the Quiver-Loc system is my back-up and is particularly valuable in strong cross-winds. It also works brilliantly with backleads, although that hasn't figured in my tench fishing yet.

The Line-Aligner

As the tench in our waters inevitably became wise to the side-hooking rig, its effectiveness declined and so did the big, sailaway bites associated with it. As a result Bill and I were back to square one, trying to connect with 'microscopic' twitch bites. Then through the big fish world's grapevine came news that some of the top carp boys had something new in rigs that was really very good, and had accounted for many, very big fish from some of the country's most difficult waters, waters which are heavily fished and where the carp, like the tench Bill and I were fishing for, had seen it all before. After the briefest discussions, an investigation was instigated.

We began our quest for the relevant information in hostelries frequented by the said 'top carp boys'. Fortunately, some of the more famous (or should it be notorious!) of these, such as the Horse and Barge, the Fisheries and the Royal Oak are situated in the Colne Valley, not far from the 'Tench Lake'. Bill thought it a splendid arrangement, muttering something about 'having our cake and eating it'. After the 'oiling' of many dry and dusty carp fishers' throats, which I assure you is not something to be undertaken lightly if you have any respect for money, tongues began to loosen and snippets of information began to slip

forth. Piecing together, a pattern began to emerge. As far as we could ascertain, the new rig relied for its success on a particular shape of hook, and that the shank needed to be longer than was usual. Later on, after even more expense, we learned that this was the bent-hook rig.

Bent-hook rigs now have the reputation of damaging fish and so are banned on some waters. Although I've yet to see any discernible extra damage to tench caused by a bent hook, I don't now use it; as similarly any caring angler should abhor the thought of using anything that might injure fish unnecessarily. The current development on the bent-hook principle incorporates straight-eyed hooks and Jim Gibbinson's clever idea: the line-aligner (apart from doing away with the bent-hook itself, Jim's line-aligner works on very much the same principle, is even more effective and it does not damage fish.

The arrangement is as follows: before the hook is tied on, just thread the hooklink through the tube with a needle. The tube must be rigid and a tight fit on the hook-eye, and the hooklink exits the front of the tube. Using good braided hooklinks the hook will turn and catch every time, so long as the bait is mounted in exactly the right place (*see* below).

It is probably as well to understand the reasons why this type of rig was invented in the first place: some big, wary carp had been observed feeding on boilies thrown in as free offerings. After each bait had been picked up, the carp would move slowly backwards, in low reverse gear so to speak, whilst keeping their mouths open. If a hookbait was encountered, the resistance of the tackle resulted in it being gently pulled out of the mouth. The

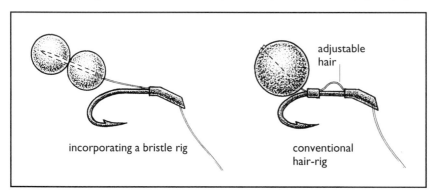

incorporating a bristle rig

adjustable hair

conventional hair-rig

Gibbinson line-aligner.

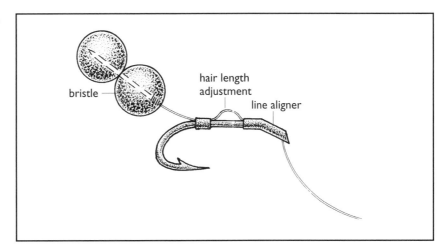

Adjustable-hair line-aligner (with bristle-rig).

principle of the line-aligner is that no matter how carefully the fish moves backwards, the hook will usually turn and prick the inside of the mouth.

Experience with the line-aligner has indicated that two vital factors must be considered: the bait needs positioning accurately; and it must stand as proud as possible from the hook, yet be firmly fixed to it. We use the bristle-rig as a quick and easy way of attaching the boily to the hair. This clever but simple idea of Bill's is a real time-saver and will be fully described later in this chapter. Here I'll just say that there are no needles needed, no threading, and no messing about with fiddly little stops. So long as the bristle doesn't go right through the boily so destroying the vacuum effect, it is surprising, just how much force is needed to dislodge a boily mounted this way.

After the bristle has first been tied to the hair, the hair is then tied to the eye of the hook. Then after tying on the hooklink, a small piece of the narrowest diameter silicon rubber tube (an almost transparent version is available) is slid over the hookshank and the hair, followed by a more rigid piece of tube, 1mm diameter by about 20mm long. After the boilie(s) is mounted on the bristle, the rubber tubing is slid tight to the bait,

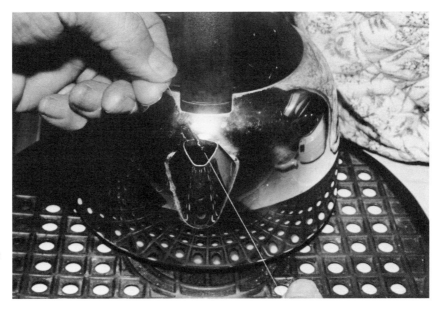

Steam from a kettle being used on shrink tube on a line aligner; so much more controllable and you can see what you are doing.

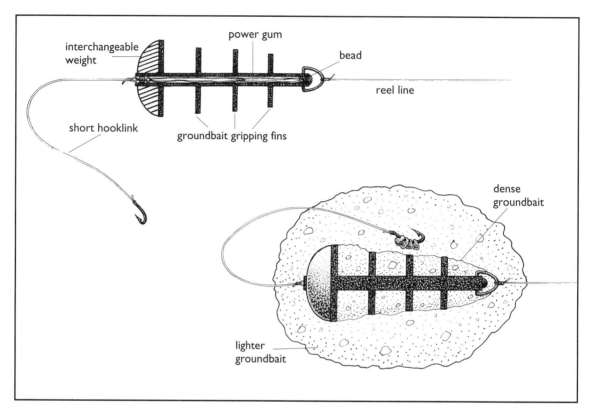

'The Method' rig.

holding it firmly in place. As I say, the correct positioning of the bait on the hook is critical, especially if consistent success with shy-feeding tench is to be enjoyed. It needs to be close to the original bend and at the back of the hook, although very small adjustments can be made to suit particular circumstances, or bait size.

Jim Gibbinson recommends that the aligner itself (the stiff tube) be made from shrink tube, and that it should be shrunk by means of steam from the spout of a kettle. Some queried the wisdom of this procedure, thinking the steam might adversely affect some braids used for hooklinks. However, Jim put a selection of braids to the test and found no deterioration. He goes on to warn (*Carpworld* magazine, December 1995) that dry heat such as that from a hair-dryer should never be used because it will cause hooklinks to wrinkle and curl which results in serious strength loss.

Pop-up Baits This rig works very well with pop-up baits. To solve the problem of mounting pop-ups which have become hard, it is only necessary to soak them first. I now keep pop-ups permanently in liquid for three reasons:

1. Extra flavour can be added to the water, which compensates for that lost when the baits were baked.
2. By squeezing the pop-ups under the surface of the liquid after they have been mounted on the rig, it is possible to obtain the exact buoyancy to counterbalance the hook and so on, without resorting to split-shot, lead wire or anything else.
3. This critical buoyancy balance will be maintained long after casting. If, on the other hand, 'dry' pop-ups are used, the balance will alter as the bait absorbs water, ruining the intended presentation.

The Method

The Method has revolutionized match fishing during the past couple of years, but its origins go back much further than that. Bob Buteux was using a primitive version back in the 1960s, his aim being to ensure 100 per cent tangle-free casting. He moulded groundbait around his bomb and stuck the hookshank into it, and it proved a very effective, tangle-free rig.

Recently the Method has been the subject of much thought and experimentation, and matchmen use it mainly for carp; however, it works well for tench, too. The rig is quite simple to make: drill a hole through the lead weight on the base of a frame feeder. Take a loop of power-gum, and slide on a swivel and leger bead. After threading the gum through the drilled hole, tie it to the top of the feeder, with the bead tight against the base. Tie the reel line to the top swivel and the hooklink to the bottom swivel, and the rig is complete.

The frame feeder is then packed with a stodgy inner groundbait, which takes about ten minutes to break down after casting. A larger ball of lighter-textured groundbait is moulded around the feeder, also enclosing the hooklink and bait. The fish attacks the ball of feed, eventually mouthing the bait, getting pricked by the hook in the process. It then bolts, and the resistance posed by the heavy feeder drives the hook home. The stretch of the power-gum protects fine hooklinks.

A 5–6lb hooklink between 3in and 12in (7.5cm and 30cm) long would be a good place to start; choose the hook size to suit the bait being used. Maggot and worm are good choices for bait because their movement helps to break down the groundbait quickly. Of course, incorporate some hookbait samples in with the groundbait mix as well.

Method feeders are available from commercial suppliers which are specifically designed for this style of fishing, in three readily interchangeable size weights: small, medium and large. And the grit-free elastic/power-gum system can be varied to protect whatever the chosen hooklink strength.

Anti-Tangle Rigs

Exposed hook rigs are notorious for tangling, particularly when long casting is necessary and/or when super-soft hooklinks are used. Again, we must thank the carpmen for solving the problem. The secret is to prevent the reel line and the hooklink from twisting together. This is achieved by the simple expedient of covering the final few inches of the reel line, above the link, with tubing. The tube needs to be longer than the combined length of hooklink plus hair. I use two versions; one is 'in-line' and employs the Smith Bomb; the other is the 'helicopter rig'.

The 'Smith-Bomb' Rig

The Smith Bomb has been specifically designed to ensure the fish is hooked before it notices any resistance or slight movement which could make it suspicious and result in it rejecting the bait. This has

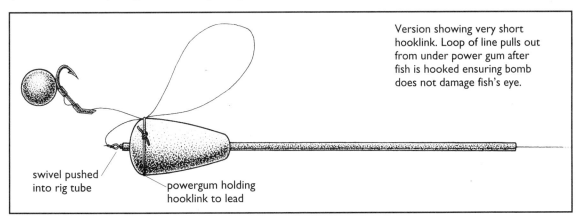

Version showing very short hooklink. Loop of line pulls out from under power gum after fish is hooked ensuring bomb does not damage fish's eye.

swivel pushed into rig tube

powergum holding hooklink to lead

The Smith-bomb rig.

been achieved by ensuring that the resistance comes from the end nearer the hooklink, the heavy end. Its cunning shape ensures that there is very little likelihood of the lead coming to rest in any position other than that intended by the designer. These leads have the line passing directly through them (in-line) and are therefore aerodynamic and practically tangle free, two extra bonuses.

Fishing with the new leads, which come in 2oz, 3oz and 4oz sizes, is simple. With pointed scissors or similar, open out the hole at the heavy end until it will accept the size of swivel you intend to use. Poke flexible plastic tubing through the hole in the lead, ensuring that the tube's bore is large enough to allow any knot in the tackle to pass through. This point is vital: any obstruction, such as a leader knot, must pass through the tube with ease. In the event of a break-off, a hooked fish will not then become tethered.

Cut the tubing, leaving about ⅟₁₆in (1mm) protruding at the big end of the lead, and the other end cut longer than the combined hooklink/hair length. After threading the mainline through the tube, tie to the hooklink swivel. Then it's just a case of holding the mainline in one hand and the lead in the other, thereby pulling the swivel into the short end of the tube. Don't pull it in too tightly; the fish should be able to free it easily, should the lead get snagged. (any problems of supply, contact Roger Smith direct, *see* Useful Addresses).

The Helicopter Rig
The helicopter rig is one of the most successful rigs ever developed for tangle-free, long-range casting. Some anglers tell me that they have problems getting the necessary components for constructing these rigs, however, I have always found them all readily available from Drennan.

Cut some 1mm rig tube a bit longer than the required length, cutting one end at an acute angle, like a point; this will allow tight-fitting ³⁄₁₆in (5mm) shock beads to be threaded on easily, by gripping the end of the 'point' with the fingernails, and pulling the tube through the bead. Don't forget to put on a small Drennan ring before the second bead. There should be a gap of about ⅜in (10mm) between the tight-fitting beads, and the first one should be about 1in (25mm) from the pointed end of the tube. When both beads and ring are in position, trim the pointed end of the tube square.

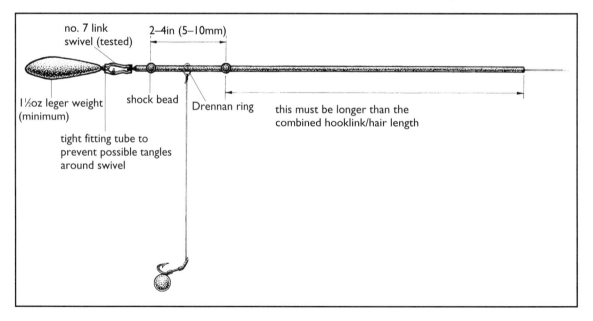

The Helicopter rig.

Use a grinner or some other reliable knot to tie the hooklink to the ring. You can leave this until you arrive at the water, when you can make up your mind exactly what length you need for the session. But don't forget that the combined hooklink-hair length must not be longer than the tube above the bead. Thread the reel line through the tube – a special line threader saves a lot of time – and tie a strong size 7 Berkley type link-swivel to the end of the line. The knot must be reliable and the swivel top quality, because the whole strength of the rig depends on these points.

Finally, attach a suitable leger weight to the link and pull the tube over the eye of the swivel. You will find this a tight fit, but not so tight that a lost fish couldn't shift it, should the leger become snagged. A further refinement is to cover the link-swivel with a small piece of silicon tube to lessen the chances of that snagging or tangling.

Also essential – and this is vital for the well-being of any lost fish – is that any knots in the tackle above the rig must be small enough to pass through the tube easily. Attention to this detail

will prevent a lost fish becoming tethered and suffering for hours. Attention to detail when tying up rigs and hooklinks will save time in the long run, as well as put more fish on the bank.

The Quinlan Bristle-Rig

Versions of anti-eject type rigs are being used nowadays which some anglers, including my friends and I, consider unacceptable on ethical grounds. Unfortunately one of the rigs of this type is known, in some circles, as the 'bristle-rig'. However, this is not the kind of rig I would use, as the principle behind them is to be abhorred. The bristle-rig described here is quite different and Bill Quinlan and I, as well as others of our friends, have used it to great effect on both carp and tench.

Many anglers still use baiting needles and various bits of plastic as bait stops, for mounting boilies on hair-rigs. However, there is a much quicker and more reliable way of mounting boilies on the hair, invented several years ago by Bill Quinlan: the bristle-rig. With this rig, a short

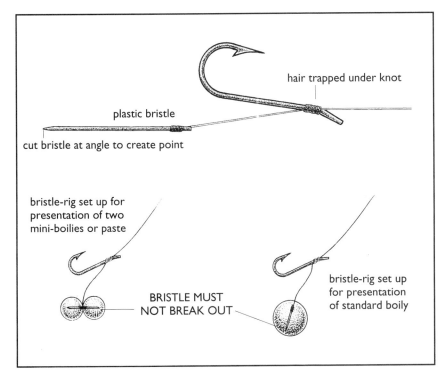

The bristle-rig.

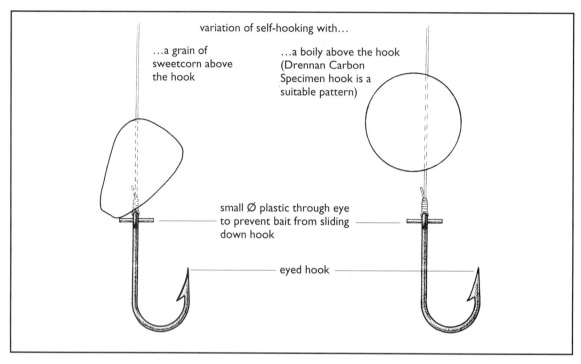

variation of self-hooking with...

...a grain of
sweetcorn above
the hook

...a boily above the hook
(Drennan Carbon
Specimen hook is a
suitable pattern)

small Ø plastic through eye
to prevent bait from sliding
down hook

eyed hook

Sweetcorn-above-hook-rig (left) and boilie-above-hook-rig (right).

length of small-diameter plastic is tied to the hair, and boilies are mounted on it simply by pushing the bristle into, but not right through, the boily. Because of the vacuum effect, the boily won't fly off, no matter how vigorous the cast.

There is also a product known as the 'Boilie-Bayonet'. This has transformed the small, simple piece of plastic so the business end is equipped with micro-engineered barbs, and a stretchable tail attached (in effect the hair) for adaptable presentation. I usually tie mine directly onto the hook's eye, but there are any number of different ways of fixing it. The Boilie-Bayonet is also ideal when using pop-up baits, but they must be pre-soaked.

To get the best from a pop-up or critically balanced bait, it must remain mounted on the back of the hook, away from the point. The conventional hair-rig is always prone to looping around the back of the hook, consequently ruining presentation. This is impossible with the Boilie-Bayonet, which ensures the bait is exactly where you intended it to be, every cast.

The Bait-Above-Hook-Rig

A successful variation of a self-hooking bolt-rig entails mounting the bait above the hook. It looks crude, but it works. When we first tried it, we used a needle to thread the bait (usually sweetcorn in those early days) onto the line, the hook being tied on afterwards. Both Bill and I caught seven-pounders on this rig, and it also accounted for my first-ever eight-pounder; moreover the bites were big, bold and beautiful. This is an effective rig, however; when we described it to another angler we had great difficulty in convincing him it was so successful; he just couldn't accept that anything that looked so crude could outwit the wily tench. Eventually, however, we did convince him, and hope he caught a few 'biggies' as a result.

The effectiveness of corn fished above the hook proved quite short-lived, and we thought this kind of rig was finished. However, used in conjunction with midi-boilies it is now proving successful all over again. There is, however, a slight difference in the set-up: for two reasons we

A boilie mounted above the hook accounted for the author's first 9-pounder.

Ritchie MacDonald is more than a carp-only specialist as this 9lb 1oz tench amply illustrates.

The Hair-Rig

Contrary to what was supposed when the rig was invented, the 'hair' of the hair-rig does not have to be tied in very fine line. It now seems obvious that if a fish is frightened by the sight of a baited hook tied, say, to 6lb line, hanging a piece of fine line on the end of the hook is not going to reassure it. However, even relatively recently it was generally supposed that this indeed was the case, and that the hair-rig had to be formed from extremely fine and flexible material to maintain its effectiveness.

Some go as far as to say that with a better understanding of the mechanics of the hair-rig, actually using a stiffer hair gives improved bite-to-hooked-fish ratio. Now, some anglers apply super-glue to braided hairs to stiffen them, and others use quite heavy monofilament for the hair. I have no experience of this so am not in a position to comment; but depending how the rig is tied, I think I can see the logic. Personally I find that Jim Gibbinson's line-aligner proves very effective, and has an almost perfect record of converting bites into hooked fish. So when fishing boilies at least, this remains my current first choice in conjunction with the hair-rig.

The Multiple Hair-Rig

Several hairs tied to one hook, and each hair mounted with small baits, can be a devastating rig for tench. The hairs can be tied to the hook's shank, or to the eye or the bend, or even just above the hook on the hooklink. All knots should be secured with a dab of super-glue, applied on the point of a cocktail stick to ensure that no

now employ a round-bend eyed hook, because it allows boilies to be threaded on without splitting too many, and a small piece of plastic through the eye prevents the bait being forced back onto the hook during casting.

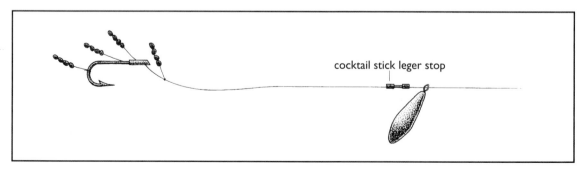

cocktail stick leger stop

Multiple hair rig.

Pete Frost had returned this 7lb 10oz specimen. However, lying with its head under some weed did not prevent the author from scooping it out to take its picture.

excess glue seeps into the braided hooklinks; if it does, it will ruin the braid's flexibility.

The multiple hair-rig is very fiddly to tie so is not used as frequently as its effectiveness warrants. I usually resort to the adhesive product known as 'Bogey' for mounting seed baits – although I will let you into a little secret: before Bogey became available, I used chewing-gum for the purpose, and very successful it proved.

MAGGOTS AND FEEDER FISHING

Maggots and/or casters fished in conjunction with a swimfeeder is a deadly combination and one with which I have had enormous success. There is, however, more to it than just filling a blockend with maggots and chucking it out. More often than not maggot/feeder combination is fished in conjunction with swingtips. I know it means sitting close to the rods and striking bites but, funnily enough, I actually prefer fishing like this, rather than lying on a bedchair waiting for a buzzer to scream out. Though again, if conditions dictate or a situation arises where the swingtips are a liability, I will of course resort to other methods of bite indication. For example, swingtips are of little use when fishing off high banks, such as those at Wilstone Reservoir.

A swingtip-armed rod has the reputation of being difficult to cast with, but this is unfounded. It just demands the correct technique, and once mastered this is never forgotten. To avoid tangles and achieve accuracy, the cast must be made with a smooth, overhead action; the slightest snatch or jerk will result in frustration. There is nothing else to it, but you do need to practice. At first, on some days you'll be better than others, but don't get discouraged.

Undoubtedly tench prefer fresh, soft maggots, and the only way to be absolutely sure of getting them is to breed them yourself. But if, like me, you don't have either the time or the inclination to go to that bother, there is a reasonable alternative: find a good local tackle shop – one that supplies a number of matchmen is a safe bet – and fresh maggots will almost certainly be delivered at least two or three times each week. A shop like this will be bound to 'turn' their own casters as well.

When using maggots on a session of a few days' duration, they must be looked after if you are to get the best from them. They need constant riddling, and a change of bran every few hours. I don't discard the used bran, it all goes in the groundbait bucket, as do any dead maggots. Any resulting casters are kept in water in a separate container, the floaters being used to counterbalance sinking maggots. By putting maggots in a container, the bottom of which is barely covered with water, you can get them to float as well. Flavour can be added to the maggots via this water too (see below). Let me warn you that wet maggots can climb up the sides of the deepest containers, so keep the lid on!

Suitable Tackle

The angling press perpetuates the myth that ultra-fine tackle has to be used with maggots, but this is nonsense. Matches are often won on the flimsiest of tackle, but then how many times do we read of lost fish, especially big ones? My aim is to land every fish hooked, and however good the angler, there is no chance of landing even the majority of tench on 1lb line and a size 24 hook. The lightest tackle I would generally

recommend for big tench is a 3lb hooklink and size 16 hook. Of course, more times than not, I myself would fish far stronger; maggots fished on size 8 hooks and 5lb line still catch plenty of tench, and it isn't always necessary to scale down the tackle to get a better response when bites are petering out. Believe me, the reverse often works, and more times than most would credit. I think it is often just change, any change, that works the oracle.

Over the years it has been demonstrated repeatedly that a new bait, or an old bait used in a new way, will catch well educated fish. It seems the fish get more wary of baits than they do tackle. I remember one example clearly, where the tench on a particular pit were proving very difficult to catch on conventional baits; in fact, unless very fine tackle was used you were completely wasting your time. Then I tried pineapple-flavoured maggots. What a revelation! The action was so hectic that only one rod could be fished, and to combat the weed, I increased my tackle to 7lb double strength hooklink and No 6 hooks so the fish could be landed quickly and safely. This happy situation did not last long, but important lessons had been learned, and my approach now recognizes that fish (and not just tench) eventually become very wary of a particular bait. And when a new successful bait is found, I don't shorten its effective life-span by fishing it on fine tackle from the start.

Flavouring Maggots

In those early days flavouring maggots was a slap-dash affair, the flavour being added straight from the bottle. Although that approach undoubtedly worked, it was impossible to standardize even roughly. However, flavour is now added to maggots accurately and methodically: for standard strength flavours, a good starting point is 5ml per pint of maggots; then you can experiment each side of this until the ideal is found.

Floating maggots are intended for hookbaits only, so an extra 5ml is added to the water which makes them float; this ensures that at least some of the flavour is carried inside the maggots, and not just on their skin. I also believe that floating maggots help to neutralize the weight of the hook, and stops them burrowing into the mud or silt. Whatever the truth of the matter, flavoured floating maggots are a very good edge to have up your sleeve.

A flavour that works on one water will not necessarily be as effective on another, and this may have something to do with water temperature (Archie Braddock certainly believes so, see his book *Fantastic Feeder Fishing*). Certainly it is clear that one flavour's effectiveness declines as the water cools, and another's increases, which is why it is preferable not to fish with the same flavour on both rods at the same time; it is important to compare one with another as often as possible, Archie considers that sweet, fruity, creamy flavours work best in warmer water; hot, spicy flavours being better as it cools. This is good advice. Successful summer flavours include pineapple, strawberry, maple creme, plum, scopex, hemp, sweet peanut, chocolate malt and tutti frutti – but really, the list is endless. And maggots aren't the only bait worth flavouring, luncheon meat, sweetcorn and bread being obvious examples.

A point worth mentioning is always to check the maggots on the hook after each cast, because it is pointless recasting crushed or damaged maggots. Furthermore, if you are getting bites you are not seeing, you need to change tackle, bait, or something.

FEEDER RIGS

Rigs for use with feeders are many and varied, and range from simple to more complicated set-ups. Reliability coupled with versatility are the key words, and I like to keep everything as simple as possible. Thus the rig I use most often has the feeder sliding on the line between two power-gum stop knots, an arrangement which permits instant flexibility because the hooklink length, and the distance the feeder can travel on the line, can be altered at will; it only takes a few seconds to change from a sliding link-leger to a bolt-rig, for example.

Where it is necessary to incorporate some form of shock-absorber to protect the hooklink, well known matchman Peter Brownlow showed me his way, without any need for power-gum or pole elastic. This is how it is tied:

1. Take the end of the reel line between your right index finger and thumb. About 6–8in (15–20cm) up the line, do exactly the same with the left hand.
2. Without letting go, move your hands until you are looking at both thumbs, and you have a loop of line pointing upwards and away from you.
3. Twist the line by moving both thumbs in the same direction, it doesn't matter whether to the left or right, whichever you find easiest.
4. Continue until the line is twisted together

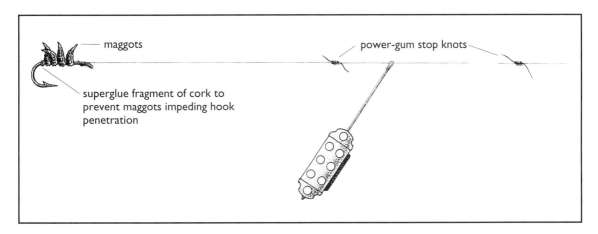

Feeder rig incorporating two power-gum stop knots.

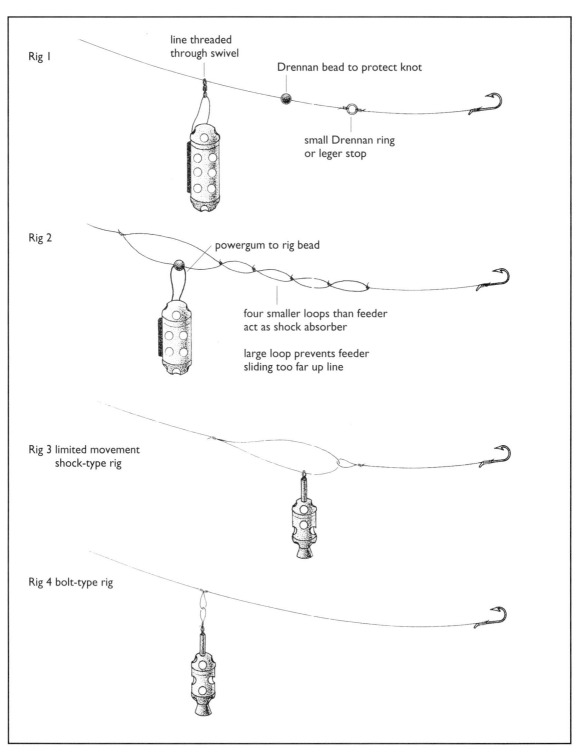

Rig 1

line threaded
through swivel

Drennan bead to protect knot

small Drennan ring
or leger stop

Rig 2

powergum to rig bead

four smaller loops than feeder
act as shock absorber

large loop prevents feeder
sliding too far up line

Rig 3 limited movement
shock-type rig

Rig 4 bolt-type rig

Four useful feeder rigs.

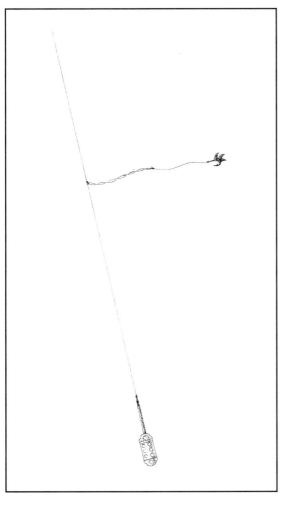

Brownlow fixed paternoster rig.

along a 3in (75mm) length, leaving a small loop at the upper end.

5. At the end of the twists, away from the loop, tie off with a double overhand knot, and add a dab of super-glue for security.

6. After joining the hooklink loop-to-loop, the twists will provide quite a good measure of elasticity.

If you prefer to use a fixed paternoster, leave a tail of sufficient length, onto which is tied the feeder (or bomb). This has the added advantage of keeping the hooklink well away from the reel line during casting, reducing the risk of tangles.

I also use maggot and feeder in conjunction with a float, because what could be better for ensuring bait samples are in the same vicinity as the hookbait? And the weight of the feeder draws the hookbait quickly through any small fish feeding off the bottom. Of course the feeder must be fished on a sliding link, and in the event of a bite the float will only go in one direction – down.

The weight of the hook may also be balanced using rig foam, or a sliver of cork or polystyrene glued to the back of the hook. But perhaps the most popular method is with a chip of breadcrust, or a fragment of breadflake.

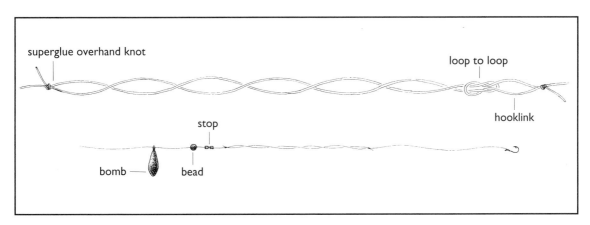

Peter Brownlow rig.

7 ESTATE LAKE FISHING
by Bill Quinlan

In the course of many fishing hours I have reached a few conclusions about estate lakes which may be of interest and benefit to all those who seek tench. To my mind, bolt- and anti-eject-type rigs are out of place on old estate lakes, so I make no mention of these, concentrating solely on the methods I normally use.

Estate lakes have weed growth that varies from year to year. The tench feed fairly regularly during seasons of prolific growth and vice versa when weed is less prominent. Despite the tench's alleged love of weed, many are caught in open, weed-free water up until perhaps the end of July. At about this time of the year the weed begins to recede.

Open-water tench are then more difficult to locate and are, in the main, confirmed 'twitchers'.

However, to begin at the beginning: 16 June usually finds the tench well dispersed and feeding confidently on big baits early in the morning. Most of the females have not yet spawned, and therefore heavy fish are quite common. The males have invariably partially spawned, are smaller, and also appear to outnumber the females.

Tench are caught from both deeper and shallower areas, though the fish in the latter seem more temperamental feeders. The fish in the shallower swims will only feed well for the first two or three hours of daylight. Chances of a

Blenheim action.

An estate lake male, caught by Bill Quinlan.

tench after 8am are small, and one is usually fishing for twitchers long before this.

Without a doubt the most consistent early season pitches are the deeper ones. Tench in these areas will 'hang on' a couple of hours longer, until perhaps 10am.

Evening fishing for tench in estate lakes is usually a 'chancy' business in any swim though, again, deeper water is the more consistent.

LEGERING

A first-light start (approximately 3.30am) will, with luck, find the tench feeding well on conventional baits (sweetcorn, crust, flake, etc.) fished on hook sizes 2–6. A dough-bobbin pinched on the line above the tip ring is a reliable indicator, and much more efficient than one positioned between reel and butt ring. It needn't weigh a pound, either: a ¼in (6mm) ball of paste is visible without the aid of binoculars, and bites are

detectable in combinations of quite strong wind and drift.

The best way of all to detect bites when legering in calm conditions is to watch for line movement. Expecting good bites on big baits, you should allow plenty of slack line between the tip ring and water. A word of warning: when watching for line movement, should the line between tip ring and bait be lying over weed, a drop-back bite won't be properly indicated because of the drag. The remedy is to use a dough-bobbin (or float).

Except in weedy areas, it is usually necessary to cast well out, say 25–30yds (23–27m), although fish can be found much closer in first thing in the morning. Therefore on arrival, enter the swim as cautiously as possible, and tackle up well back from the water's edge.

Baits

Should bites not be forthcoming, or if they are indecisive, or both, it is probably a case of either using the wrong bait or, more likely, the wrong bait size. (We will ignore the possibility of wrong pitch, bad conditions and so on.) Say, perhaps, that the time is 5am and the bites are hesitant and spasmodic: it is then a waste of time to persevere with big baits, as the tench are probably only mouthing them. Scaling down to a size 10 or 12 hook will usually produce better bites and will certainly offer a better chance of connecting. Tench are more likely to take a small bait inside the lips.

Sometimes perfect bites on big baits will be missed time and time again. Scaling down again often provides the remedy. Failing this, lobworms can be tried. When using lobworms allow the fish to take a few feet of line before striking, more fish being hooked thus. Lobworms can, however, be a very uncertain bait on estate lakes, especially after 6am, and I would always try scaling down first.

Maggots

All the usual baits can be satisfactory when using small hooks, but here, I feel, the maggot really comes into its own. Two or three maggots on a size 10 or 12 hook, preferably with a chip of flake on the hookbend, is probably the best all-round bait to use after 6am.

Maggots tend to work down the shank and lodge on the hookbend where they probably impede penetration. To counteract this I put maggots on first, slide them up the shank, and use a small chip of crust or flake beneath them, to prevent them crowding on the bend.

On and off during the summer, the lake may become green with suspended algae. Under these conditions maggot is nearly always the best bait to use, and I usually start off with them on fairly small hooks, say size 8 or 10. I think big bunches of maggots on big hooks make for risky hooking, and therefore never use them on a size 6 or bigger without the above-mentioned pad of crust or flake on the bend.

Combination Baits

Maggots and flake bring me to combination baits, a relatively unexplored and an exciting field. For more years than I care to remember I have been taking tench quite consistently on hooks holding two, three or even more different baits, and it is difficult to prove that orthodox single baits wouldn't have produced these tench. But, having on many occasions had one or two fish on combination baits when the tench were, to all intents and purposes, seemingly right off the feed, makes me think there must be times when tench take them out of preference.

There are probably numerous reasons why this should be so; however, the likely ones are that the different colours of say cheese, maggots and a small redworm are more eyecatching, and/or that the tench take them out of curiosity. There is enough evidence to suggest that tench are a nosey and inquisitive species. Take dragging a swim for instance. This can work so well sometimes that it is obvious that it didn't just induce tench already in the swim to feed. No! they came from all over the place to see what the rumpus was all about. So, if we offer tench something 'different' and 'eyecatching' they will probably pick this up out of curiosity, even if they have no need to eat it.

My friends and I have spent much time experimenting with unusual and/or combination baits and have proved, to our own satisfaction, that not only does the theory work and on many diverse waters, but they also produce the bigger specimens more consistently than do the usual baits. It is a pretty safe bet that big tench, in old estate lakes especially, will have had plenty of painful experience of conventional baits. So on this score alone it is probably well worthwhile to persevere with unusual and/or combination baits.

Coloured Baits

Are tench colour-conscious? Fred J. Taylor once pointed out that many successful tench baits are pink or red, and having taken tench on sweetcorn and bright yellow paste, I am inclined to think that yellow is also attractive to them. Bob Buteux and I use yellow baits, dyed with different colouring agents, and on numerous occasions have caught fish while other anglers have remained biteless.

TWITCH BITES

'Twitchers' aptly describes the bites you can expect from estate lake tench for 75 per cent of the time during the summer months. I apply this term to bites ranging from short, quick pulls to barely visible movements of the line (or swingtip) where it enters the water. With short, quick pulls, a lot depends on your tackle layout and your reflexes. Provided these are suitable, a fair proportion of twitchers will be hit. With minute line movements, however, luck is probably the deciding factor.

Twitchers and two rods rarely mix! The resultant divided attention produces less fish in the long run.

Technique and Tackle

I like to sit with the rod between my knees and strike sideways with both hands. This is much snappier and more direct than the usual one-handed upward strike, which introduces considerable and undesirable water resistance or drag.

Peter Drennan acts as Neil Pope's ghillie.

A rare 5-pounder from Henlow Grange.

Tackle drag should be reduced to a minimum, bearing in mind weeds and snags. A lighter line will nearly always result in better twitches, but even in clear-water swims I think it unwise to drop below 4lb line, as a powerful, two-handed sideways strike is so direct, that breakage on connection when using light line is an ever-present risk.

What you gain on the swings you loose on the roundabouts! A 3lb line gives better bite indication than a 5lb line, but at 25yd (23m) range the increased line stretch of the lighter line probably cancels out most of that advantage. Line stretch is a great disadvantage at longer ranges, and at extreme distances it pays to increase line strength considerably whilst retaining small hooks.

How small a hook? Having taken many tench on sizes 14 and 16 hooks (and lost plenty, too!) baited with just one or two maggots, I thought this was the answer. However, I now use the same baits on short shank, thick wire size 12s and found no difference, except a reduction in lost fish! I will never use such small and unsuitable hooks again. Tench appear so un-hook-conscious (provided the hooks are not finished with luminous paint) that now I rarely go below size 12, even when using a single maggot. When trying to deal with twitchers, more important factors are bait size and tackle drag.

FLOAT FISHING

Due to wind and drift, and the distances involved, it is not always possible to use float tackle, specially on exposed, shallow estate lakes. When it is possible, however, this is by far the best method to employ for twitchers. Small line

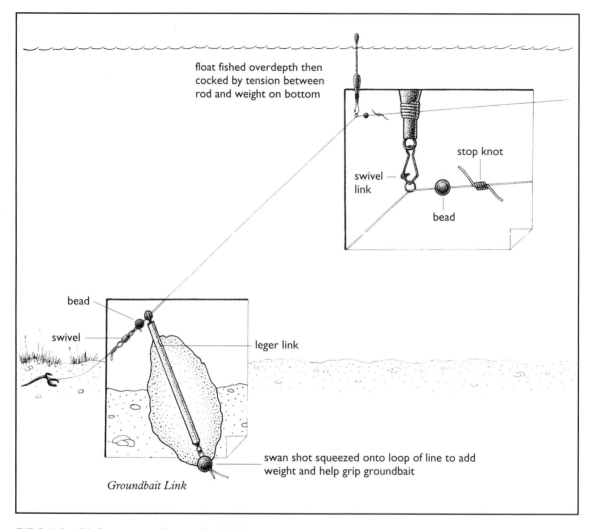

float fished overdepth then
cocked by tension between
rod and weight on bottom

stop knot

swivel
link

bead

bead

swivel

leger link

swan shot squeezed onto loop of line to add
weight and help grip groundbait

Groundbait Link

Bill Quinlan lift-float set-up with groundbait link.

movements on leger gear usually become good
pulls or lifts on an antenna float which is as light
as conditions will allow. Before suitable commercial antenna floats were available I made
a selection of floats myself, from balsa wood
and cane. Points to bear in mind with these floats
are:

1. The body shouldn't be too near the lower end;
   approximately a third of the overall length is
   about right. Otherwise, too much lead is
   required to cock it, thus sluggish 'lift' indications will result, and it will be unstable in ripple.
2. The visible section should ideally have a sight-

bob, because this reduces eye-strain at ranges
of more than 20yds (18m).
3. Pre-load the lower end of the stem with lead
   wire so the float is on the verge of cocking; this
   will reduce the amount of weight needed to
   hold bottom, and is most important.

The best colours for the tip and/or sight-bob
are fluorescent flaming orange, and when the sun
is behind the float, matt black. Most useful
lengths are from 10–15in (25–38cm).

I usually fish these floats with a terminal load
equivalent to a swan shot; this is fixed to a short
link, 2–3in (5–7.5cm) from the hook. Should

conditions demand more than a single swan shot to hold bottom, then wave action will probably render the float invisible anyway. The reason for using a link, rather than pinching the shot directly on the line is that a ball of groundbait is required to achieve the necessary distance. Should a potential twitcher happen along before the groundbait dissolves, an orthodox float-leger bite will result, that is, the float will disappear.

Line should be completely submerged between rod top and float, and a vigorous two-handed side-strike used to counteract the inevitable amount of slack line present.

GROUNDBAIT

There is no doubt that a properly planned and carried out pre-baiting programme can produce excellent results. The angler arriving for a single morning's fishing, however, is probably best advised to groundbait as little as possible, at least at first. Groundbait often attracts hordes of small fish into the swim, and small roach and perch can prove an absolute menace. And even big baits such as large lobworms, are not immune to their attentions. There are perhaps four partial solutions to the small fish problem:

1. Move swims (or lakes!).
2. Use a heavier weight to get the bait down quickly.
3. Use very little, if any, groundbait.
4. Use enormous amounts of groundbait to try to feed the little blighters off!

If you can spend three or four consecutive days at the water it does pay to groundbait quite heavily, and stick to the same swim. With luck, this will attract numbers of tench to the swim. Given settled conditions, this type of concentrated fishing should produce fair bags of medium-sized tench for a couple of days, followed by a decreasing number of higher-than-average-sized fish.

As good a groundbait as any is a fifty/fifty mixture of plain breadcrumb and sausage rusk, although I add ground hemp, trout pellets and flavour. I also add dye to make it less conspicuous; I just can't believe that wary tench will feed

confidently over great white patches of groundbait. The groundbait should be mixed just enough for it to hold together.

CONDITIONS

From about mid-July onwards, tench can be very difficult to locate in clear, open-water swims and are then best sought in shallow, weedy swims. It is asking for trouble to use light tackle in such swims and I start, at dawn, with 8lb line and size 2 hooks. Early morning feeders frequently give good bites and seem oblivious to such coarse tackle. If bites turn finicky, as they are wont to do, I scale down to 7lb line and strong size 10 hooks used on float tackle. The use of float tackle is nearly always possible in these types of swim as tench can be caught at quite close range, say around 10–20yds (9–18m). Odd fish can also be caught right through the day from these swims, particularly from August onwards. Personally, I would not use a line of less than 7lb in these weedy swims, since breaking-off and leaving tackle in fish is totally unacceptable. Furthermore, I am beginning to think more and more that the very largest tench feed at odd hours throughout the 24-hour period. Also that they won't feed very far away from heavily weeded areas.

Many anglers avoid the shallow swims in rough conditions, or later in the year, because they feel the tench should be in deeper, warmer water. Much nonsense is talked and generally believed as regards temperature and its effects on tench, even by experienced anglers who should know better. I have kept records of temperature, wind direction and so on for a very long time, and might just as well not have bothered. There are so many other factors involved, that to work out the movements of tench in one water alone is enough to give you a blood clot! Let us take a typical scenario.

You have fished through the night without a bite until 3.25am. At 3.30am bite follows bite. Now, the water didn't suddenly warm up sufficiently in five minutes to bring the tench madly on the feed – water temperature doesn't go up and down like a yo-yo. Much more likely, they just moved into the swim or even just felt like feeding; but not because of water temperature.

As the day grows older and bites become less frequent, temperature is blamed again; however, it is much more likely that the fish are just full up. These remarks apply to small variations or even gradual changes of 7°F to 8°F (about 2°C): sudden freeze-ups and the like are another matter entirely. The point I am trying to make is that the effect on tench of a small, or even a quite large but gradual temperature variation, is quite unpredictable and, I think, we would be better not to worry about it.

A sudden large drop in temperature will have a noticeable effect, however. A drop of 5° to 6°F (about 1½°C) in the course of a few hours, (easily possible when strong cold winds strike a shallowish lake), will generally put fish off the feed all over the lake. Should such conditions occur in late morning or early afternoon, you can be reasonably sure that the tench will feed that evening and on into darkness, even though the temperature is falling. This has happened so often that I feel sure the tench sense that the following morning will prove unfavourable, and are having a good 'stodge-up' in advance. Any tench caught at all the following morning will usually take only a small bait, and probably do so just out of habit.

It is rather difficult to decide when tench fishing in estate lakes finishes for the season because summers vary so much – so much so, I have often taken tench as late as November, although in some years it hasn't been worth the effort after the end of September.

POSTSCRIPT

Two more thoughts have occurred to me:

The implement intended for raking tench swims should not be equipped with tines or prongs. Weed and rubbish catches round the prongs and are a nuisance and difficult to remove. Much better is a plain steel rod with an eye attached to its centre for tying the rope to.

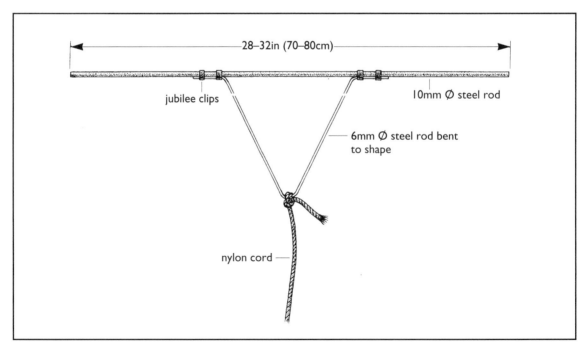

Tine-less rake.

Bill Quinlan dragging his tench swim.

Weed slips off this easily after retrieving, saving much time and effort.

I've recently experienced a demonstration showing how 'unsensitive' common leger rigs can be. This event actually occurred on a gravel pit, but the principle remains the same whatever the water type. We wanted to see if we could find out the secrets of a particular hotspot about 60yds (55m) from the bank, so Ritchie MacDonald donned snorkel gear and swam out. He discovered a shallow bar, covered by about 4ft (1.2m) of water, and actually found my hookbait. Despite Ritchie giving the terminal tackle quite

violent tugs, the swingtip only flickered. To get the tip to lift any appreciable distance he had to move the bait sharply over a full arm's reach. The terminal was a simple sliding link-leger set-up, but I think results would be similar with a fixed paternoster.

I can only think that the reel line ran up and down over weedbeds and so on, and that some of the resulting 'bends' in the line had to be taken up before the swingtip moved. The moral is clear: keep the bite indicator as close to the bait as possible, so whenever you can, fish with float tackle.

8 THE QUALITY DOZEN

A brief comparison of the accompanying lists, one recording the current twelve top tench caught in the British Isles, the other from 1989, underlines how massive the change has been over the past seven years. In 1989 I recorded twenty-four top tench, the final fish being Ron Chant's 9lb 15oz specimen – although in fact Ron's entry was really the twenty-fifth because Steve Scales' Wilstone 10½lb fish, caught in 1986, had unfortunately been overlooked. Today's entry at number twenty-five weighs over 1lb more (11lb 1oz, caught by S. Lambard from a Hertfordshire gravel pit), therefore representing a more than 10 per cent increase.

1989 LIST OF BRITAIN'S HEAVIEST TENCH

Weight	Captor	Bait	Location	Year
14.3.0	P Gooriah	worm	Wraysbury 1	1987
12.8.11	A Wilson	sweetcorn	Wilstone Reservoir	1985
12.8.0	R Blaber	worm	River Kennet	1951
12.0.0	Found dead		Burnham-on-Sea	1947
11.9.0	Found when pond drained		Thornville	1801
11.6.0	C Wylot	lobworm	Home Counties	1988
11.3.0	M Perkins		Kent Water	1988
11.1.0	S Lambard		Herts Pit	1985
11.0.0	D Laing	breadflake	Wraysbury Pit	1959
10.13.0	A Wilson	mag/flake	Wilstone Reservoir	1988
10.10.0	J Darville	worm	Herts Pit	1984
10.10.0	A Willis		Oxford Pit	1987
10.10.0	D Kelly	maggot	Cheshire Mere	1981
10.6.0	D Penny	boilie	Berks Pit	1988
10.4.0	R Francis	worm	Wilstone Reservoir	1981
10.4.0	P Stone	sweetcorn	Oxford Pit	1985
10.3.0	G Mills	sweetcorn	Herts Pit	1985
10.2.8	P Cardozo	special	Herts Pit	1985
10.2.0	E Edwardes		Oxford Pit	1982
10.1.4	A Chester	worm	Wilstone Reservoir	1981
10.1.2	L Brown	worm	Peterborough	1975
10.1.0	K Ferguson		Johnson's Pit	1985
10.0.0	A Wilson	mag/flake	Wilstone Reservoir	1988
9.15.0	R Chant	boilie	Long Life Pit	1985

Apologies to S Scales for omitting his 10lb 8oz fish caught in 1986.

Now compare the average weight of the twelve heaviest fish from both lists: the difference is almost incredible, the figure being approximately 10½lb per fish for the 1989 list, and around 12½lb for the current crop – give or take a few ounces, a 20 per cent increase! It could be argued that, since the most recent fish in the earlier list was caught in 1988, this gives a span of eight years, but who's quibbling? From any standpoint a 20 per cent increase, even in eight years, is still remarkable.

It is also true that the ultimate weight other species may attain – carp, barbel, bream and chub for example – appears to be on the increase, too; but I doubt any come close to matching that of tench. Furthermore, tench weight escalation has been going on for a very long time, twenty-five years at least, and rather than slowing down, it still appears to be gathering momentum. Whilst most tench specialists agree that this is a good thing, the big questions are: for how long will it continue? Will there be any cost? And if so, what is that cost likely to be? The evidence seems to

suggest that the 'big tench bubble' remains some way from bursting. If we anglers, or the tench themselves, are going to suffer in the long run, it is difficult to see how. Every year more big tench are caught, and from an increasing number of waters – even a few very old estate lakes and meres are producing bigger tench than ever before. But of course, it is mature gravel pits and reservoirs that provide most of the front-runners. And I urge all tench anglers to take advantage of this situation now, because it may prove a fleeting phenomenon, never to be repeated in our lifetime.

This past summer (1995) two Colne Valley pits I know very well both produced their first-ever double-figure tench. However, neither of these fish were reported and therefore don't figure on any list. The controlling clubs, not the anglers, are responsible for this cover-up because they frown on publicity of any kind, not allowing the fish to be reported even if the name and location of the water are kept secret. Any infringement of the rule usually results in the miscreant being called before the committee and

TOP TWELVE TENCH (NOVEMBER 1995)

No.	Weight	Captor	Location	Date
1	14.7.0	G Beavan	Herts Pit	Sept 1993
2	14.4.0	G Newman	Bury Lake	Aug 1994
3	14.3.0	P Gooriah	Wraysbury 1	June 1987
4	14.0.0	A Wilson	Wilstone Reservoir	June 1992
5	14.0.0	G Beavan	Herts Pit	Sept 1993
6	13.7.0	G Newman	Bury Lake	Sept 1994
7	12.15.0	G Newman	Bury Lake	Sept 1994
8	12.13.0	D Franklin	Wilstone Reservoir	Sept 1995
9	12.8.11	A Wilson	Wilstone Reservoir	June 1985
10	12.8.0	R Blaber	River Kennet	Feb 1951
11	12.8.0	C McCorkell	Startop Reservoir	June 1990
12	12.6.0	A Wilson	Wilstone Reservoir	June 1993

1	Current record
3	Previous record
9	Previous record
10	Not accepted due to abnormal condition

My sincere thanks are due to Marsh Pratley of NASA, and to all the members of the Tenchfishers for allowing me to quote from their list.

ultimately expelled from the club, so serious do they consider this offence to be.

This is the sole reason behind my decision not to provide further details about these captures: I'd hate to get anyone into trouble. Personally I believe the 'no publicity' rule is a shame, besides being something of a farce. It is a shame, because some historically valuable fish will never be generally known about, or appreciated by future generations. And it is a farce, because the big-fish world's grapevine is so good that everybody interested enough makes quite sure they learn about all notable captures anyway. In fact representatives of the angling press often refer to these 'secret' (sic) captures, some obliquely, others

more blatantly, the motive behind these revelations I suspect being just to let their readers, or their competitors, realize they know that these whackers have been caught. In more than one case, however, it has caused much grief for the captor: believe me, I know!

I understand only too well the need to keep some things quiet, specifically the name and location of the waters where the fish are caught. The reason for this is that the fish themselves are the most important consideration, and subjecting them to excessive pressure, especially from inexperienced anglers, is not in their best interests. Some will undoubtedly accuse me of hiding behind this reason because they think I want to

You'd need a tench over 2lb heavier than this magnificent 10lb 4oz specimen, caught by Peter Stone, to figure in 'The Quality Dozen'.

keep waters quiet for my own selfish ends. However, this just isn't true and my motive is as stated, nothing more.

The lists graphically illustrate just how localized are the waters producing these exceptional tench. Though not familiar with 'Bury Lake', I've heard that it isn't very far from London, and the remaining nine fish also come from Home Counties' waters; in fact every tench, right down to and including number twenty in the current list, was caught within about 40 miles (64km) of London. Of course, some of these are repeat captures; for example Gordon Beavan's was the same fish caught on two separate occasions. Nevertheless, the dominance of this area is clear to see, albeit far from easy to explain. Five fish from the top twelve were caught in June, which comes as no surprise, but a further five, including the record fish, were caught in September! Is this mere coincidence? Again, I have little idea. Eleven of the twelve have been caught in the past ten years, with no fewer than nine coming in the 1990s, giving even more weight to the argument that tench as a species continue to get bigger.

There is only one river fish in the lists: Blaber's 12½lb tench from the Kennet. Six of the top dozen are reservoir fish, and five come from gravel pits, and there is nothing untoward in that. But the current top fifty tench list (*see* Chapter 1) clearly shows the dominance that gravel pits have, with as many as thirty fish coming from these; this is twice the number from reservoirs, which have fifteen representatives, and twelve of these come from one water – Wilstone. Natural meres come third, with four entries.

The baits on which these fish were caught are interesting, but on the whole not really surprising, four coming on boilies, three on worm, three on maggots, and Gordon Beavan's record and Alan Wilson's ex-record of 12lb 8oz 11dr on sweetcorn. I'd have thought bread and casters would have figured, and prominently.

These lists are as accurate as possible and fairly comprehensive. But they still leave many questions unanswered, such as what time of day were these fish caught? And what line strength and hook size were used? What was the water temperature? And was it rising or falling? And so on... From what I have been able to glean from press reports and suchlike, every one of these top fish gave a big sailaway bite – so perhaps I'm wasting my time twitcher-hitting after all!

The fact that three anglers figure more than once in the top twelve underlines how important location is. You can't catch fish that aren't there. Gordon Beavan has two entries, the record at 14lb 7oz, and the same fish again at 14lb. Gary Newman has three fish listed, 14lb 4oz, 13lb 7oz and 12lb 15oz (it is reputed these were repeat captures too). Alan Wilson is also represented three times: 14lb, 12lb 8oz 11dr, and 12lb 6oz. Plenty of other anglers fish these same waters, but without anything like the same achievements. However, results such as these are not due to luck: they are the result of dedication, confidence and sheer hard work, and I heartily and sincerely congratulate all three of the anglers mentioned above.

The first fully authenticated capture of a double-figure tench was only twenty years ago (Lewis Brown, 10lb 1oz 2dr, 3 August 1975), so why is it that more than fifty 'doubles' have been recorded since? Chapter 1 carries a detailed hypothesis of possible reasons. Yet another possible reason is that, because of the good summer of 1976, there was a particularly good survival rate, and that these are the big fish we are catching today. Personally I cannot subscribe to this idea: on the contrary, I think the survival of too many baby tench would have an adverse effect on optimum sizes because the competition for the food available would surely increase. But wherever the truth lies, the trend still continues. Thirty-four of today's top fifty have been caught since 1990, and assuming the peak has not yet been reached – and from the lists it doesn't seem likely – these statistics bode well for the foreseeable future. Furthermore, from reports in the angling press, and from the stories continually buzzing around the big-fish world's 'jungle-telegraph', it appears there is no shortage of back-up fish either. And don't forget that for one reason or another, we don't hear of every fish; for example many carp anglers don't even weigh the big tench they catch accidentally. For this reason and others, more big tench go unrecorded these days than ever before.

For the now sadly defunct magazine *Big Fish World*, editor Kevin Clifford asked me what I thought the chances of a new record tench would be. My reply appeared in the June/July 1991 issue:

> Since Phil Gooriah's fish was caught a lot of people think the tench record is beyond reach. However, I don't necessarily go along with that. For instance, there is a large gravel pit in the Colne Valley which produced some double-figure tench quite some time ago. If night-fishing was allowed on this water, thereby encouraging motivated anglers to fish it seriously, I think we could be in for a few surprises. I also think Wraysbury 1 could still break the record. It is those sorts of fisheries that have areas where tench live most of their lives without seeing an angler's bait, that offer the best chance. I have been reliably informed of tench being caught which were 28–29in in length. If one of those fish was caught carrying a lot a spawn it would annihilate the record.

Well, it's very nice to be proved right sometimes! More to the point, I still believe the chances of surpassing Gordon Beavan's 14lb 7oz record are good. And I continue to believe that the Colne Valley provides the types of water from which a record tench is likely to come. And in no way is the Thames Valley to be discounted, either.

Another reason for optimism is this: in April 1990, one of my favourite haunts of old in the Colne Valley – known as Longfield in my day, and Fox Pool latterly – was netted, and amongst the big carp landed was a monster tench weighing in excess of 11lb! However, I was probably one of the few anglers not surprised when this fish turned up because a long time ago Dave Short and I had actually seen it from the sandbar-

bank, or, at least, a tench of very much the same size! It has been said that this fish was virtually devoid of spawn, so you can imagine what it might weigh in the middle of June! I am told that the proprietors, Leisure Sport, put this huge tench into another of their waters in the area and, as far as I know, it hasn't been caught since.

From the foregoing you might think that big tench are plentiful and easy to catch. However, this just isn't true and I don't wish to give the impression that it is. Thousands of anglers fish for big tench every day of the week in summertime, and it is only a very small minority that succeeds in landing big ones: relatively speaking, big tench remain rare creatures.

A common question is, what constitutes a big tench? Well, it depends on the waters you have available, your attitude to angling, and whether you believe all you read in the papers or not. Thus a 5lb tench is still a big fish, especially coming from a canal or river, and a 5lb male deserves a photograph. Having said that, if you are on a water that produces seven-pounders on a regular basis (and there are a few that do), then your sights must be upped accordingly. Eight-pound female tench and 7lb males are monsters, and many of today's specialists still have to catch one or the other.

My next aim is to catch a 'double', which I think now represents a realistic target for any big-fish man. However, I have no ambition to fish 'circuit waters', so my task is that much more difficult. But I wouldn't have it any other way: when I finally catch my ten-pounder it will certainly have been worth the effort – and I sincerely hope I'm swingtipping at the time. If you really want the chance of catching a record tench, the list names the top waters. Outside these, a large deep pit, lake or reservoir that produces only a few tench, but big ones, is a likely venue. And to give yourself the best chance, you will probably be legering with sweetcorn, boily or maggots, in such a water, within about a 50-mile (80km) radius of London.

9 THE CARE OF BIG FISH

BASIC CODE OF PRACTICE

- Don't keep specimen fish out of water for longer than is absolutely necessary.
- Unhooking should be done on an unhooking mat.
- After unhooking, place the fish back in the water in your landing net while you sort out your weighing equipment.
- Never put a specimen fish in a keepnet; a sack is far more humane.
- A dark-coloured sack incorporating a weigh-sling is much preferred; don't forget to wet it.
- Put the fish in the sack/weigh-sling and weigh it as quickly as possible.
- Choose a deep shady place to site the sack, out of direct sunlight, and in at least three feet of water. You may need to wade to reach deeper water, and if you get wet in the process you must not mind.
- Find a suitable sacking site before you catch your specimen.
- Before leaving the sack for whatever reason, tie it securely to some fixed object such as the branch of a tree or a bank-stick.
- Make sure that the fish is upright and that it is breathing satisfactorily by gently feeling its movements through the sack.
- Ensure that the sack is big enough for its occupant, and that it has sufficient and adequate water flow; too many holes for water circulation is far preferable to too few. (*See also* the National River Authority's requirements for retention of sacks in Chapter 4).
- Each sack must contain only one fish.

Remember to keep checking the situation, and the fish's breathing; when you are certain that it is perfectly happy, only then can you leave it to do whatever you have to do, such as set up the camera gear. Keep all this as close as possible to where you have sited the sack. If it is necessary to keep the background unidentifiable; use an umbrella to hide it or have it blanked out in the final picture, but don't carry the fish further from the water than is necessary simply to disguise the venue.

Do everything you can to minimize the time the fish is out of water: you should aim for less than a minute, and I know that this is realistic, because I have often done all that is necessary in less time than this. For example, mark out where photographs might be taken before you unsack the fish, and roughly focus the camera; if a tripod is to be used, even critical focusing can be carried out. Ensure that there is sufficient film in the camera; it is quite unacceptable to keep a fish out of the water while a film is replaced.

Only carry a fish in the landing net or in a sack; it is notoriously difficult to carry a fish in your bare hands, and if you drop it, you could cause it permanent damage. I have discussed this topic with people who handle live fish every day of their working lives, and without exception, they all say that fish are liable to be dropped when carried by hand, no matter how experienced the person. For the same reason, keep fish as close to the ground as possible when taking pictures – and it won't hurt you to get your knees wet in the process.

Be sure that a fish is fit enough before you bring it out of the water for weighing and/or photographing. Strong body and gill movements are essential, and it must be sturdy enough to stay upright of its own volition. If there is any doubt at all, it should not be removed from the water,

Ron Chant is one of the anglers who knows how to care for fish. Together, this brace weighed more than 16lb.

and if there is ever any sign that it is becoming weak as a result of its stay in the sack, release it and do not remove it from the water again. It is infinitely preferable to go without pictures than to have the death of a big fish on your conscience, a death which, quite apart from all other considerations, will prevent other anglers from experiencing the thrill of catching that particular fish.

Most mistakes as regards a fish's welfare are made at the moment of release. Understandably anglers will want to return a fish as soon as possible, but it should not be released until it is strong enough to swim away of its own volition. If a fish has been removed from the water for photographing, it should be carried back in the wet sack. It should be held upright in deepish water even if you have to wade to get to such an area and get wet in the process. Pick some suitable places before you even start fishing, so saving valuable

time. Once the fish is back in the water and out of the sack, it should be nursed for however long it takes for it to regain its strength; signs to look for are regular, even gill movements that become steadily stronger. Eventually it will swim out of your hands. However, this is not the end of your responsibility: you must still keep an eye on it in case it turns belly up. If it does, retrieve it with the landing net and begin the nursing procedure anew; although if the preceding guidelines have been observed, this is rarely necessary.

It is now well known that carp are extremely long lived; fifty years is not exceptional. What is less well known is that other fish, too, live to a ripe old age. So the message is clear: if you want to catch specimen fish, take the trouble to look after them properly – and there is much more to know than is described in this brief summary. Don't be afraid to ask experienced anglers their views: they will be only too pleased to help and advise you. Moreover if you should see someone not doing the right thing, do not be afraid to advise them. And don't take offence in the unlikely event that you are verbally abused for your advice; everything is worthwhile in the interests of, and the care of specimen fish.

UNHOOKING MATS

The days of laying fish on the bank to unhook them are gone, as is using 'make-do' unhooking mats such as carpet underlay. Commercial unhooking mats are so well designed there is absolutely no excuse not to use one; in fact many fishery owners and controllers now insist they are used: no unhooking mat, no fishing. This is one regulation that I feel makes complete sense and should be stringently enforced.

ANTISEPTIC

An essential addition to any tackle bag is a bottle of antiseptic, to clean and sterilize any wound(s) the fish may have. Several companies supply bottles of

Knotless mesh is essential for specimen fish. Here, Tony Arbery has landed a 7-pounder for Keith Griffin.

specially formulated antiseptic, small enough to be carried in a pocket, which will treat hundreds of fish and last for years. I use 'Remedy', the best available anti-bacterial solution suitable for all species of fish. This will treat torn fins, ulcers, sores, spawning lesions and wounds, and will speed up the healing process. It is formulated as a sticky,

Returned undamaged.

viscous solution and is most effective because it clings to the affected areas and won't wash off before the antiseptic penetrates and does its job.

Squeeze a small amount onto a bud of cotton wool and smear it onto the affected area(s), although avoid the fish's eyes, its throat and its gills. After hook removal a dab of antiseptic solution will sterilize the area and accelerate healing.

ARGULUS

Occasionally tench are caught and found to be carrying a skin parasite called argulus, a type of freshwater louse. At first sight these resemble small greyish/green pimples, but they are actually little animals adhering to the skin. They can be removed easily with the corner of a towel first moistened with a saline solution. To make up, dissolve a pinch or two of table salt in a small quantity of water, using any convenient clean container.

10 TENCH FOR THE MEMORY

In this chapter, friends have been invited to relate some of their most memorable tench-fishing experiences: we have accounts written by Bob Buteux, Tony Arbery, Pete Jackson and Bill Quinlan; also the story of Gordon Beavan's record tench, and a few of my own experiences, too. As Bob Buteux's Southill piece goes back the furthest, I'll start with that.

SOUTHILL MEMORIES by Bob Buteux

If anyone asked me which water has given me the most pleasure in the many years I have fished, I would say, without hesitation, Southill Park in Bedfordshire. As I write the memories flood back. There was nowhere else I wanted to fish: surrounded by trees that cut out all outside noise, to me it was a little world of its own; and with big tench to be had, what more could a keen tench fisher want?

The way I found out about Southill was quite unusual: one afternoon in June 1959 I was fishing the King George Reservoir for big roach, and while I leaned against its steep sloping bank, I spotted another angler some 60 or 70yds (58–67m) around the curve of the concrete bank. During the afternoon his friend arrived and they began to chat, and I could hear every word just as if they were next to me, an effect created by some peculiarity of the overhanging coping stones. 'Had a 6lb tench yesterday.' My ears pricked up. 'Where?' came the obvious reply from his mate. 'Southill Park.' 'Where's that?'... and so on. I had all the details in my notebook inside a few minutes – tickets were 2s [10p!] a day from a Mr Malloy, the estate agent, obtained by writing.

Within a fortnight three tickets had arrived and plans were laid. My close friends at the time were Bert Dell and Cliff Wood: they arrived at my house at midnight in Cliff's old 'Y'-type Ford, in torrential rain. We bundled everything in the back. 'I'm afraid it's got a leak,' called Cliff as we pulled away. And so it had, right in my lap. It was the first and only time I have ever had to put up my umbrella in the back of a car.

Off we chugged. We were stopped twice by the police about the lights on the car; they were certainly dim, I had to agree, barely glowing, and that was headlights! But we made it. Finding the entrance after locating the estate took ages, but eventually we squelched onto the lake side just after 3am – giving an average speed for the journey of 16mph!

As it became light the rain stopped and I looked around; with only one minor road close by, all that broke the silence was the sound of wildlife on and around the lake. We could only fish one end of the lake, which was about 30 acres, but there was enough room for the dozen or so anglers allowed each day.

None of us had a bite that day, but I knew I'd come back for more of this tranquillity – and so I did, hundreds of times. Subsequent visits were made on my old Triumph 110 motorbike. The ride down through the twisting lanes was usually uneventful, until a mile or so from the lake when on a particular bend my headlight would pick out perhaps a dozen rabbits on the road. They were always there. As I slowed they would zigzag away in all directions, and at each visit I managed to miss them, except once when one ran under the back wheel. I gave it to old Ernie Wakelin, the bailiff – alas, now deceased. His eyes lit up when

Bob Buteux lands a big Southill tench.

trees to the lake by the boathouse. One particular, morning, at 3am, it was pitch black and I had forgotten my torch. I had to find my way in the dark, and to make matters worse, the night before there were reports that a dangerous criminal had escaped from a mental hospital and was at large in the Bedford area. You can imagine my thoughts as I felt my way along the path with only the sound of my boots on gravel to guide me. When at long last the hole of light showed at the end of the trees I ran as fact as my legs would carry me, arriving hot and out of breath.

It was strictly an early morning water. In the first few weeks of the season bites faded out by 8am; come 9 o'clock I invariably had the water to myself. So, eating most of my sandwiches and drinking half my tea, I would sleep for as long as I could during the day. There were very few who

Bob Buteux and Bill Quinlan at Southill Park more than thirty-years ago – a friendship that has endured to the present day.

he saw it, for it would provide him with two or three meals. Ernie lived in a small stone building called 'the Temple'. His meagre income hardly kept him going, but he was a complete and utter gentleman who, on his old bike, would ride around at the same time each day to check tickets. Not a penny would he take; I tried to get him to supply tickets on the bank, but not Ernie: a more honest man I never met.

The entrance in those now far-off days, was some little way from the stretch we were allowed to fish, and a gravel path led under a canopy of considered it worthwhile fishing during the evenings as I did, but as a fish or two came my way, usually at dusk, it was worth it.

My old favourite, breadflake, caught most of my fish, but swan mussels had to be tried because there was a profusion of them in the shallows. There was a shallow weedy area near the Temple, so one morning I gathered half a bucket of mussels, chopped them all up, mixed in mashed bread and stirred up the horrible mess before slinging the lot in. I then gave the lake bed a good raking, all the time thinking any self-respecting tench would be miles away. But within minutes of casting I had a screaming run, which I missed because it took me so much by surprise. It turned out to be the only bite of the day!

It was in the same swim, one morning in July 1962, that I hooked a tench which bogged down in thick weed. I was in a bit of a state when a fellow angler picked up my net and waded out and got it for me. This turned out to be Bill Quinlan, and it was the start of a friendship which has endured to the present day.

There were some very good anglers fishing Southill at around that time, and I learned bits and pieces of information from all of them. Frank Guttfield was a regular, living locally at Arlesey; Bob Rutland, too, enjoyed Southill, as did Dick Walker and Peter Thomas in the earlier years.

The main quarry at Southill were tench and rudd, and there were also a lot of small pike and a few roach and perch. According to the Tench-fishers, the tench were of the highest average size from any water they knew of, and they could have been right. My personal average was 3lb 14oz. Five-pounders came occasionally, although a 'six' was rare; 7lb exactly was the record for the

Bob Buteux fought this battle for over half-an-hour before the hook straightened.

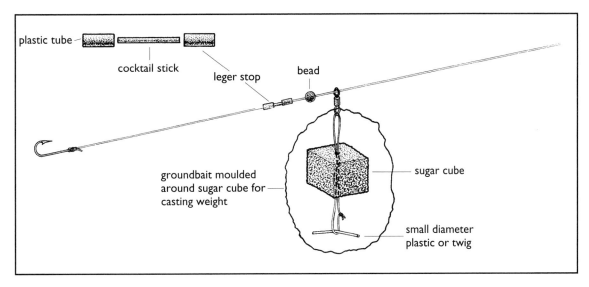

plastic tube

cocktail stick

leger stop

bead

groundbait moulded around sugar cube for casting weight

sugar cube

small diameter plastic or twig

Bob Buteux' sugar-cube link-leger.

water. After groundbaiting heavily Bill and John Simpson fished the opening of one season together. They caught fifty-one tench with an average weight of 3lb 15oz, topped by a 5lb 12oz fish to Bill; an exceptional bag in those days.

There used to be something very big in Southill that was hooked from time to time, though to my knowledge it was never landed. On two occasions during the years I fished there I myself hooked something large; the first time whatever it was screamed off and never stopped, probably an old carp left behind by a livebaiter. The other was the complete reverse, a very slow, ponderous fight that went on for over half an hour before the hook straightened. It felt so big I think it could have only been a large pike, foul-hooked; but I shall never know!

In later years Bill and I tried various methods to induce better bites. I remember making special pastes, including sausage rusk, flour, sugar and yellow groundbait. The very first tench on it was well over 5lb and I thought we had 'cracked' it – but no, the rest were average size. Another idea was to drill a hole in a cube of sugar, put it in place of the bomb on the link and squeeze groundbait around it for casting weight. I had experimented by dangling a cube of sugar in a glass of water, finding it took around eight

seconds to dissolve, and so I judged that within thirty seconds of casting I would be fishing free-lined flake at 50yds (45m). But that didn't produce any better bites, either, or any better fish.

Meanwhile Bill tried float fishing at long range, but had problems with wind and drift. The Southill tench were reluctant to feed close in, and Bill eventually fished small baits using orthodox leger tackle – and it worked! One of his favourite baits he called a 'cocktail', any combination of two, or even three baits, all very small. It could be flake and maggot, or worm and crust, in fact anything. The idea was to strike at any movement, and his success rate rose dramatically; he became really quite adept at hitting these 'twitchers', as they came to be called. He also showed Jack Hilton and Roger Smith how to catch carp at Brooklands using the same ruse.

As most waters, Southill gradually changed. The roach proliferated and became a nuisance, and the rudd practically disappeared; I am told that nowadays, small bream have taken over. When, in the 1970s, the tench all over the country put on weight, the Southill fish stayed the same, for years; but I did hear that eventually they had caught up, although they had become 'football jobs' rather than big-framed fish – for example in 1981 Frank Guttfield landed a 9lb

6oz tench that wasn't any longer than the 'fives' we had caught twenty years earlier.

It is many years since I last saw my Shangri-La. I keep saying I will return just to have a look around and revel in the memories; but I suppose that would spoil them all. I even heard 'Southill Margaret' has retired – so Bill will never go back!

GREEN GODDESSES by Tony Arbery

I'd spent a lot of time tench fishing a Surrey pit, and after setting a new record for the water, my sights were now set on the next step up the big-fish ladder. A water in the Colne Valley was my intended destination; the same pit then being fished by my dad and his friends.

On arriving at the lake for my first visit I soon found dad and Bill Quinlan sharing a swim. They had been fishing for a couple of days but with little in the way of tench to show for it. As I set up in the next swim to Bill, he mumbled to Dad, 'He's not having any of my digestive biscuits,' this remark immediately followed by a distinct click as the padlock snapped shut on his coolbox. I pretended not to notice. After setting up, and before casting out, I joined them for a cup of tea. I brought along my own cup and my own water, because hadn't I learned long ago not to accept the tea Bill usually reserves for guests? I am convinced this consists of water out of the lake, served in the cup he keeps his false teeth in!

Dad was working nightshift at this time and soon had to leave the lake, although he would be back just after midnight. He suggested I fish his pitch with his rods until he returned. At this, more mutterings could be heard emanating from the ramshackle canvas shed which Bill called a bivvi. 'No more peace and quiet!' and, 'Lots of tea, and he'll be into my biscuits,' were the more printable ones. As I was re-casting Dad's rods, two of Bill's friends arrived to see how he was doing; he told them how he and Dad were fishing for little return. 'New blood is needed to sort them out,' I joked. And no more than fifteen minutes later the left-hand swingtip sailed

serenely up! It would, I'm sure, have gone on for ever, but my strike arrested its progress and the rod took on its battle curve.

Soon the tench lay in the folds of the landing net, a beautiful 'green goddess' of 7lb 9oz. To rub salt into Bill's wounds, I asked him to do the honours with his camera, making out mine had been left in the car.

With the photographing ceremony over and the tench returned to its watery world, Bill's friends left with the parting remark, 'You'll be OK now Bill, now you've got somebody to show you how it's done!' I just asked for a biscuit and a cup of tea. Although no more bites were forthcoming. I really enjoyed that evening's fishing and looked forward to much more of the good-natured banter that Dad and his fishing friends are fond of. Dad returned soon after midnight and the three of us tried to get a few hours sleep.

He woke me up with a cup of tea a little before 4am. In the first glimmer of daylight wreaths of mist were curling lazily up from the water; the sky was clear, and not a breath of wind ruffled the surface of the lake – a truly beautiful summer's dawn. To my mind this is the best time of day, and one which so many people miss. It was all very peaceful and tranquil, the only sounds coming from wakening birds and from coots fussing about in the margins.

As I sipped the hot, sweet dark brew which Dad calls tea, I studied my surroundings. About 50yds (45m) out and slightly to my left was a small island. From this, running diagonally to my right, was a weed-covered bar under about 3ft (0.9m) of water, culminating in another even smaller island, quite close to the bank. I decided to cast my left-hand rod as close as possible to the island on that side and leave it there, and to position the other bait on the bar's near drop-off; this one I would move to a different position at hourly intervals along the bar if bites were not forthcoming, the idea being to search the bar thoroughly for feeding fish. Bait was a single 14mm Richworth boilie on a short hair-rig, and I catapulted a few midi-boilies around the left-hand bait; a stringer holding four midi-boilies was added to the other. Line was 6lb, and

Another big male for Tony.

like Dad and Bill, I used swingtips for bite detection.

Almost an hour passed uneventfully and I was about to recast the right-hand bait according to my plan, when a big tench rolled silently within about 5yds (4.5m) of it. So I decided to leave well alone. Everything was nicely settled and I didn't want to risk disturbing any feeding fish. Ten minutes later a big tench rolled again, much closer to the bait, and now I had one of those feelings that

things were going to happen; and they did! But no twitcher this, the tip flew up and I was 'in'. The hooked fish kited away from the island and the bar, and also the weed, which I didn't mind at all. It fought with a constant heavy pull, which suggested just one thing: a big fish. Steady and even side-strain eventually took its toll and as the fish slipped over the cord and into the net, I could see it was a beauty. Gently laying it on the unhooking mat the folds of the net were parted to reveal an absolute beauty, certainly a new personal best. The scales confirmed this: 8lb 12oz.

After first slipping the fish into the sack, I crept round to inform Dad and Bill of my prize. Pictures were duly taken and the fish returned. Bill said he was horrified to learn that the lake held more than one idiot fish, and suggested that they were in fact the same individual and that I'd weighed it wrongly the second time. No chance!

The morning wore on with no further action so I popped round to see if the other two had had any bites. It seemed that they hadn't, for they were both in bed, sound asleep. Life at the top is tough! Tea seemed in order to me, so I woke them up. As soon as the kettle was on they both recast, and not long afterwards lightning struck: this time it was Bill's buzzer which cried out. There was a mad dash for his rod and tea went everywhere, but by the time he picked it up the hooked tench had made the most of the delay and

Not seen every day; a 6lb plus male and an 8lb plus female, both caught by Tony Arbery. Dad holds the male.

had visited more weedbeds than Bill visits pubs! And who'd have thought the lake was that big! After much heaving and handlining, a large clump of weed surfaced not too far out. 'Net it!' ordered Bill. 'Net what?' I enquired. 'All of it!' he shouted. So I did. Amongst 1/2cwt (25kg) of weed, a search revealed a male tench of about 3lb! Dad and I made the most of that!

Later in the day Dad landed a nice female of 7lb 4oz. I had to pack up the following morning so was fishing again soon after dawn. It was another lovely day, but I had to wait two hours for my first bite. There was no rolling or any other sign of fish when the left tip lifted an inch and held, the answering strike met solid yet living resistance, and believe it or not, another eight-pounder was soon in the sack.

I didn't have much of a wait before I successfully connected with a similar bite on the other rod. This fish travelled faster than any other tench I'd ever encountered, and because of this I convinced myself it was a carp. Its first run took it almost the full length of the bar in front of me, and there was no way I could stop it, or pull it off

A 7lb 4oz for Dad.

A right pair – the tench, of course! Son Tony and Keith Griffin return a pair of whackers.

course; the more pressure I applied the harder it fought, and the more line it took. Why it didn't swim over the bar to almost certain freedom, I've no idea, though I'm not complaining! Luck was obviously with me and inevitably the pressure eventually told. By this time Bill and Dad were by my side and one of them finally had it in the net.

This proved to be yet another personal best, a male tench of 6lb 14oz. As this and the 8lb 4oz female were being photographed they certainly made a lovely sight. And I knew I'd be back for

more of these green goddesses and all the rest of the fun that goes with it. Bill said I couldn't but I knew he didn't mean it!

ON MY OWN TERMS by Bob Buteux

The success we had enjoyed on our first assault on the water wasn't to be repeated in the following years. A few good fish still came, but in the main it was much slower fishing, and the tench weren't up to the same standard. It is so easy to become blasé after the capture of a few good fish; five-pounders that would have made us jump for joy a few short years back were rarely even weighed. Big fish certainly learn fast.

Experimenting with baits and rigs worked to a degree, but after the first fortnight, two or three bites were as much as I could expect from a long weekend. And, don't forget, it wasn't a relaxing sort of fishing, but intensely concentrating on two tiny bobbins, waiting for that 1in (2.5cm) lift! So it was a satisfying feeling when, after a few hours' waiting, a tiny bite was 'dotted'. However, a five-pounder wasn't worth the effort now; what we needed was a new venue, and once again, Len came up trumps.

I clearly remember my first impressions on being shown round these two lakes in the close season, they were beautiful, as mature gravel pits often are, and everything an angler could ever want: fairly secluded and only lightly fished by a

Pete Frost with a 'Martins' cracker.

club whose members were friendly and well behaved, large enough to retain some mystery but not so large that they lost that intimate feeling – and of course they held tench, a big one rolling right in front of me on that very first visit.

I chose to fish the lake that looked to me as though it was hardly fished at all, Peter Frost christened it Martins. It was shared by a yachting club, but if past experiences were anything to go by, the tench fishing would be all over for the day before its members got on the water. I missed the start of the season, and being the 'stick in the mud' that I am, chose to use the tench-fishing tactics that have served me so well over so many years: link-legering breadflake or sometimes sweetcorn, and 50/50 breadcrumb and sausage rusk groundbait, 'cupped' around the link for casting weight.

My tranquil solitude was shortlived, however. Shortly after settling in, cars started arriving at the yacht club immediately behind me – and then the music started. I like music, but this was deafening 'heavy-metal' which just doesn't gel with the gentle art of fishing. Besides which I couldn't kip! It was long after midnight before the racket eventually subsided, and for long after that a succession of cars illuminated the inside of my bivvy. The ribbing I was subjected to was all very good-natured, but frankly, I could have done without any of it!

Needless to say I overslept, the buzzer waking me eventually. I scrambled out of bed to land a plump 6lb 10oz female. Not a bad start, and a big bite; things were looking better. I had more tench during the day, too, including another six-pounder at dusk. There were no bites at dawn the next day, however, and then the wind got up, a strong cold easterly which hit me in the left ear and blew directly into the bivvy. Worse though, all the bits of weed stirred up by the yachts drifted onto my lines. Rearranging the tackle, time after time, made little difference; even with the top joints completely submerged I couldn't keep a bait out for more than a few minutes. Something had to be done. Finally I found a large dead branch and dragged it the 200yds (180m) or so back to my swim. It took hours to get it posi-

Mick Voller's 8lb 10oz specimen took maggots.

tioned just right so that it collected all the drifting rubbish and protected my lines. When at last everything was done, darkness had fallen; I recast for the night, and though lathered in sweat, climbed into bed and was soon 'well away'.

It must have been about 2am when I was rudely awoken by someone shaking me and a voice in the dark said, 'Come on Uncle. Wake up, wake up!' It was Pete Frost. I staggered out. Through bleary eyes I could see he looked very pleased with himself. 'What's the matter?' I asked him. 'I've arrived just in time,' he said, and went on, 'I've just pulled out a bloody great branch that was about to tangle with your lines. Wasn't it lucky I came along when I did?'

Despite what I thought, I said nothing, except thanking him for saving my gear. I value his company too much to upset him. Whilst he set up in the next gap, I made us both a cup of tea.

Next day there was another angler fishing not far from us, and although he didn't seem too keen for a chat, I just had to go and see after he landed what looked like a very big tench. This angler turned out to be Mick Voller, and the tench was more than just big – it was huge, weighing no less than 8lb 10oz and the biggest tench I'd ever set eyes on. After photographing, it was returned straight away.

Not long afterwards Len turned up. For once he'd missed the start of the season, having been to the Isle of Man for the TT motorcycle racing. He nipped along to congratulate Mick Voller, but in short order returned. 'Mick is packing up and said I could fish his swim,' he panted. And, without saying another word, he roared off on his motorbike to get his gear. And believe me, it didn't take long!

All was quiet and we sat together drinking tea; Len had decided not to cast out until dawn. At about 10pm I had a very slow take on the bread-flake rod; this turned out to be a dustbin-lid of a bream, which Pete weighed for me at exactly 10lb. A personal best. Then just before midnight I hit into a similar bite on the same rod. At first it came in easily and was very nearly netted, but then it found renewed strength, and despite firm pressure the fight lasted no less than *ninety minutes*. There was much conjecture as to what sort of fish was responsible; Len even went to fetch the outsize landing net from his van, just in case. And do you know, it turned out to be an 8lb bream foul-hooked in the cheek. If it had slipped the hook, it would have been another of those 'monster-that-got-away' stories!

Next day Bill Quinlan came on a visit and to 'crow' about the fantastic brace of tench he'd just

Who needs enemies with friends like this? Bob Buteux helping(?) the author.

a tench of 7lb 1oz – but then Len rubbed salt into my wounds by going back to the other lake and getting his first eight-pounder. My life just wasn't worth living after that, both of them continually crowing of being members of the exclusive '8lb tench club'. Then in later years when they both got 'nines' it became even worse, neither of them missing and opportunity to remind me that no tench under 8lb counted. They were joking of course, but at the time I thought I would just creep off, find a new swim and catch a monster to shut them both up.

I found a promising area on the opposite bank, and while I watched them landing one big tench after another, I hooked a very big fish; it took a lot of line and 'hung out'. Eventually it rolled, showing a great golden flank. I nearly died: it was truly monstrous! I netted it out – to find a yellow-

caught from the other lake, 8lb 6oz and 7lb 13oz: his first tench over the magic 7lb mark. I couldn't resist much of that sort of persuasion, and decided to join him. When we arrived back at Bill's swim the late Alec Lewis had arrived and was setting up in 'the boat swim', the very place I had in mind. So I settled in not far from Bill. You've guessed, of course: Alec landed a string of big tench, including an 8lb 6oz. He was only staying the one night, however, so as soon as he left, I moved in, rubbing my hands with glee as I did so.

Yet another of our little group (the Herts-Chiltern Anglers), Bob Carter, then arrived and fished the swim I'd just vacated... and promptly landed an '8–12'. I wanted a shoulder to cry on, but all Bill and Len did was joke about my misfortune! Slight consolation came in the shape of

An 8lb 12oz specimen for Bob Carter.

Ken Bingham nets a Sywell tench for Janet Jackson.

coloured mirror carp of 13½lb! *Never* was I so disappointed with such a beautiful fish.

I have managed to catch a few more 'sevens' but haven't yet qualified for the 8lb club, let alone the 9lb club. And Bill and Len both assure me there is no such organization as a 10lb bream club.

I feel sure my failure is due in no small part to my stubbornness. I insist on using my old tactics and bait, which Len is continually trying to persuade me to give up. But it is important to me to catch fish on my own terms. It doesn't happen very often these days, but when it does, it's the greatest feeling I know.

AN EARLY BREAKFAST
by Pete Jackson

Along with Janet, my wife, and a couple of long-time friends, I was starting the new season on a little lake not far from home. The water held big tench, but the fishing was so hard it put off all but a few hardy souls.

We had set up during the afternoon on the eve of the new campaign. Towards evening the first bottle of well chilled Lambrusco was opened to go with the food Janet had prepared. She is a true heroine of tench fishing: at the drop of a woolly hat she conjures up feasts fit for a king right on the bank – by the time the second bottle had disappeared we had relived the great days and nights

among the tench. Manea to Southill to Sywell, and many more stops in between, were recalled, and then, with steaming mugs of tea in hand, we spoke of our hopes for the coming 'opening day'.

'Loads of big'uns.' said the ever-optimistic Rob Brace. 'I think I'll just wait and see what happens,' said the ever-cautious Janet. For myself, I pondered a little, before resurrecting a phrase often heard at Sywell in the early seventies: 'A brace of 'sevens' and an early breakfast will do nicely for me.' After a brief pause everybody agreed that that would indeed do nicely. Of course in those Sywell days we were talking tongue in cheek, because one seven-pounder would have been an event, let alone two! Even now, in much headier times, seven-pounders are still not that common.

By now the 'bewitching hour' was fast approaching and our little party broke up, each individual heading for his or her own already pre-baited swim. My first cast dropped in a shallow silty area, below a gravel ridge; a favourite spot. 'Oi! it's not the sixteenth yet,' called Rob, 'there's still two minutes to go!' (If the truth be known, he had probably cast out and was in bed already!) The other rod was cast into deeper water to my left. I turned toward by comfy bed in the bivvy.

I'd taken but one step when my buzzer screeched, the right-hand Mitchell spinning madly. The fight with the first fish of the season is always an affair fraught with tension, for the outcome seems an omen for the remainder of the season: a lost first fish drops me into a pit of misery that seems to last for months. But I needn't have worried for everything went according to plan. A 6lb-plus female was landed, weighed, and then quickly returned. The boily, still on and seemingly undamaged, was obviously a good one, so it was repositioned in exactly the same spot. After recasting I sat on the grass and looked out over the water for signs of fish activity; it looked like polished slate, so I went to bed.

Dawn was just breaking when the buzzer squawked again. This was obviously a fish with a lot of weight behind it. Line was gained, then with an angry clatter was pulled off the reel again.

For a couple of minutes it was stalemate, then I gained the upper hand and pulled it straight into the net first time: a cracking tench of 7lb 14oz. 'That'll do for me,' I said to myself as I recast once more.

All seemed quiet with the others; Janet was still asleep, and Rob was frying bacon for a breakfast sandwich. How does he keep his figure with the amount he eats?! I crept back to my swim. The left-hand rod hadn't stirred since casting out at midnight, so I contemplated, over a cup of tea, whether I should move it; but decided to leave it where it was.

With the sun just breaking through the trees I thought my chances were just about gone for the

Pete Jackson's set up.

day; this venue was really a 'night-only' water, and it was rare for it to produce this late in the morning. And then the previously stationary bait was away: with the rod up and well bent, this was obviously another big tench. 'If it's another 'seven', it's an early breakfast for me!, I thought. The fish and I battled it out, and after a few fraught moments when it ran under some marginal tree branches, I soon had it in front of me and close to the net. But just when I thought it was under control, the hooked tench dived deep, yanking the rod top under water. 'This shouldn't happen,' I thought, 'The fish should have been ready for the net.'

Like one of Zane Grey's marlin the line angled up, out of the water as pressure caused the fish to surface and wallow. Closer it came and closer; now steady; and it was mine! Instinctively I knew it was the biggest tench I'd ever seen on the bank. I weighed it straight away, and very nearly fainted as the 11lb balance bottomed out; however, it eased back a little to settle at 10lb 5oz. Janet came round and confirmed the weight, so less the weigh-sling, the fish actually weighed 9lb 13oz.

I recast, but not with any real conviction; nevertheless, half-an-hour later the same rod produced an '8–2'! The start of the season had never been so kind to me before; I'd caught more than two 'sevens' and so deserved... *my early breakfast.*

THAT CERTAIN FEELING
by Len Arbery

In those days my job allowed Monday mornings free, and in summertime I used to take advantage of this by going tench fishing. One Sunday afternoon I was preparing my gear for such a trip, when I started to feel uneasy. I recognized the feeling straight away, for I've experienced it several times: my instincts were telling me to get to the lake without delay, and not to wait until tomorrow morning.

From time to time in the angling press we read accounts written by respected anglers, telling of their experiences of certain feelings, or premonitions, which let them know when and/or where to

'Within the hour I was on the bank'.

fish. Richard Walker wrote about the 'sixth-sense' he developed whilst carp fishing, a sense which proved utterly reliable. Then Roger Baker relates how when he was fishing for (and catching) some big tench, the 'feeling' came to him that he ought not to be tench fishing, but out on the river Ouse in search of a big barbel. Roger obeyed his instincts, and that very evening caught his biggest barbel to date, 12lb 2oz!

I, too, have felt the same sort of irresistible urge to fish, come what may. In my case this 'feeling' is not totally reliable – yet the following account is, I assure you, perfectly true, and the 'feeling' on this occasion did not let me down. June, my wife, understood the situation and within the hour I was on the bank of the tench lake setting up. This chore had hardly been started when another angler, struggling under an enormous load of tackle, inquired whether I was packing up. When I told him I'd just arrived he looked disappointed, and stomped off into the gathering gloom without uttering another word. I never did find out who it was. Thank goodness I got here poste haste, I said to myself.

Everything was soon sorted out: rods lay in their rests with the swingtips set so the tips only just touched the surface. Don't ask me why, but I didn't start fishing immediately. I just catapulted out a sprinkling of midi-boilies, then made a cup of tea, before getting my head down for a few hours' sleep.

I was up at dawn, just in time to greet Tony, my son, who was keen to share the swim with me after his mother had told him of my premonition the night before. However, three biteless hours later it looked as if the 'feeling' had let me down, and Tony left to go to work. He could hardly have locked the gate behind him, and driven back into the outside world, when my swingtip indicated the first bite. An unspectacular fight ended with the landing of a 6lb 9oz female tench. It was almost as if the fish had been waiting for me to be on my own.

For the rest of the day the swingtips were hardly ever stationary, and by lunchtime my bag consisted of no fewer than fifteen tench, five of which were over 7lb apiece! The heaviest was a gorgeous creature, containing not a single ounce of

One of the five over 7lb – 7lb 9oz.

spawn: weighing 8lb 11oz, it was my personal best at that time, and although I've since caught heavier specimens, it remains my most memorable.

If you are not to miss out, you must learn to rely on your natural instincts sometimes. Dick Walker said, 'If *I've* got it, everybody else has got it too!' So as long as you culture and cultivate it, I promise you, one day you won't regret obeying 'that certain feeling'!

GORDON BEAVAN'S RECORD
by Len Arbery

Gordon Beavan set off for a week's tench fishing at a 60-acre (24ha) Colne Valley lake, accompanied by only his faithful black labrador, Joe. This was Gordon's second visit to the venue, and he was fishing by courtesy of a guest ticket. The planned seven-day stint was then unexpectedly extended by two days when Joe was knocked down by a car, and Gordon was forced to stay at the lake while the dog recovered at a local vet's.

Bolt-rigged boilies fished in a relatively clear channel between two weedbeds produced a few carp to 18lb 9oz. Later Gordon noticed some fish movement very close in, so he switched to a cutdown porcupine quill float, equipped with a Mini-Nightlight. Because of the carp being present, together with strong dense weed, he decided not to compromise on tackle strength; he therefore chose 15lb mainline and a 8lb Silkworm hooklink, tied to which was a size 10 hook.

Fishing a rod length out, over an area already heavily baited with hemp and corn, Gordon lost a number of good fish, including one enormous tench. After experimenting with hook sizes, he eventually presented a single grain of sweetcorn on a size 14 hook, and sat back to wait events. Sure enough, when darkness had closed in the Nightlight on the float disappeared; after a hectic ten-minute battle, a giant tench was landed. In Gordon's own words: 'It was the middle of the night and I was alone on the lake when I caught it. At 10.30pm it weighted exactly 15lb, less 8oz for the weigh-sling. I immediately sacked it and

called out two witnesses with two more sets of scales. At dawn my mates Danny Hopcroft and Dean Martin witnessed the fish, and all three sets of scales put it at 14lb 8oz. I've since had my scales examined by Weights and Measures officials who have confirmed they are accurate within 1oz up to 22lb 8oz.'

Gordon went on, 'All my mates thought the fish an ugly freak, but I thought it was beautiful. It wasn't spawn-bound, and didn't have a boily-belly, so I've no idea how it grew into that shape.'

The significance of the fish wasn't at first realized. Gordon believed that the tench record at that time stood at over 16lb, and it wasn't until two days later that he realized he might be able to claim Britain's top tench spot. He then applied for record status for the huge tench. The *Angling Times* reported:

Gordon was devastated when he received an official application form demanding witnesses for weighing *and* capture.

'Nobody witnessed the capture because I was fishing alone,' said Gordon 'How can they expect me to have witnesses?' I know I've caught the record fair and square, but if they reject my claim because no one saw me slip the net under it, I'll be absolutely gutted. Let's face it, millions of anglers fish alone every year. You can't expect every bloke to have a chaperone just in case he catches a possible record. It's about time all these rules were sorted out so there's no chance of any angler being done out of a rightful record.'

But Brian Crawford, the then secretary of the National Association of specialist Anglers' (NASA) Record Fish Committee, said:

There are rules in place for such contingencies. I've asked Gordon to fill out an affidavit saying he caught the fish fair and square, and we are looking forward to receiving his claim.

Gordon's claim was received first by NASA and the National Federation of Anglers (NFA), and subsequently by the full British Record (rod-caught) Fish Committee, and was unanimously accepted, although it was adjusted down by 1oz to 14lb 7oz because of the error in his scales, as found by the Weights and Measures inspector.

Two weeks later Gordon caught the same fish again, this time weighing 14lb exactly.

Postscript

I can now reveal that Gordon's record tench was caught from Bury Lake, the same water that produced tench of 14lb 4oz, 13lb 7oz and 12lb 15oz for Gary Newman. We are able to release this information because there was a massive fish-kill at the water in 1995; I have been reliably informed that 95 per cent of the water's stock perished, two full, large skiploads of dead fish being taken away. I have no precise knowledge of what caused these fatalities, so can only speculate: the summer of 1995 was long and hot, with very little rainfall, and under these conditions dissolved oxygen levels can fall disastrously. It is therefore likely that the fish suffocated. What a terrible shame!

MY TENCHING YEARS
by Bill Quinlan

It all started when I was about sixteen, when I met a much older angler called Albert: He was a mean old 'so-and-so'; he used to buy the *Angling Times* for a 'tanner' (2½p!), and after he'd read it he would sell it to me for half price! But he took me and a couple of pals to Stockers lake in the Colne Valley.

Every weekend I and my fishing friend Pete would hurry down to Stockers, piking during the day and setting up for bream just before 9pm. And it was just as if a switch had been thrown to turn them on, the bobbins flying on all the rods. Then one day Pete caught a fish we'd never seen before. We thought it was some kind of tropical fish, and took it to be weighed at the bailiff's hut-cum-teahouse run by a Mr and Mrs Edwards. Oh!, it's a tench they said. It weighed 3lb 8oz, and that event started us wanting to catch tench

by design. But in spite of trying for years, I never did catch a tench from Stockers.

We would arrive very early – on motorbikes by this time – because we'd heard tench were dawn feeders. So we'd begin fishing before dawn and get one or two bream, before the bites petered out as it got bright. We concluded the bream were feeding all night, so we had to try, even though night fishing was banned. The very first night we tried it, the bream bites petered out at about 11 o'clock – and shortly afterwards we heard, 'Now then! Now then! What's all this 'ere!' It was Jim the bailiff, and despite all our protestations he barred us.

After this we tried other lakes in the area, but even though we caught comparable-sized fish, it wasn't the same. I eventually swallowed my pride and went back to see the Stockers' bailiff: 'Please Mr Edwards, let us back in?' To his eternal

Bill Quinlan's 3lb 6oz tench from Moor Lane.

credit he relented, and we never night fished there again.

I was mad keen to catch tench, and at about that time Don Wray was writing about the big catches of quality tench he got from Moor Lane fisheries. I found out where Moor Lane, was – it is now under the Staines by-pass! – and started 'haunting' the place, fishing it night after night, but without so much as a bite. Then I got three fish in one night, up to 3lb 6oz. By this time I'd got a Heron buzzer, but was using a rod made from an ex-army tank aerial. And then it was tench, tench, tench. Now knowing how to do it (or so I thought), I went back to Stockers – but I still couldn't get one there!

My next venue was North Met Pit, a water I learned of from a little book by Ken Sutton called *Fishing for Londoners*. At this time my close fishing mate was Reg – who later tragically died – and we heard North Met contained tench so started going there in the summer. I'd go there for a week at a time, on a motorbike – and let me tell you, it's a *very* long walk from where you park, carrying all the gear necessary for a week along the tow-path. I'd trudge backwards and forwards, what must have been literally miles, and set up my tiny tent to fish this little point. But I started catching tench quite regularly, and landed another 3lb 6oz fish, equalling my best.

In the summer of 1957 we went to Ireland: John Roberts, whom I'd read about fishing Redmire, used to advertise these fishing holidays on a beautiful, unspoilt Irish lake, stuffed full of great big tench, and called, I think, Reynella. Reg and I organized our affairs and booked.

We sailed for Ireland on my twenty-first birthday, 8 June 1957, and it was the most miserable twenty-first anyone ever had! It was a real rough crossing and I was violently sick all night. When at last we arrived, we *ran* down to see the lake, only to find this great expanse of water completely stuffed with weed. Well, we'd never come across weed like it, and were so disappointed we asked for our money back. But John insisted the big tench were there to be caught, and wouldn't give us a refund. We tried to argue, saying the water was unfishable (because to our eyes and

our experience it was), but he remained adamant. Eventually he persuaded us to consider our decision over a meal. There were some other English anglers in the room, one of whom was certainly Frank Guttfield, and overheard them talking about very big tench at a water called Southill Park. I remembered the name from Dick Walker's writings, and the information was duly filed in the memory.

Stuck in Ireland still, Reg and I debated what to do, but we really didn't fancy fishing Reynella, so left the same day without a refund! At this point in my life for reasons I don't want to go into, I stopped fishing altogether for a couple of years. Then one day I decided to take my Triumph motorbike for a trip out into the countryside to 'blow away the cobwebs'. I had no particular destination in mind, but was just following my nose. I came to a signpost to Hitchin; 'Well!' I thought to myself, 'Walker lives here!' I carried on. All of a sudden another signpost said Arlesey: Arlesey Lake is where Walker caught those giant perch. Then Maylin's café with the pool behind, which I'd also read about, where Don Wray had caught carp. Shefford: I'd heard of that, too; the The Airman, which had been mentioned in *Angling Times*. And finally I came to another signpost with that magic inscription, Southill.

I reasoned this just had to be Southill Park because it was in the same area as all these other renowned waters. So I followed the signs and did, eventually, find Southill Park. It was a beautiful lake, and I fell in love with it at first sight. An angler there told me how to obtain permission to fish, and for me it was a new beginning.

I clearly remember my first visit. I caught two fish, a 1½lb rudd and a tench: guess what weight? That's right, 3lb 6oz! For some reason this fish confirmed I was in the right place – the place where Pete Thomas had lost a 'record' tench when his leger weight had slipped down and knocked the hook out. Of course, from that moment on I began 'haunting' Southill Park.

There was one particular character in this scenario who always arrived before me, and I was there well before dawn. His motorbike would

A Southill specimen caught by John Simpson.

always be leaning against the tree that I liked to lean my bike against; and I knew he'd only just beaten me because his bike would still be 'spitting and crackling' as it cooled down. I'd go in and he'd usually be asleep; he'd be waiting for the dawn. I'd have to tread over him on the way round the lake, and he'd be absolutely dead to the world, despite only arriving a few minutes before me. I actually landed a fish for him one day when he got into a bit of trouble with a snag. This character proved to be Bob Buteux: we started fishing together then, and have remained firm friends ever since. (This was almost certainly 1962).

Largely as a result of Walker's writings, I'd long done away with my inadequate gear.

Twitcher-hitting at Southill brought its rewards.

Walker advised MkIV rods, and he also recommended a manufacturer: B. James & Son, of Ealing. So that's where I went, eventually becoming very friendly with Mr James, as I always called him; I always had great respect for him and called him nothing else. Later I learned his real name was James Bruce, but I didn't know that then. He was so good. A split-cane Mk IV in those days cost about £10; this seems cheap, I know, but most of us just didn't have that sort of money. So Mr James would let us have the rods and allow us to pay whatever we could when we had it. We didn't have to sign anything: he just kept a record in the back of a book; yet nobody ever let him down. He was such an obliging man. Bob Southwell was building the split-cane for B. James in those early days, and those early B. James' rods were very, very good: excellent materials, and first-class hand-finishing – in fact, better than Walker said they were. I bought a pair of Mk IV Avons for tenching, before buying the carp rods.

At Southill I met a whole host of good anglers in the early to mid-sixties, people such as Alan Brown, Frank Guttfield, Bob Rutland, Roy Pinnock, John Coxhill, Dave Hugill and Bob Carter, as well as Bob Buteux and John Simpson.

John Simpson, or Simmo as I used to call him, was certainly a character: he lived and talked as though in a mediaeval time warp, using such words as 'damsels' and 'gadzooks', and be really living in the past. Perhaps this came about because of his job: he was a restorer of antiquarian books and manuscripts. In fact Simmo was, and still is as far as I am aware, a leading authority on that sort of thing; his collection of old fishing books is second to none; and he possesses volumes that aren't even in the British Museum library.

The tench fishing at Southill in those days largely followed a set pattern: a few big bites very early in the morning, petering out as it got brighter; the final indications would be the occasional flip, dig or small pull. I tried to deal with these 'twitch bites' as they came to be called, and it almost drove me crazy. But you could catch tench on and off all day if you were prepared to concentrate hard and slash away at those tiny bites. It was no good using a dough-bobbin between the reel and the butt ring, as you would early on; we found very small bobbins on the line in front of the rod much more sensitive.

I considered float fishing might be an even better alternative, in spite of the fact that the tench were quite a long way out, and started experimenting. Eventually I developed a range of floats that could be fished at long range. These were home-made antenna floats, and there were plenty of failures before I got the design right. But when I did, I could fish very sensitively as far out as I could get my groundbait, say 60–70yds (54–64m). Because of this range and depth, the mainline wouldn't go to the bottom of the float, it went about half-way between float and hook.

The main advantage in this arrangement was beating the sub-surface drift: Southill was notorious for drift, and you'd submerge the tops of the rods as well.

Another successful ploy to defeat the twitchers was using small 'cocktail' baits such as maggots and flake, maggots and crust, worm and paste. It was also vital to keep varying the bait, alternating between one or the other, a lesson I learned from John Simpson. And with the benefit of hindsight, I now realize we were catching the same fish over and over again. So obviously it was, and presumably still is, easier to fool the same individual tench by changing the bait.

Indirectly the tench fishing at Southill was responsible for the formation of that most famed group, the Herts-Chiltern Anglers. For me it all started on 3 April 1964 when a workmate pointed out a notice in *Angling Times*. This said: 'Wanted – Bill the Bike, who fishes Southill Park and Henlow Grange'. It was sent in by Roy Pinnock and John Coxhill, two characters I'd chatted to for hours, so it was a good chance they were referring to me. As I got home that evening Bob was on the phone; he'd also seen the notice in *Angling Times* and also believed it referred to me.

Bill the Bike

Will Bill (?) whom we first met tench fishing at Southill Park and later at Henlow Grange, Bedfordshire, and who arrives from the London area on a motorcycle, please write to us at this address:
R. Pinnock, 61 Kingsdown Ave., Luton, Beds.

The Angling Times *letter*

Their idea was to ask Bob and I to join the Chiltern Specimen Group. It had been founded in 1957 by Roy and John, together with Derek Smith and Gwyn Williams. After contact was made, Bob and I met Roy and John and we joined. More anglers followed, and at the last count, as far as I remember, the names were: Roy

Pinnock, John Coxhill, Tony Williams, Gwyn Williams, Derek Smith, Alan Brown, Dave Hugill, Bob Carter, Bob Buteux and myself.

Some of us were constantly fishing with members of the Herts group, too, as most members of both groups fished waters such as Southill and Henlow Grange, and it became clear that, rather than have divided loyalties, it would be preferable to amalgamate. Hence the Herts-Chiltern Anglers was formed, I think in May 1965. This brought in people such as Jack Hilton, Roger Smith, Pete Frost, Frank Guttfield, Bill Keal,

Alec Lewis, Roy Wickes, Kenny Ewington and Ron Taylor. As some members lost interest and left, others were invited to join, but there had to be a unanimous vote from existing members before the invitation was extended. Later members of the Herts-Chiltern included Tony Dixon, Trevor Hutchins, Dave Boothroyd, Dave Cheshire, Tony Abbot, Harry Green, Pete and Janet Jackson, Kerry Barringer and of course, Len Arbery.

During the course of the next few years I became increasingly involved in other species,

Is this really you, Bill?

notably carp, barbel and chub, but not to the exclusion of tench. In the early 1970s I was still tench fishing at Southill Park, although at this time it was exclusively at night because the place had become overrun with little roach, and it was pointless fishing during daylight because they wouldn't leave the bait alone. However, night fishing was the reason for my being thrown out of Southill, not because it wasn't allowed but because the bailiff, Ernie Wakelin, never saw me! He refused to renew my permit, saying that as I wasn't using the facility, it was better if someone else was offered my ticket. But I *was* fishing! He didn't see me because he was ninety years old and tucked up in bed during the hours of darkness!

At about this time Yateley came up; this was long before it became the carp complex it is now. Pete Cranstoun put us onto the North Lake, and he was probably the first specialist angler on the water. Pete told me about the Yateley tench; these gave only tiny bites on corn that he rarely hit. I suggested he tried lobworms at night, and this produced a big one, a 'seven'! This was inducement enough for us to fish the North Lake. We used to feed the carp but didn't fish for them; all we were interested in were the big tench. Then, of course, someone caught a 20lb-plus carp, followed soon after by Kevin Clifford's '30'. We managed to keep it quiet for a little longer, but then the bubble burst and we were

Ralph Wylie offered to drive the author to a fishing club interview, an unselfish act which proved sufficient to get him 'black-balled' too! The tench is a 7lb plus male.

A place where we could fish in peace with no stupid bans.

driven away by the hordes of carp anglers that descended on the place.

We wanted to fish other waters, but had a great deal of trouble because clubs wouldn't accept us as members. I tried to join some clubs just to fish for tench, but they'd think I was after carp, even if there weren't any carp in the water! They'd say, 'Oh, he's Jack Hilton's mate, they're going to bring all their carp-fishing cronies down here!' They wouldn't stop to think there was no carp in the water. Nor was this an isolated event: it happened many times over.

Towards the end of the 1976/7 season we finished at Redmire, and spent much more time after tench. Clive Diedrich and the late Malcolm Winkworth found this tench water not far from Heathrow Airport. It was very little fished, very weeded, and extended to about twenty acres (8ha). Clive and Malcolm baited heavily with corn, eventually catching some quality tench

including a couple of six-pounders. Now, six-pounders were still very big fish in those days, and as they were late summer fish – hence no spawn – they were very big fish indeed.

The controlling club was one of the few in the area that hadn't heard of us, so we joined with no trouble. This was a revelation, harking back to the old days: a place where we could fish in peace and where no pointless bans were in force. The first weekend's fishing, in September, produced several quality tench including a '5–12', which equalled my best at that time, Len soon eclipsed this, upping his personal best to 5lb 15oz in the process. This fish was particularly significant because it was our first using a swingtip.

We opened the new 1977/78 season here and virtually had the place to ourselves. Being good boys, we sat up talking until it was time to cast out at midnight. Len scored first, and what a fantastic fish it was: 7lb 6oz, and without a trace of spawn, it was huge! Then a couple of nights later, along comes Bob Buteux, plonks himself down in the most comfortable swim, and soon gets a '7–13'! There just ain't no justice! There were Len and I desperately slashing away at twitchers, and Bob, who only fished in daylight, getting great big bites, landing seven-pounders: he caught four 'sevens' that weekend! I had my first 'six', but after Bob's achievements this was small beer!

We were using sweetcorn more or less exclusively on this water, and did our best to keep it secret: our bait buckets had black adhesive tape wrapped round them so no inquisitive eyes could penetrate their secret, and we baited up by wading, or covered the grass with groundsheets to prevent any loose grains being found. Then Kevin Clifford was invited to join in the fun, and blew it straightaway; he left corn around everywhere! Suddenly Ken Smith, whom we first met on this water, was catching regularly, so we knew he was using corn as well now. Our 'edge' being blown, our search for new waters once more intensified.

In about 1980 I started fishing another large pit with a reputation for big tench. It was a lovely water. I picked a likely looking swim and fished it for twenty-four hours, but the 'tufties' drove me mad; it was completely 'tuftie'-infested. The next day I caught three tench, including one at 6lb 6oz, and was well pleased with myself; this was obviously another good tench water and hardly fished at all. But it was hard, *hard* fishing, and I came to the conclusion that there weren't many tench in there – although what few there were, were quality fish.

In March 1981 I was struck down with tuberculosis and spent several months in hospital. Len and Bob reported eight-pounders coming from the water, and I was desperate to get out; but they didn't release me until August. I went down there straightaway and had it virtually to myself, most of the regulars having given up by then. The fishing was almost impossible, yet I got a few tench, including one at 6lb 9oz. One of the few who was still tench fishing was Ron Chant: he'd had weekend after weekend without tench. I put him onto the 'maggot-and-feeder' ploy and he ended up with about twenty-six including a seven-pounder!

I couldn't fish in the 1982–3 season, but 1983 was truly outstanding for me, when all my years of hoping for a seven-pounder (my best had been

Blabber-mouth Clifford.

a pair of 6lb 12oz fish) were realized. The tackle I used included swingtips, with maggots and feeder, fished on 4lb line, the water being almost weed free. On opening day I knew there were tench in the swim because the tips showed little 'nudges', and the few tentative strikes I had came back with tench scales on the hook; but I couldn't figure out why they wouldn't really take the hookbait, particularly as they were obviously feeding on my free offerings.

On the 17 June I could think of nothing else but to reduce the line still further to 3lb; this was the minimum I considered feasible to use in this particular swim. But the transformation was immediate, and my first fish of the morning weighed 8lb 6oz! Moreover the next bite, half-an-hour later, was a fish of 7lb 13oz with no spawn: a monster, to my mind! (The 8lb 6oz tench was carrying quite a bit of spawn). I had a really good year, catching thirty-eight tench before the weed became too prolific, obliging me to come off the 3lb line.

Funnily enough I remember reading a couple of articles by Tony Miles at about this time, in which he related experiences on his waters which replicated those of Len and myself. Len was fishing another water further up the valley and catching some big tench, including an eight-pounder. However, I didn't think that the potential size of tench in Len's water was as high as mine. He was trying to get me to fish up there with him, whilst I was trying to persuade him that it would be better if we joined forces on mine. Len's lake had one advantage: it was so difficult that *nobody* else fished there. But Len eventually tired of blanking and we got together at my lake, in June 1984.

We decided to give a 'new' area the 'maggot-and-feeder' treatment, and it worked like a charm, both of us often catching big bags of quality tench. By this time we knew of the hair-rig, and although Len had caught a 'seven' on it the previous year, I still held to the traditional belief of being bitten off; for this reason I was using a 4in (10cm) long hair! Ridiculous, when you think about it! I'd get these steaming runs but never hook anything!

Len remembers 1984 as being the best summer's fishing he'd ever had: not only was it exceptionally productive, it was also in the best of

'Len eventually tired of blanking'.

company, and in the best of styles. Fishing adjacent swims we could work out different strategies between us, and consequently stayed one step in front of the tench all summer long. We did have a break though, when I had to concentrate on work and Len took the opportunity to go carp fishing with Ron Chant. Then one day I heard that a tench had been caught from our pit on a boily, and I immediately contacted Len; as the weather was more conducive for good tench fishing, we decided to try boilies the following weekend. Len would bait up every morning to give the tench the 'message'.

This strategy worked, and the tench went berserk on them. They were 'woofing' them down, so much so that they were all hooked well back in the mouth. It was so good that that summer, in spite of the long lay-off in the middle of the season, I ended up catching no less than 111 tench! Sixty-four were over 5lb, twenty-eight over 6lb, nine over 7lb and two over 8lb, 8lb 10oz being the best. Len couldn't put in as much time as me, but even so he caught more than seventy tench, and had the biggest at 8lb 11oz. This was another enormous fish containing no spawn.

'... that bearded chap at Wilstone, Alan Wilson, goes and gets a 12lb 8oz, which took the wind right out of our sails.'

We made plans for the following season and Len carried out the pre-baiting programme in the close season. We really went to town that year. We didn't catch so many tench, my total being seventy-four, but out of this number, sixty were over 5lb, forty over 6lb, nineteen over 7lb, eight over 8lb...and seven over 9lb! Which was incredible fishing. I knew by then that there were at least two spawn-free 9lb fish in the water, and was fairly sure there was a further one. The 'record' at that time was about 10lb 8oz, so either of these 'clean nines' with the addition of spawn were potential eleven-pounders and obviously potential record-breakers.

Then, of course, that bearded chap at Wilstone, Alan Wilson, goes and gets a 12lb 8oz, which took the wind right out of our sails. We knew our water was good, but it wasn't *that* good!

Another interesting fact about that year was that at one time I had caught ten tench between 7lb and 8lb, yet none of them held any spawn at all, not even the early season fish! And of these, seven were over 7½lb, therefore potential nine-pounders when carrying spawn. But in the following summer I realized the water was passing

Bill's 8lb 6oz and 7lb 13oz brace.

its best, because I caught exactly the same number of tench as the previous year: seventy-four. Fifty-four were over 5lb, twenty-eight over 6lb, ten over 7lb, and two over 8lb; but only one of

'. . . even if you can't catch as many big tench as I do!!!'

the 'sevens' was over 7½lb. So to my mind the water had peaked.

This period was really a purple patch: between 1983 and 1986 I caught 203 tench over 5lb, of which 111 were over 6lb, forty-seven over 7lb, thirteen over 8lb and seven over 9lb, the best being 9lb 7oz – tench fishing of a quality that I am absolutely sure I will never equal again. They were extremely enjoyable times, not just because there was the chance of catching a 'double', but because the circumstances and whole ambience were so pleasant. For example we had one memorable weekend when Fred J. Taylor came down as a guest. True to form the tench wouldn't oblige when we really wanted them to, but we never stopped talking and the whole weekend was a real treat.

As you have seen, I've spent a lot of time fishing the Colne Valley mainly for tench – my first love – and have met more fishing notables per square inch in that area than anywhere else. I can't mention them all, but would like to take this opportunity to thank them all for being the very best of fishing companions – even if you can't catch as many big tench as I do!

APPENDIX

RECORDS

I am indebted to the National Federation of Anglers (NFA) and to the National Association of Specialist Anglers (NASA) for making the following notes available.

The British Record (rod-caught) Fish Committee

Aims and Objectives

The committee exists to recognize and publish record weights of freshwater fish caught on rod and line, by fair angling methods, in the waters of England, Wales, Scotland and Northern Ireland.

To provide an adjudicating body to which freshwater anglers may submit claims for record fish taken by fair rod and line angling.

To investigate all such record claims to the fullest possible extent and maintain a permanent record of such investigations.

To establish and maintain accurately a list of British freshwater fish of record size and to publish this list frequently and make it available to all interested persons.

The activities of the committee are voluntary, and claims are considered and adjudicated upon, only on the basis that the committee shall be under no obligation whatsoever to claimants, that its decisions shall be final, and it shall not be obliged to give reasons for its decisions. Halliday House, 2 Wilson Street, Derby. DE1 1PG. Telephone: 01332 362 000

How to Claim a Record Fish

As soon as possible on capturing a potential record fish, contact any one of the committee members below:

Phil Smith, secretary
        (West Midlands) 01203 687 780
Neville Fickling (Lincolnshire) 01427 837 31
Dr Bruno Broughton
        (Nottinghamshire) 01602 841 703
Len Arbery (London)   01895 271 009
Kevin Clifford
        (North Humberside) 01430 440 624
Bryan Culley (Leicestershire) 01509 413 797
Tony Miles (West Midlands) 01203 544 704

Rules

The committee needs to be satisfied beyond all reasonable doubt that the fish was correctly identified and weighed accurately, and was captured by fair angling. It reserves the right to accept, reject or delete any fish from its list without being compelled to give reasons for so doing.

The committee will use its discretion to examine claims, subject to the following requirements:

1. Photographs of the fish must be available which should be of good quality and preferably in colour. They should include shots of the angler holding the fish in the normal manner, and the fish lying on the ground next to an identifiable object.
2. The weighing scales and/or a Weights and Measures/Trading Standard Department certificate must be presented for inspection.
3. The weight must be verified by two independent witnesses who, for example, should not be relations of the claimant or a member of his

club or party. NASA representatives are available as witnesses and can be contacted by phoning one of the committee.

Verification Procedure

1. Upon catching a potential record, contact one of the committee.
2. This member will scrutinize the national list of representatives and contact by phone the person living nearest the place of capture. If he can't be contacted, the next nearest will be contacted.
3. He will attend as soon as possible, and should be aware of the rules regarding claims.
4. After his visit, during which we hope he will have verified the necessary details, you should then make a formal claim to the British Record (rod-caught) Fish Committee via the NFA (Tel: 01332 362 000).

How to Weigh Potential Record Fish

1. Wet the weigh-sling-bag and squeeze out excess water.
2. Put the weigh-sling-bag onto the scales and zero to '0' as near as possible, but ensure the needle can still move and is not 'bottomed'. (Scales must be in a vertical position and held by the handle, not by the body.)
3. After zeroing, the scales should not be laid flat but kept in a vertical position.
4. The fish should be transferred to the weigh-sling/bag and suspended from the scales.
5. Have the reading on the scales witnessed in both cases (zeroing and weighing the fish).
6. Subtract the zeroed weight (if not actually at '0') from the total weight.

7. In case of scales that have a pointer that rotates several times, you should repeat the weighing of the fish several times, counting the rotations carefully.

Submitting a Formal Record Fish Claim

(Write out the following data)

1. Fish species.
2. Weight in pounds and ounces (plus drams for small species). (Note scales used must be appropriate for size of species: do not use 32lb or 40lb scales for bleak or gudgeon, for example.)
3. Length (from tip of nose to fork of tail).
4. Maximum girth.
5. Location of water (will be treated in confidence).
6. Date and time of capture.
7. Description of bait and tackle used, including name of rod, reel, etc.
8. Name and address, postcode and phone number of claimant in block letters.
9. Any other relevant details.
10. For roach, rudd, chub, dace, silver bream, give numbers of scales in the lateral line, plus count of rays in dorsal and anal fins. (I would also advise including good quality close-up photographs showing relationship of dorsal and pelvic fins, head etc. LA.)
11. Names, addresses, postcodes and telephone number of independent witnesses, plus their statements, if not witnessed by an official NASA representative.
12. Send application to the NFA.

BRITISH RECORD COARSE FISH LIST (AS AT 31ST DECEMBER 1995)

Species *latin name*	Weight					Date	Captor and Location
	lb	oz	dm	kilo	gm		
BARBEL *Barbus barbus*	16	2	0	7	314	1994	P Woodhouse River Medway, Kent
BREAM (COMMON) *Abramis brama*	16	9	0	7	152	1991	M McKeown Southern Water
CARP *Cyprinus carpio*	55	4	0	25	061	1995	A White Mid-Northants
CARP, CRUCIAN *Carassius carassius*	5	11	8	2	594	1994	D Lewis 6 Acre Surrey pond
CARP, Grass *Ctenopharyngodon idella*	23	14	0	10	829	1991	G Wallis Canterbury lake
CATFISH (WELS) *Silurius glanis*	57	4	0	25	968	1995	R Coote Withy Pool
CHUB *Leuciscus cephalis*	8	10	0	3	912	1994	P Smith River Tees
DACE *Leuciscus leuciscus*	1	4	4	–	574	1960	J L Gasson Little Ouse Thetford, Norfolk
EEL *Anguilla anguilla*	11	2	0	5	046	1978	S Terry Kingfisher Lake Nr Ringwood, Hants
ORFE, GOLDEN *Leuciscus idus*	7	7	0	3	381	1995	D Smith Horton, Bucks
PERCH *Percia fluvatilis*	5	9	0	2	523	1985	J Shayler Furnace Lake, Kent
PIKE *Esox lucius*	46	13	0	21	234	1992	R Lewis Llandeggfedd Res. Pontypool, Gwent
ROACH *Rutilus rutilus*	4	3	0	1	899	1990	R N Clarke Dorset Stour
RUDD *Rutilus erythrophthalmus*	4	8	0	2	041	1933	Rev. E C Alston Thetford, Norfolk
TENCH *Tinca tinca*	14	7	0	6	548	1993	G Beavan Herts Lake
WALLEYE *Stizostedion vitreum*	11	12	0	5	329	1934	F Adams The Delph Welney, Norfolk
ZANDER *Stizostedion lucioperca*	18	10	0	8	448	1993	R Armstrong River Severn

Species under 1lb							
BREAM (SILVER) *Abramis bjoerkna*	–	15	0	–	425	1988	D E Flack Grime Spring Lakenheath, Suffolk
BLEAK *Alburnas alburnas*	–	4	4	–	120	1982	B Derrington River Monnow Wye Mouth, Mons.
CATFISH (BLACK BULLHEAD) *Ameiurius melas*	–	2	15	0	085	1993	G Green Lake Meadows, Billericay, Essex
GUDGEON *Gobio gobio*	–	5	0	–	141	1990	D H Hull River Nadder Salisbury, Wilts
MILLER'S THUMB *Cottus gobio*	–	1	0	–	28	1983	R Johnson Bramley and Shamley Green River
MINNOW *Phoxinus phoxinus*	–	–	13	–	023	1981	R Merrifield River Calder Nelson, Lancs
PUMKINSEED *Lepomis gibbosus*	–	4	9	–	129	1987	D L Wallis Whessoe Pond Darlington, Co. Durham
RUFFE *Gymnocephalus cernus*	–	5	4	–	148	1980	R J Jenkins West View Farm Cumbria
STICKLEBACK, 3-SPINED *Gasterosteus aculeatus*	–	–	3	–	12	1995	M Drinkwater River Calder

Notes

A. The committee confirms the decision taken at its last meeting when it considered the recent trends, especially in respect of the introduction of non-native species to UK waters. These fish, by law, should not be introduced without a Section 30 Consent Certificate as issued by the NRA for the transfer of fish. It was agreed that claims for non-native species (other than carp; wels catfish; golden orfe; and rainbow trout) would not be considered unless a valid consent for introduction to the water concerned is produced by the owner of the fishery. The Committee agreed this decision would not be retrospective.

B. Claims for new records for the grass carp by Mr M. Plank and Mr D. Smith were deferred pending the clarification concerning Section 30 Consent Certificates.

C. The Committee wish to make it known their appreciation of the continued sponsorship of Messrs J. Barbour & Sons Ltd who not only sponsor the official British Record Fish List, but who also provide, free with every record claim accepted by the BRFC, a Barbour waxed cotton jacket of the record holder's choice.

BIBLIOGRAPHY

BIBLIOGRAPHY NOTE

Beside providing extremely good reading, there are other good reasons for the following bibliography to contain some old and out-of-print titles. For far too many years I did not read old fishing books: what, in the way of stimulus, I asked myself, could such works offer the modern progressive angler? The answer is much, as I shall explain.

Most big-fish anglers will no doubt agree that the most significant development in bait presentation was the invention of the hair-rig. Understandably, most anglers consider this a relatively recent innovation, for it was Lennie Middleton and Kevin Maddocks, working in the late 1970s, who worked out the effectiveness of the hair-rig when fishing for carp. However, it is no less true that similar devices have been used by anglers of the past. In at least two well loved old fishing books something similar to the hair-rig had been described. Here, within those dust-laden pages, they waited for someone to rediscover and exploit them. This may be difficult to believe, but perhaps you won't be so sceptical after perusing the following two passages (in both cases the italics in the excerpts are mine). The first is taken from Hugh Tempest Sheringham's *Coarse Fishing*, published in 1912.

> I believe water-snails, and fresh-water shrimps, and things like that, are the barbel's natural food. The trouble is putting them on a hook. Shrimps are tiny little things, and barbel hooks have to be pretty stout in the wire. Perhaps you could use some sticky stuff like seccotine, and simply stick four or five shrimps to the hook. Snails might be *tied on with fine thread.* Frenchmen use aniseed cake for many kinds of fish, and they *tie it to their hooks with thread.* They call it 'La noquette'; we don't know everything about fishing in England, though we think we do.

If it seems eighty years is a long time for the hair-rig to have been in existence, the following snippet is even more interesting: 'Some have directed to cut the cheese into thin pieces, and toast it, and then *tie it on the hook with fine silk.*' Believe it or not, this quotation is taken from a 1907 facsimile reprint of the first edition of Izaac Walton's *The Compleat Angler*, published no less than 340 years ago, in 1653! Since this is one of the most widely read books in the English language, surely at some time during the course of the past three and a half centuries, someone must have read these words and benefited from them. My only regret is that their experiences are not recorded.

BIBLIOGRAPHY

Arbery, Len *Catching Big Tench* (David & Charles, 1989)

Bailey, John *The Great Anglers* (David & Charles, 1990)

Bailey, John *In Visible Waters* (Crowood, 1984)

Barnes, Tag *The Exploring Angler* (Eyre & Spottiswoode, 1945)

'BB' (Denys Watkins-Pitchford) *The Fisherman's Bedside Book* (Eyre and Spottiswoode, 1945)

Bickerdyke, J. (C.H. Cook) *The Book of the All-Round Angler* (The Bazaar, Exchange and Mart, 1912)

Braddock, Archie *Fantastic Feeder Fishing* (Pisces, 1992)

Buckland, Frank *The Natural History of British*

Fishes (Society for Promoting Christian Knowledge, 1883)

Church, Bob *Catch More Tench* (Wolfe, 1974)

Clifford, Kevin and Arbery, Len *Redmire Pool* (Beekay, 1984)

'Faddist' (Edward Ensom) *Memorable Coarse Fish* (Burlington, 1953)

Falkus, Hugh and Buller, Fred *Freshwater Fishing* (Macdonald & Janes, 1975)

Foster, David *The Scientific Angler* (Bemrosse and Sons, 5th ed c1893)

Foster, Fred *Swing Tipping* (Cassell, 1976)

Geen, Philip *Days Stolen for Sport* (T. Werner Laurie, 1907)

Gibbinson, Jim *Modern Specimen Hunting* (Beekay, 1983)

Gibbinson, Jim *Tench* (Beekay, 1990)

Guttfield, Frank *In Search of Big Fish* (EMAP, 1964)

Guttfield, Frank (ed) *The Big Fish Scene* (Ernest Benn, 1978)

Head, Len *Tench* (Crowood, 1986)

Hilton, Jack *Quest for Carp* (Pelham, 1972)

Ingham, Maurice and Walker, Richard *Drop Me a Line* (Macgibbon & Kee, 1953)

Linnaeus, Sir Charles *Natural History, vol XI* (Encyclopedia Londinensis, c 1805)

Marsden, Graham *Advanced Coarse Fishing* (A & C Black, 1980)

Marshall-Hardy, Eric *Angling Ways* (Herbert Jenkins, 4th ed, 1956)

Martin, J.W. *The Nottingham Style of Float Fishing and Spinning* (Sampson, Low, Marston, Searle & Elvington, 1882)

Martin, J.W. *Coarse Fish Angling* (Brendon and Son, 1908)

Martin, J.W. *My Fishing Days and Fishing Ways* (J. Brendon & Son, 1906)

Martin, J.W. *Roach, Rudd & Bream Fishing in many Waters* (Albert Frost & Sons, 2nd ed, 1905)

Miles, Tony *The Complete Specimen Hunter* (Crowood, 1989)

Miles, Tony *Big Fish Angling* (Crowood, 1990)

Norman, John *Coarse Fishing with the Experts* (Allen & Unwin, 1956)

Parker, Capt L. *This Fishing: or Angling Arts and Artifices* (Cleaver-Hume, 2nd ed, 1960)

Rickards, Barry *Angling: Fundamental Principles* (Boydell, 1986)

Rickards, Barry and Webb, Ray *Fishing For Big Tench* (Rod & Gun, 1976)

Roberts, Bob *The Complete Book of Legering* (David & Charles, 1993)

Rogers, Pete (ed) *Red Letter Days* (Crowood, 1994)

Sheringham, H.T. *Coarse Fishing* (A & C Black, 1912)

Sheringham, H.T. *An Open Creel* (Methuen, 1910)

Sheringham, H.T. *An Angler's Hours* (Macmillan, 1905)

'Silver Doctor' (Lewis-Smith) *Angling From Many Angles* (Mrs E.G. Lewis-Smith, 1946)

Smith, Phil *Rainbow's End* (Ironbridge Publications, 1987)

Sosin, Mark and Clark, John *Through the Fish's Eye* (André Deutch, 1976)

Stone, P. *Come Fishing With Me* (Pelham, 1973)

Stone, Peter *Gravel Pit Angling* (David & Charles, 1978)

Taylor, Fred J. *Tench* (Macdonald, 1971)

Taylor, Fred J. *Fishing For Tench* (Stanley Paul, 1979); an updated version of the previous book.

Taylor, Fred J. *Angling in Earnest* (Macgibbon & Kee, 1962)

Taylor, Fred J. *Favourite Swims* (Macgibbon & Kee, 1961)

Taylor, Fred J. *My Fishing Years* (David & Charles, 1981)

Taylor, Fred J. *Reflections on the Water* (Buchan & Enright, 1982)

Travis-Jenkins, J. *The Fishes of the British Isles* (Frederick Warne, 2nd ed, 1958)

Turnbull, Chris *Success With Big Tench* (David & Charles, 1992)

Vaughan, Bruce (ed) *Top Ten* (Beekay, 1983)

Walker, Richard *Still Water Angling* (Macgibbon & Kee, 1953)

Walker, Richard *Walker's Pitch* (Allen & Unwin, 1959)

Walton, Isaac *The Compleat Angler* (numerous editions since 1653)

Yates, Chris *The Deepening Pool* (Unwin Hyman, 1990)

Yates, Chris, James, Bob and Miles, Hugh *A Passion for Angling* (Merlin Unwin, 1994)

USEFUL ADDRESSES

THE ANGLERS' CO-OPERATIVE ASSOCIATION

Let's suppose you come to your favourite fishing water and find it hideously polluted, with hundreds of fish floating belly-up on the surface... We hope it never happens to you, but there is always the chance that it might, both stillwaters and rivers face pollution. Suppose, again, you are 99 per cent sure that the source of the pollution is a large factory some miles upstream, a factory owned by one of the world's wealthiest multinationals. Now ask yourself these questions: whether you are an individual riparian owner or act for an angling club or syndicate, could you afford to sue such a powerful opponent? Would you be able to hold out, financially, against the manoeuvres of a defendant with an almost bottomless purse? Do you know what scientific evidence is needed to convince a court of law, and would you have the necessary facilities to obtain it? The Anglers' Conservation Association can, and does, many times every year.

The ACA now also incorporates the Pure Rivers Society, and we have been fighting the polluters of Britain's waterways since 1948. Such is our reputation that most of the cases we take up are settled out of court, with due compensation paid by the offenders. If you care about the environment, put your support behind the ACA.

ASSOCIATIONS

Anglers' Co-operative Association (ACA), 23 Castlegate, Grantham, Lincs NG31 6SW. Tel: 01476 61008; Fax: 01476 60900; Mobile: 0860 432714.

Carp Society, 33 Covert Road, Hainault, Ilford, Essex, IG6 3AZ.
National Association of Specialist Anglers (NASA), Marsh Pratley, c/o Orchid Lakes, Abingdon Road, Dorchester, Oxon OX10 7LP.
The Tenchfishers, Paul Thompson, 28 Middle Meadow, Chalfont-St-Giles, Bucks HP8 4QS.

RECORD FISH CLAIMS

See Appendix.

ANGLING PERMITS

Orchid Lakes: Mainly specimen carp and tench to double figures. Day tickets from: Marsh Pratley, Abingdon Road, Dorchester, Oxon OX10 7LP.
Christchurch Angling Club, c/o P. Reading, 17 Mayford Road, Branksome, Dorset, BH12 1PT.
Leisure Sport Angling Club, Thorpe Park, Staines Lane, Chertsey, Surrey, KT16 8PN.
Reading & District Angling Association, c/o Reading Angling Centre, 69 Northumberland Avenue, Reading.
Ringwood & District Angling Association, c/o J. Levell, 4 Forestside Gardens, Poulner, Ringwood, Hampshire.

ROD LICENCES

National Rivers Authority (NRA), 30–34 Albert Embankment, London SE1 7TL.

Note

The National Rivers Authority announced that a single national rod licence covering all species of fish would come into effect in England and Wales from 1 January 1992. This replaces the old system of over 100 rod licences in different parts of the country, which is 'divisive and expensive to operate'; it also obviates the need for anglers to have separate licences to fish either for salmon and sea trout, or for all other species. As at 1996, the new licence allows anglers to fish with two rods throughout England and Wales, where rules and byelaws permit, at no extra charge. Young anglers aged from twelve to sixteen, the disabled and OAPs (aged sixty and over) will only have to pay roughly half price. Anyone who goes fishing in fresh water must have an NRA licence; these are available from Post Offices.

BAIT SUPPLIERS

Streamselect Ltd: manufacturers of Richworth products (i.e. frozen boilies, shelflife boilies, blast-frozen deadbaits, etc.). Island Farm Avenue, West Molesey, Surrey KT8 0UZ.

John Baker: 'High Trees', 4 Dark Lane, Wargrave, Berks RG10 8JU.

Hinders Specialist Bait Centre: Ermin Street, Stratton St Margaret, Swindon SN3 4NH.

SPECIALIST TACKLE MANUFACTURERS

Drennan International Ltd: Bocardo Court, Temple Road, Oxford.

The Edward Barder Rod Company (Makers of finest split-cane fishing rods): Ham Mill, London Road, Newbury, Berks RG13 2BU. (Tel: 01635 552916).

The Roger Smith Bomb Supply Service: 31 Willowmead, Hertford, Herts.

Kryston Advanced Products: Bolton Enterprise Centre, Washington Street, Bolton BL3 5EA.

Gardener Tackle: 2 Pepper Box Lane, Palmers Cross, Bramley, Surrey.

Shimano Reels: Unit B2 Lakeside, Phoenix Way, Enterprise Park, Llansamlet, Swansea SA7 9EH.

Solar Tackle: 35 Sutherland Road, Belvedere, Kent DA17 6JR.

Swallow Centre-pin Reel: Dave Swallow, Bridge Farm, Iford Bridge, Nr Ringwood, Hampshire.

SUNDRIES

Fish Carvings: Brian Mills, 3 West Dumpton Lane, Ramsgate, Kent CT11 7DG.

Fish Artist: John Grant, 17 Woodyard Close, Kentish Town, London NW5 4BU.

INDEX